". . . Portrays with heartrending poignancy an American tragedy in which an anguished mother found atonement through outer-directed love and the rebuilding of private faith. [A] stellar, crucially significant narrative. . . ."

   —*Publishers Weekly*

"Particularly effective in drawing connections between adolescent suicide and the anguished struggle that gay teenagers may undergo as they begin to realize and acknowledge their homosexuality. Urging parents to understand and accept rather than reject and harangue, Mrs. Griffith speaks, through Mr. Aarons, with clarity and compassion."

   —*The New York Times Book Review*

"A passionate, gripping book . . . so raw with pain and intense love that it is difficult to read without tears and at the same time, nearly impossible to put down."

   —*Marin Independent Journal*

"[Aarons] has the newspaperman's gift for letting the narrative tell itself—his sparse prose compounds the jolt of the story. This book will become an instant classic. And it will save lives of countless young people. . . ."

   —*The Advocate*

"Aarons masterfully traces Bobby's short life in this account of a young man with seemingly everything to live for who took his own life in reaction to the homophobia of his family in particular and society in general. Recommended for all library types."

   —*Library Journal*

"Painful and personal. . . . Excerpts from a diary [Bobby] kept, family photos, and letters written by Mary to her dead son make the book intense reading."

   —*Booklist*

"*Prayers for Bobby* is a powerful, contemporary telling of what has traditionally been called the 'Pascal Mystery,' that is, the story of a life, death, and resurrection. This is a story of authentic spirituality in action and of the real price paid by real families for toxic religion."

— *Creation Spirituality*

"Written with clarity and great insight, *Prayers for Bobby* [is] a contemporary American tragedy. . . . A must read for all parents, educators, and clergy who believe that life is precious and God-given to every human being."

— *Paulette Goodman, former national president of P-FLAG*

"*Prayers for Bobby* renews my passion to demonstrate to the church and society that gay love is created, inspired, and blessed by God, so that no other gay child is spiritually abused."

— *Chris Glaser, M. Div., author of* The Word Is Out:
The Bible Reclaimed for Lesbians and Gay Men

"*Prayers for Bobby* . . . is far more than a cautionary tale; it is also a story of a tragedy that marks one mother's journey to redemption. This is a book that is every parent's business, and, in fact, should be read by anyone who is interested in caring for children."

— Robb Forman Dew, *author of* The Family Heart

"I hope this book will help religious people everywhere face their complicity in the evil way gay and lesbian children have been treated. Perhaps then the religious world can repent, apologize, and welcome all our children into the love of God that we proclaim."

— The Rt. Rev. John S. Spong, *Bishop of Newark and author of* Rescuing the Bible from Fundamentalism

"This book about how the Griffith family's love contributed to the suicide of their son is also the story of Mary's growing up. Bobby's death led her to new ideas and experiences that have transformed her into a mature adult. It is a transformation we all need as Americans confused about homosexuality and our concept of family values."

— Mitzi Henderson, *President, P-FLAG (Parents, Families and Friends of Lesbians and Gays)*

Prayers for Bobby

Prayers for Bobby

A MOTHER'S COMING
TO TERMS WITH THE SUICIDE
OF HER GAY SON

LEROY AARONS

HarperOne
A Division of HarperCollinsPublishers

HarperOne

PRAYERS FOR BOBBY: *A Mother's Coming to Terms with the Suicide of Her Gay Son.* Copyright © 1995 by Leroy Aarons. All rights reserved.

HarperCollins books may be purchased for educational, business, or sales promotional use. For information, please e-mail the Special Markets Department at SPsales@harpercollins.com.

HarperCollins Web site: http://www.harpercollins.com

HarperCollins®, ■®, and HarperOne™ are trademarks of HarperCollins Publishers.

Library of Congress Cataloging-in-Publication Data
Aarons, Leroy
Prayers for Bobby : a mother's coming to terms with the suicide of her gay son / Leroy Aarons. — 1st ed.
ISBN: 978–0–06–251123–2
1. Griffish, Robert Warren, 1963–1983.   2. Gay men—United States—Diaries.
3. Gay men—United States—Suicidal behavior.   4. Gay men—United States—Family relationships.   5. Parents of gays—United States.   6. Homosexuality—United States—Religious aspects—Christianity.   7. Religious fundamentalism—United States.   8. Homophobia—United States—Religious aspects.   9. Parents & Friends of Lesbians and Gays.   I. Title.
HQ75.8.G75A25   1995
305.38'9664'092—dc20   94–45141

ScoutAutomatedPrintCode

To Josh Boneh, who believed

CONTENTS

Contents

PHOTOGRAPHS

Photographs

All photographs printed courtesy of the Griffith family and friends, unless otherwise noted.

Acknowledgments

ACKNOWLEDGMENTS

My first acknowledgment is reserved for Mary Griffith, who reached into the darkest corners of her life to make this book possible. My gratitude to her for her cooperation, hard work, and friendship is boundless. I am also indebted to the Griffith family—Bob, Joy, Nancy, and Ed—for their contributions, as well as other family members and friends who were completely candid and helpful.

Thanks to the following for their help in reading various stages of the manuscript and suggesting improvements: Charles Kaiser, Juan Palomo, Belinda Taylor, David Harris, Micha Peled, Beth Smith, and Pat McHenry Sullivan. And, of course, my beloved Josh, who read and encouraged me every step of the way.

Thanks to researchers John Sullivan and Kate Newburger.

My gratitude to my editor, Kevin Bentley, who saw the potential in this story early on, was instrumental in Harper San Francisco's decision to publish it, and who honcho'd it all the way.

Acknowledgments

Thanks to Pam Walton for permission to use transcripts of interviews conducted for her important video documentary *Gay Youth*.

Finally, to Bobby Griffith, whose living spirit permeates this book and much of my life.

Prayers for Bobby

I first learned of the Griffith family in a 1989 article in the *San Francisco Examiner*. The piece, written by staff reporter Lily Eng, was part of a mammoth sixteen-day series on gays and lesbians in America. The *Examiner* was commemorating the twentieth anniversary of the Stonewall incident, considered the birth of the gay civil rights movement in America. (The Stonewall Inn was a Greenwich Village bar whose clientele on a warm summer night in 1969 defied a squad of police raiders, repelling them with bricks and debris and attracting hundreds to the scene in a protest that stirred gays and lesbians to action around the nation.)

I was deeply stirred by the story of Bobby Griffith's suicide, saddened by the waste of this young man's life. The scalding self-hatred contained in the excerpts from his diary included in the account was indeed painful to behold. My instinct was to grab hold of the boy who was writing these words and shout, "No, Bobby! You've got it all wrong. You're okay. It's the others who are crazy with hatred and ignorance!"

But, of course, it was too late. Unable to reconcile his gay sexual orientation with his family's religious and moral beliefs, Bobby had leaped to his death from a freeway bridge in 1983.

Other gay kids were committing suicide. In fact, some statistics maintained that gay teen suicide was approaching an epidemic level. What made the Griffith story unique was not only the daily record contained in Bobby's diaries over four years, but the companion tale of his mother, Mary, a blue-collar suburban housewife.

Included in the *Examiner* package was a confessional piece by Mary Griffith in which she told of the religious fanaticism and fear of gays that had led her to wage a relentless campaign to get her son to overcome his homosexuality. She had been too committed to her deep-rooted beliefs to notice that her rejection of Bobby was contributing to the self-hatred that ultimately culminated in his death.

The death of her son brought into question Mary Griffith's most basic beliefs. "Looking back," she wrote, "I realize how depraved it was to instill false guilt in an innocent child's conscience, causing a distorted image of life, God, and self, leaving little if any feeling of personal worth."

The story went on to document Mary's belated change of heart, her rejection of her religious doctrine, and the beginning of her crusade to help save the lives of other gay and lesbian children. Now she could say, "What a travesty of God's love, for children to grow up believing themselves to be evil, with only a slight inclination toward goodness, convinced that they will remain undeserving of God's love from birth to death."

This extraordinary conversion touched me as deeply as the tale of Bobby's tragic death. This woman of limited education was able to cut through a lifetime of conditioning, risk rejection by her religious peers, and embrace society's outcasts. How did she accomplish that? I wondered. What enabled her to transcend her background and perform what could only be described as acts of courage?

Like a lot of other gays and lesbians, I had my own history of rejection and self-hatred. Fortunately, I never contemplated suicide. It never entered my head as an option. My self-loathing took me in other directions—directions not quite as final, but certainly damaging, painful, and self-defeating.

I survived and, indeed, over many years, made peace with myself. But the Griffith story gripped my heart at a moment when I was taking a major new turn in my own development.

At the time the article appeared, I was the executive editor of the *Oakland Tribune,* a successful senior journalist whose gayness was known to his staff. I had come out to them, and to my family and friends, several years earlier, after a lifetime of subterfuge and lying to protect my personal and professional "image." I was comfortable being out as a gay man but, as a journalist, had no intention of ever being involved as a gay activist, beyond going to gay pride parades as an observer.

In the spring of 1989 the American Society of Newspaper Editors, the professional association of the newspaper industry, decided for the first time ever to survey gay and lesbian journalists on their attitudes toward workplace conditions and news coverage of gay issues. ASNE's executive director, Lee Stinnett, asked me if I would coordinate the study.

I agreed with some trepidation, sensing that being the author of such a national study would somehow change my life. And it did. In April 1990 I presented the results of the survey to hundreds of peer editors, and in the course of my presentation outed myself to a national audience. I remember vividly that, when I said, "As an editor and a gay man, I am proud of ASNE for doing this survey," a second sentence ran in my mind as a subtext: "Here I am, world, all of me, at last!"

Stories ran in the major newspapers and magazines: "News Executive Comes Out as Gay." I became a magnet for the aspirations of hundreds of gay and lesbian journalists, most of them closeted, urging me to form a support organization. I did so, creating in the summer of 1990 the National Lesbian and Gay Journalists Association, a pretty pretentious name for a group with six members. But the moment was right. Within months, hundreds of mainstream journalists from all over the country had joined. The gay story was catching the public wave, and with it came the willingness of gay and lesbian journalists to stand up and be heard. NLGJA thrived, capturing the attention of mainstream news organizations and ultimately affecting how gays are portrayed in the national and local press.

I felt a new and heightened sense of integration, a coming together of my professional and personal lives beyond anything I'd experienced. I could still be a journalist, yet also be *for* something without giving up my professional integrity. I could influence change on behalf of my fellow gays, yet remain consistent with the tenets of good journalism.

Meanwhile, the *Tribune* had run into severe economic trouble. I made the momentous decision to leave newspapers after thirty-three years and devote my time to NLGJA and to my lifelong dream of being a "serious" writer.

But a writer needs a subject. In mid-1991, the *Advocate,* a national gay newsmagazine, ran an item on Mary Griffith. Josh Boneh, my life partner, saw it and said, "Why not write about her? It's a great story. It fits the direction you're going in. And she lives right here in Walnut Creek [a town a few miles from Oakland]."

Of course! Josh's reminder brought back the story with all its emotional charge. I scrambled for my saved copy of the *Examiner* article, phoned Lily Eng to get the Griffith telephone number, and soon was on my way to Walnut Creek.

Mary and I hit it off. Though she was initially shy, I immediately sensed strength and determination. She had wanted to write a book, but hadn't gotten anywhere with it herself. I asked what she hoped such a book would accomplish.

"I'd like to give kids enough courage to continue their lives," she said, "until they come to that point where they are able to accept factual information about their sexual identity."

Mary spoke calmly, but with a current of urgency. She also wanted to reach parents, teachers, the churches—all of the targets she already had in her sights regionally. A book could accomplish that on a national level.

We began a series of detailed interviews over many months. It became clear that Mary had another reason in mind for the book. Nearly a decade after Bobby's death, she still carried a burden of guilt for her role in the tragedy. Laying it out in a book for the world to witness would be an act of expiation.

Mary was hard on herself. She seemed to relish telling stories about dumb or thoughtless acts she committed regarding Bobby. She told them with the zeal of a convert. As she said, she was amazed at her stupidity.

But as I got to know her, and the rest of the Griffith family—Mary's husband, Bob; her son Ed; and Ed's sisters, Nancy and Joy—I came to realize that this was a story not of brute rejection, but of ignorance. The surviving Griffiths love one another with an intensity that few families can match. It became clear to me they had loved Bobby with that same magnitude, and he them.

Most gay suicides occur among youngsters who were disowned by their families—cast out and cut off. One of the ironies of this story is that the Griffiths acted from love. What they lacked was information and comprehension, and any knowledge of how to go about getting them. What they relied upon was the limited vocabulary of response they had available to them. It was as if they lived in a sealed bubble, unable to grasp the consequences of their actions. The events unfolded as they did with a tragic inevitability.

Through his diaries and his family, friends, and coworkers, I came to know Bobby as well as it is possible to know someone who is no longer living. He was a tender soul from the beginning, vulnerable to slights, eager to please, shy. At the same time he had a vibrant life force, reflected in his open, smiling map-of-America face. He took pleasure in nature, in things artistic, in comic hyperbole, and most tellingly in his writing, which for someone so young had elements of eloquence and promise.

The contortion of that promise, that life, which I traced exhaustively, was all the more painful in the context of what should have been a supportive and loving environment. The internal family psychosis that often clicks in when homosexuality is a factor is one of the cautionary themes of this book.

As I dug deeper, another subtext asserted itself. What I was discovering was more than the story of Mary's overcoming prejudice; it was also the story of her liberation as a thinking, adult woman, at age fifty. Mary had grown up with a deep-seated insecurity, clinging to the approval from her husband, her mother, and her church. The awful impact of Bobby's death undermined all of her old assumptions. She had to start over. In re-creating herself, she not only found justification for Bobby's life (and death) but learned to value herself.

In working with Mary and developing the story, I came to think of the scene from *The Miracle Worker* in which the young Helen Keller has a furious temper tantrum, spilling a water pitcher at the supper table. Her teacher, Annie, ignoring the pleas of Helen's parents, drags her roughly to the courtyard and forces her to refill the pitcher from the pump, at the same time repeating over and over the hand signal for *water* in Helen's palm.

Suddenly, after months of drilling and helpless noncomprehension, Helen gets it. Water! That's how you say *water!* Things have words attached to them, and words are the way out of the tunnel. Helen is spontaneously transformed—a seeing, hearing, talking butterfly soaring from the chrysalis. It is a moment of supreme grace.

That moment, the triumph of the human spirit, lives for me in this story. It is not merely about gays, or religion, or suicide, although it is about all of those things. It is about family, about redemption. But, in the end, it is about a victory of the human spirit that transcended tragedy. That, I realized, is what I always wanted to write about.

Leroy Aarons

The Plunge

AUGUST 27, 1983
PORTLAND, OREGON

Bobby Griffith left the Family Zoo lounge about midnight and walked northwest through downtown Portland, past office buildings and lofts that still bore the ornate imprint of another century. It was a warm but cloudy western night in late August 1983. Blond, green eyed, six feet tall, and muscular, he wore a light plaid shirt and green fatigue pants, and walked with a deliberate, loping gait. To a passerby he would have looked like any other young man on his way home after a night out.

He headed up a hill and onto a plateau through which sliced Interstate 405, the main north-south artery. From this vantage point one could see most of the city, aligned on either side of the Willamette River. Lights flickered in the foreground, yielding to patches of darkened residential neighborhoods where most of Portland slept. The steady roar of freeway traffic played counterpoint to the still night.

Bobby approached the Everett Street overpass. Once on the bridge he could see the 405 traffic rush by, then disappear beneath the concrete span. The fragrance of diesel and petroleum hung in the air.

What was he thinking? Perhaps he voiced the silent wish, often repeated in his journals, to lift off, set sail to the heavens, forever drifting. Perhaps the familiar dark depression engulfed him, strangling hope.

"My life is over as far as I'm concerned," he wrote in his diary exactly one month before. "I hate living on this earth. . . . I think God must get a certain amount of self-satisfaction watching people deal with the obstacles he throws in their path. . . . I hate God for this and for my shitty existence."

He must have seen the large tractor trailer approaching from under the Couch Street overpass and timed the jump. Bobby executed a sudden and effortless back flip and disappeared over the railing. The driver tried to swerve, but there was no time.

Two witnesses later reported they at first thought it was a prank. They rushed to the railing expecting to see Bobby dangling. No. He had descended twenty-five feet directly into the path of the trailer, which tossed his body fourteen feet under the overpass.

The impact had ripped away most of his clothes and strewn them on the highway. Beneath his body paramedics found a two-dollar bill and seventy-seven cents in change.

The medical examiner said later that Robert Warren Griffith, age twenty years and two months, had died instantly of massive internal injuries.

TWO

"What Went Wrong?"

Bob and Mary Griffith's stucco-surfaced wood-frame house is part of a 1940s tract, built in the sleepy days when Walnut Creek had both walnuts and a free-flowing creek. The northern California town had graduated from a bucolic suburb to a flourishing nexus of service businesses and clean industry. Just twenty miles east of San Francisco, Walnut Creek had the conveniences of a bedroom community with the gloss of an increasingly sophisticated and congested city.

Still, there remained quiet streets and charming neighborhoods. Except for a disquieting rise in traffic fed by a massive freeway a few blocks away, Rudgear Road was that kind of street. Mary and Bob and three of their four children enjoyed what appeared to be an idyllic life in their compact three-bedroom ranch-style home with a swimming pool out back.

The night of August 26–27, 1983, Mary Griffith, forty-eight, sat up late sewing in her kitchen. Her neatly styled brown hair had begun to assume gray highlights, but she was still slim, in scale with her five-foot, three-inch frame. She had a pleasant but ordinary face with a rather blunt nose and soft hazel eyes hidden behind oversize clear-frame glasses. When she spoke, her speech had a faint midwestern cast, although she had been brought up in Florida and California.

Favorite pictures of her four kids adorned a buffet in one corner of the living room: Joy, the oldest, now twenty-two, large boned and serious; Ed, twenty-one, square jawed and muscular; Nancy, the baby, age thirteen; and Bobby, a tousle-haired Tom Sawyer.

She sewed and chain-smoked Carleton menthols, surrounded by familiar icons of her faith. Next to the telephone was a crammed wooden box of index cards inscribed with Mary's favorite Bible verses. On the kitchen wall hung a ceramic cross with a little child nestled asleep on the horizontal bar. On the table was another cross, of wood, and a bookstand supporting Mary's weathered and dog-eared personal Bible.

Bob was asleep in the bedroom. Joy, Nancy, and Ed were out tripping around in Joy's old truck. Mary loved these rare moments of solitude, feeling safe in an ordered universe in which the rules and regulations had all been codified two thousand years before and bequeathed to humanity for all time. It was like living in a giant compound guarded by angels: the world was an alien and dangerous place, but if you had faith and played by the rules, you and your loved ones were okay.

Her home reflected the warm simplicity and unpretentiousness of a blue-collar family that had made it to the suburbs: reproduction prints on the walls, doilied tables, family pictures on the refrigerator; in the kitchen, white walls and pink cupboards. Bob, an electrician and a proficient carpenter, had built the kitchen table of plywood and tile and trimmed it in mahogany stain. Behind the house, in a large, cluttered backyard, was a "doughboy" pool—in effect, an oval-shaped ground-level tank of water.

The one jarring note in Mary's life was the constant nagging worry about Bobby. Since that day more than four years earlier when he acknowledged to them that he was gay, Mary had rarely known a moment free from anxiety. The Bible repeatedly warned that homosexuality is a mortal sin; clearly gay people were doomed to perdition. If Bobby did not repent and change, there would be no reunion in heaven.

The promise of that reunion with her loved ones at the end of earthly existence was at the core of Mary's faith, the deal she was willing to make with God. Without the prospect of rejoining her family in some celestial paradise, life would have little meaning.

Mary couldn't help feeling frustrated. Bobby seemed to be getting more and more miserable. She had prayed and badgered him relentlessly, but nothing was happening. She would often ask, "I've been praying for four years for Bobby. The change, the healing, Lord, when is it going to happen?" Then, with the knowledge that the deity does not reward impatience, Mary would add, "Not my will, but thine be done."

She yawned and looked at the clock. It was half past midnight, and the next morning—Saturday—was a workday for her. She rose to go to the sink for a glass of water. As she walked back to the table, an odd thing happened: something flicked inside her, like a light switching off. For an instant a cold blackness whooshed through her, darkening her spirit. Then it passed.

"Lord, what does *that* mean?" she wondered.

Mary shrugged it off and readied herself for bed, joining Bob in the back bedroom, which he had added to the house a couple of years before.

She uttered a silent prayer, the same one she'd been saying for years: "Dear Lord, bless my husband and children. Hold them safely in thy merciful hand."

. . .

Joy Griffith was driving her '82 Dodge Ram D50 pickup down Bollingen Canyon Road with brother Ed beside her, and Nancy and her girlfriend Wesley in the open part of the truck.

This was what passed for recreation on a Friday night in the suburbs.

The blowing wind swept away a pair of sunglasses plunked in Nancy's hair. Joy pulled to a stop, and Nancy got out to search for them. At that moment, inexplicably, Joy thought of Bobby. The thought provoked a deadening fear, as if someone had told her she had cancer, as if a tumor had been growing inside her without her knowledge. Nancy found her glasses and they went on.

· · ·

It was Joy who picked up the receiver of the ringing phone on the wall in the kitchen the next morning. Nancy and Wesley were waiting impatiently outside. Joy had promised to drive them to Santa Cruz for a day of fun on the boardwalk. Her cousin Debbie was on the phone from Portland.

"I have something terrible to tell you," Debbie said.

"What? Is everybody okay?"

"Bobby jumped off a bridge."

"What?"

Nancy and Wesley began to walk back into the house from the backyard. Joy, fighting for self-control, said, "Nancy, get out. Go back in the backyard."

Joy turned back to the phone, hysteria rising.

"Who found him?" she asked Debbie, thinking he had jumped off a railroad trestle or something.

"Joy, it's okay. It's okay."

"He's okay?" Joy almost shouted.

"Joy, do you know what I'm telling you?"

Joy said, "Bobby's dead."

"Yes," Debbie said.

Joy began to wail involuntarily. "Oh my God! He jumped off a bridge! Daddy, come here quick!"

Bob Griffith grabbed the phone. He seemed to take the news calmly, asking for details. Then, suddenly, he let the phone drop from his hands and walked away. Reflexively, he denied the reality, trying to push it back. Underneath was the beginning of a giant maw of pain.

Joy drove the short distance to I. Magnin in downtown Walnut Creek, where her mom worked as a shipping clerk. It was a gorgeous California summer day. At the employees' entrance she numbly asked the attendant to summon Mary. "And please tell her to bring her purse," Joy added. She crouched in a corner to wait, curling herself into a ball of grief.

Upstairs, Mary got the call and assumed the kids were out of gas and needed money. When she came down and saw Joy slumped in the corner on the other side of the glass partition, a rush of fear gripped her.

"What's wrong?"

Joy blurted, "Bobby's dead! He jumped off a bridge."

Mary tried to push through the glass employees' door, forgetting it was locked. She scrambled for the buzzer, but the attendant didn't seem to hear it. Mary banged frantically on the partition.

"My son is dead! Let me out!"

The attendant released the latch.

· · · ·

On the short drive home in her truck, Joy told Mary what she knew. Mary listened and understood the words, but they did not yet connect with her emotions.

At the house, Mary and Bob embraced, weeping. "It was God's will at work," Mary heard herself intoning. She had done everything by the book—capital *B*. The prayers, the Christian counselor, the admonitions. Four long years.

After dropping Mary off at home, an already exhausted Joy drove south thirty miles to California State University at

Hayward, where Ed was at football practice. When she drove up, Ed was standing in his uniform on the sideline.

"What's wrong?" he asked. Joy couldn't speak through her sobs. Ed kept repeating, "What? What?"

Finally, Joy got her voice. "It's Bobby," she said. "He jumped from a bridge. Eddie, he's dead!"

Ed stiffened, blood draining from his face. Abruptly, he picked up his equipment from the bench and broke into a wild run, heading nowhere, just zigzagging across the field. He yanked off his helmet and kicked it. In the car, Joy followed along the running track that circled the field. She reached him and jumped out, yelling, "Eddie, please, stop. We've got to go home!" Ed slowed to let Joy catch up with him. They clung to one another. "What happened?" Ed sobbed. "I'll tell you all about it in the truck," Joy said.

Ed headed for the locker room to change. His head was pounding so hard he thought it would burst. He went to a sink and threw cold water in his face. Numbly, he dressed. Then, in a burst of pain and fury, he punched a locker and stormed out without storing his gear.

. . . .

Ed couldn't face going home. He asked Joy to drop him at the home of one of the church counselors from Walnut Creek Presbyterian, where Ed was a devout congregant. Some other kids from the church came over, and Ed started downing shots of Scotch. He was not a drinker. The others urged him to slow down, but he got roaring drunk and bawled for several hours.

He and Bobby, the two boys of the Griffith family, had a special closeness, although they couldn't have been more different. Ed the athlete, built like a truck, always playing soldier, dreaming of being a professional baseball player. Bobby, slender, not into competitive games, artistic, as a kid interested in dolls and drawing and dressing up.

Yet there was a deep bond. As youngsters Ed and Bobby had bunk beds, but every once in a while they would crawl in together and sleep, one brother curled in the other's arms like a cup in a saucer. It was to Ed that Bobby had first confided he was gay.

Lately, they had drifted apart. Bobby withdrew, set up his own room, hid out in it, and brooded a lot. Ed knew his brother was unhappy, and it troubled him. But he figured Bobby would grow out of it. He never dreamed . . .

Their last parting, when Bobby had come down for a short visit from Portland, was unusually painful. Ordinarily they separated with a bear hug. This time Bobby merely put out his hand for a shake.

For now he tried to forget it all with booze. The next morning he awoke at the counselor's house with a big hangover and finally went home.

. . .

By Saturday afternoon, Mary had worked up the courage to call her parents. She prayed that Porter would answer the phone. Her mother and father knew nothing of Bobby's gayness, which until now was the nuclear family's deep, dark secret. She had only recently confided in Porter, her younger brother, a bachelor who still lived with their parents. Almost fifty, Mary still feared Ophelia Harrison's tart tongue almost as much as she desired her approval. Porter did answer, and Mary told him what had happened. "Porter, I truly believe Bobby killed himself because he felt guilty about his homosexuality."

Something had backfired. God was supposed to heal Bobby. She had seen so many success stories on the religious channel about gay people being healed by prayer. Lord knows Bobby had prayed. She had prayed. What went wrong?

The rest of that week was like navigating through a fog. There were a million details to attend to. Family members converged and took on the mundane tasks of keeping the household going. Mary, who was finding it difficult to get motivated, even to eat, was grateful. Besides, she found the chaos and confusion a blessed distraction.

But several things absolutely had to be settled. One was the question of the details of Bobby's death. Did he jump? Did he fall? Mary called the medical examiner to confirm that Bobby was neither drunk nor on drugs. There seemed to be no question that Bobby had made a conscious decision. Bobby had killed himself.

Funeral arrangements had to be made. She and Bob had no previous experience; there hadn't been a death in the family in twenty years. They didn't even have suitable clothes for a funeral.

Mary pulled from the yellow pages the name of Oakmont Memorial Cemetery, in nearby Lafayette. One of the employees there agreed to drive to Portland to bring Bobby's body back. The funeral was scheduled for Friday afternoon, September 2.

They went to a local department store, Bob to pick out a white shirt, and Mary a dress, for the funeral.

On Wednesday Mary and Bob went to Oakmont, a beautiful site in the rolling hills above the small town of Lafayette, to choose a marker for Bobby's grave.

They picked out a coffin and the marker, a bronze plate with a relief of a placid lake surrounded by mountains. They chose the Garden of Peace area for the grave site. It was on a hill, overlooking the valley and surrounded by a neatly kept lawn. That's what he had wanted through all of this, Mary thought— a little peace.

The attendant asked if they wanted an open or closed coffin. Considering the force of the blow, he said, Bobby looked "pretty good."

"No," said Mary. "I don't want to remember my son that way." She thought with a start that she would never see Bobby to say good-bye. And yet the surreal anticipation that he would walk in at any moment haunted her all week. One night in the kitchen she was changing the bag in the trash can and felt—knew—that Bobby would come through the back door.

On Thursday, Mary's nieces Jeanette and Debbie arrived from Portland in Debbie's '73 Nova rattletrap. The Nova's narrow trunk held Bobby's few personal effects. Mary rushed out to peer into the trunk. She felt like grabbing everything in her arms and hugging it. There wasn't much there—some clothes, letters, gym workout gloves. But it was all of Bobby she had left.

The treasure of the lot was Bobby's diaries. There were four books, the first two in spiral binders, the final two hardcover journals. Years before, Mary had stolen a few glimpses of early entries when Bobby had left the diary lying around. But this trove of two hundred pages of Bobby's most intimate musings now offered both a way to commune with her dead child and a passport to his inner life. She would wait for the right moment to read them.

• • •

The funeral service was at Walnut Creek Presbyterian Church, where the Griffiths (except for Bob) had worshiped for fourteen years. Mary and Joy taught Sunday school. Bobby and Ed had been involved in youth programs. To Mary, still numb with disbelief, the once safe, familiar space seemed alien.

The chapel was crowded. In addition to family, there were Bobby's friends from school, relatives, and even some of Bobby's gay friends. One or two came up and shook Mary's hand.

To Jeanette the room seemed drenched in tears. She had never seen so much emotion in one place. Everyone cried. When not weeping, they seemed to her in shock, in a trance. Nothing hurt like the loss of a young person, she thought.

A young minister, Dave Daubenspeck, who was friendly with Ed and knew Bobby slightly, gave the eulogy. He took the orthodox Presbyterian position that holds homosexuality to be a sin: out of deep frustration—disillusioned, yet feeling trapped in the gay lifestyle—Bobby had chosen to end his life. The good news was that Bobby had accepted Christ, and despite the sins of homosexuality and suicide, nothing can separate the true Christian from the love of God. Therefore, Bobby's place in heaven was secure. . . .

The choir sang the "Hallelujah" chorus and it was over. The pallbearers, including Ed and Mary's brother, Warren, gently and solemnly did their task.

At the cemetery, Jeanette watched one of the mourners throw a shovelful of dirt on Bobby's coffin. She heard the earth hit the coffin, and a vein of grief opened. She found herself crying hysterically.

. . .

There was a small reception afterward at the home of Mary's sister Noma, in nearby Concord. Mary wept almost continuously. Her mother, Ophelia, remarked testily how she couldn't fathom the flow of tears from her daughter, who was after all a staunch Christian who believed in salvation. Noma tried to leap to the rescue. "Her son killed himself!" she said sharply. It seemed that whatever Mary did, Mom would find something to criticize.

But Mary herself hadn't realized how much the loss would hurt. You die and you go to heaven; that's the glory of being a Christian. At least that's what they teach you. They don't teach you about grief.

One of her Bible verses kept repeating itself in Mary's head like a mantra. It was from the book of Revelation, the book of the apocalypse: "He that overcometh . . . shall be clothed in white raiment; and will not blot out his name in the book of life."

The way she read that verse, it meant that the sinner who repents is promised eternal life. He who does not "overcome," who dies unrepentant, must be destined for hell. Revelation seemed to contradict what Daubenspeck had said.

This frightened her. Bobby died without repenting. If he was condemned, he was in hell for certain.

. . .

Back home that evening, Mary asked Bob, "Do you think Bobby made it to heaven?" Bob shunned religion. He had resisted all her efforts to get him baptized. True to style, he answered simply, "He's not *here*."

Mary shuddered, her voice rising. "According to the Bible, Bobby's in hell. I'm never going to see him again. Never, never, never!"

She sat up late, turning the question over in her mind. Why would God allow her son to go to hell if it was in God's power to cure him?

. . .

Days later, Mary turned to the diaries. She sat through the night, reading them page by page. Bobby had begun writing in January 1979, when he was fifteen. He wrote through 1979, for some reason skipped 1980 except for a single entry, and continued up to two weeks before his death. The entries varied from consecutive to sporadic, sometimes jumping several months.

Mary quickly discovered that another Bobby—one far more scarred than she knew—lived in the diaries. The entries dripped with self-hatred. Bobby's revulsion toward his gay nature was a constant refrain.

She read:

I am evil and wicked. I want to spit vulgarities at everyone I see. I am dirt, harmful bacteria grows inside me. . . . I was innocent, trusting, loving. The world has raped me till my insides are shredding and bleeding. My voice is small and unheard, unnoticed. Damned.

Mary had known that her son was deeply unhappy. But the diaries revealed that for Bobby each day, no matter how routine, was a Sisyphean struggle.

Gentle springtime weather surrounds me, but a fierce unrelenting storm rages within. . . . How much longer? How much more can I take? Only time and a million tears of bitterness. . . . I wish I could crawl under a rock and sleep for the rest of time.

From childhood, Bobby had embraced the faith of his mother. He had been going to Sunday school for years, when, at age ten, he came to her and said, "Mom, I want to accept Christ in my life." Mary took him to be baptized. Bobby's belief in God and God's immutable word as revealed in the Bible had all the innocence and conviction of one whose faith is shaped early in life. This showed in his diaries. But Mary was shocked by the dark, violent blasphemies also present.

"Sometimes I feel so guilty about my feelings," Bobby wrote in one entry. "Am I going to hell? That's the gnawing question that's always drilling little holes in the back of my mind. Please don't send me to hell. . . . Lord I want to be good . . . I need your seal of approval."

But that mood could change mercurially: "Fuck you God! If it's not one damn thing it's something else and a person can only take so much."

Near dawn, red eyed and exhausted, Mary approached the final passages. Closing the pages, she thought of Bobby on his last visit home, just a few weeks earlier, at the end of July. He had never before seemed so blue, so lethargic. A vision haunted her of the preadolescent happy-go-lucky Bobby of the wide grin and untroubled face.

It had been a good time, and Mary had believed those times would return. Now . . . my God, such misery. Dear Lord, did he deserve that? And what was her role in it?

THREE

Fire and Brimstone

Mary Alma Harrison arrived on October 13, 1934, at Colon Hospital in the Panama Canal Zone, the fourth child and third daughter of Ophelia Harrison and Naval Air Machinist First Class Alvin Edward Harrison. She was not a comely baby. When the nurse handed the squinchy, slippery five-pound infant to her mother, Ophelia had a hard time grabbing on.

Mary was to spend a good part of her life trying to get her mother to do just that—grab on. She felt not so much unloved as ignored. There eventually were seven children, all of them scrambling for attention from a mother who seemed more interested in the social whirl of navy wives than in nurturing her young brood. For Mary, childhood was an exercise in finding ways to stay out of the way.

Ophelia, not given to stroking, ruled with an iron hand. There were few hugs and kisses to go around. On the other hand, father Alvin, when he was around, offered warmth, affection, and fun, acting as a buffer between the kids and Mom. He didn't talk much, but he made the children feel cared about. Once, when they lived in Jacksonville, there was a rare heavy frost. Alvin drew pictures on the window of the bedroom Mary shared with her younger sister, Gail, and told the children Jack

Frost had come for a visit. Mary believed every word of it and was enthralled.

Ophelia Ambria Casey had met her future husband at a dance in Pensacola, Florida, when she was just thirteen. Her father, a railroad worker, chaperoned them on dates, until they were married in 1924. Ophelia was fifteen, and Alvin, a young seaman, was twenty-two. Ophelia had been a willful child, pampered by parents who grieved the loss of an earlier daughter who had died of pneumonia at eighteen months.

She was little more than a child when she married. Two of her seven children arrived before she was twenty. She greeted motherhood with the mixed feelings of a young girl who loved her children, was intensely loyal to them, but resented the responsibility they entailed. She could be biting and cruel—a lifelong habit that prompted some of her grandchildren later to dub her, half-affectionately, "Wicked Badass Granny."

To Mary, a sensitive, introverted girl, life meant keeping from underfoot. Yearning for affection, she settled for lying low —anything to escape the maternal barbs. Mary had buck teeth; she was gawky and a slow developer. By first grade she still could not print her name. Ophelia reserved one of her most hurtful terms for her daughter: she called her "lamebrain" far into adulthood.

Mary contrived to avert conflict, spending a lot of time feeling fearful or guilty. She longed for a safe space. She felt dumb. Every day, before getting out of bed, she prayed that she would be able to get through the day without doing something to displease her mother.

Her closest friend was her sister Jean, six years her senior. Mary could confide in Jean, who shared the same feelings of neglect at home. In school, Jean was encouraged because of her unusual singing voice. Once, a teacher sent a note home urging that Jean's talent be nurtured. Ophelia set the note down, and that was the end of it. Jean, also an introverted child, never brought the subject up, but it lingered as a bitter memory throughout her life.

The navy family moved around a lot during Mary's earliest years, from Panama to Jacksonville to Pensacola. They settled finally in Oakland, California, in 1941 just before America joined the war. Alvin Harrison, by then promoted to commissioned officer, was assigned a desk job at the naval air station.

The Harrisons were churchgoers. They drifted between Catholic, Baptist, and Methodist congregations. Ophelia in particular subscribed to the wrath-and-vengeance school of religion. The children learned that God was to be feared. You did what God said or risked being punished. You could burn in hell.

Whatever else he was, God was a handy instrument of control. Ophelia employed the deity as a partner in disciplining her large brood. Once, when Mary was about five, she was allowed to go to the base movie house with her siblings to see *The Wizard of Oz*. Ophelia warned her in advance, "Just sit there and do not get up, because I can see you, and God can see you. Understand?" Mary did, and believed as well.

In that environment, God and Mama merged in Mary's mind as twin keepers of a stern domain pocked with unpredictable hazards—on earth as well as in heaven. The church told her that all of us are born with a sinful nature. Damnation is a living reality for those who do not reconcile themselves with God. In that domain, Satan was a constant living presence. It was a struggle to stay within the narrow safety zone. Mary once dreamed of a God with a giant hand coming to get her. She hid behind a rock, to no avail. God found her.

The hymns she learned in church, with their beautiful melodies and emotional lyrics, were earthy and alive, filled with vital images that spoke to her.

> *When we walk with the Lord,*
> *In the Light of His Word,*

what a glory he sheds on our way!
While we do His good will,
He abides with us still,
And with all who will trust and obey.

Trust and obey for there's no other way
To be happy in Jesus, but to trust and obey.

God represented danger, but also safety. This was a contradiction that would influence much of her life, layering it more with guilt and worry than with peace. It would dictate her response when her own son's crisis erupted.

. . .

When Mary was ten, Alvin, now a commissioned officer, went to sea and was gone much of the time for the next two years. Mary felt further exposed and more lonely than ever. At Christmas, Ophelia gave the kids the kind of gifts that would keep the children distracted and out of the way. She seemed to favor the boys: Warren, the eldest, and, born years later, Porter and Charles. The girls, especially Jean and Mary, had a harder time, it seemed to Mary.

In school, at Jefferson Elementary in Oakland, Mary felt like the ugly duckling. The other girls all seemed prettier, got good grades, and wore nice clothes. The Harrisons weren't poor—Ophelia worked to augment her husband's salary—just not sensitive to matters of style and peer competition.

Adolescence brought more trauma. When Mary started to menstruate, Ophelia seemed as upset as she was about it. "You'll start to bleed," her mother had warned her, "and if you mess with boys your belly will swell up." Sex seemed dangerous and vulgar, something you didn't talk about. Ophelia would tell her girls that a boy's kiss on the cheek could get them pregnant. Mary dreaded growing breasts; they would stick out and make her conspicuous.

She was conspicuous anyway. While other girls were setting their hair and snaring boyfriends, Mary continued to wear pigtails to age thirteen. By her teens she weighed 150 pounds and wore a coat in class to hide her bulk. This made her no less boy conscious. She obsessed over boys without fully understanding what it meant. While she envied the other girls their boyfriends, she harbored romance-magazine fantasies of meeting an older man, marrying, greeting him at the door at the end of the day . . .

She made a few friends and was allowed once to go to a pajama party, and, at fourteen, on her first date, to the movies with a boy named Louis. He kissed her a couple of times. But after the show he told her he was going to a party "where you can't take nice girls." Mary walked home alone.

For all her indifference day to day, Ophelia was possessive and fearful for her children. The world was a dangerous place. As they matured, she struggled to rein them in.

Mary as a teenager fought for a measure of independence. Her desperate quest for security obscured a strong inner will that in other circumstances would have produced a powerfully self-motivated person. That strength would show up later in tragic circumstances, but it surfaced as a streak of rebelliousness in her teens.

At sixteen, while a student at Oakland's Fremont High School, she befriended a girl named Gail, who traveled with a racy crowd. It was the postwar era, and the area was flooded with returned veterans with sophisticated ideas on how to party. As naive and impressionable as she was lonely and eager for adventure, Mary followed Gail's lead, and the pair secretly took to hanging out at bars. That didn't last long: Gail's mother discovered it and reported one of the bar owners to the authorities for serving underage kids. One day, Mary returned home from school to find state officials waiting in the living room to question her. Terrified, she confessed and was required to go with Gail to identify the waitress and owner. Once fingered, the bar owner called the frightened girls "bitches." That struck an arrow in Mary's fragile ego; she felt humiliated, and sorry to have caused so much trouble.

On another occasion, at a party Gail took her to, Mary got sick after mixing beer and whiskey drinks. She went into a bedroom to lie down. Suddenly the door opened and a man entered, leering at Mary. Gail came to the rescue. "She doesn't do that," she told the man. Someone volunteered to drive Mary home. The next day the *Oakland Tribune* ran a front-page story about a raid on a party in which the proprietress was arrested for prostitution. To Mary's horror, it was the same house, and the raid had occurred fifteen minutes after she left.

Matters deteriorated further when Mary got invited to a "tea" party, the kind that featured heroin and marijuana. Naively, Mary thought the objects people were smoking were regular cigarettes, and accepted a couple as a gift from a young man who was kind enough to drive her home. When she told her mother about it the next day, the horrified Ophelia phoned the Oakland drug squad. A day later, Mary was downtown talking to the FBI. It turned out, again to her horror, that the man who threw the party had a long police record. The authorities asked Mary to serve as a police plant at another dope party, but then failed to follow up.

She had stumbled into these situations ingenuously and out of loneliness and a desire to be anyplace but home. Ironically, while at the parties she wished she had been home, safe from the crowd she found herself among. Such events were not her style.

Things would have been far worse had Ophelia known that Mary had been intimate with a boy she'd met through a coworker while working after school at a grocery store. For Mary it was a nerve-racking and unpleasurable first experience.

Mary's view of sex and intimacy was influenced by her mother. During Mary's early adolescent years, Ophelia became obsessed with the idea that Alvin was cheating on her. With

Alvin at sea or, later, at work, she would grouse about her suspicions within earshot of the children. Mary could not tell whether her mother had evidence, or even whether the issue was ever discussed between her parents. She only knew that Ophelia was deeply embittered about it.

In later years Mary would speculate that this had been the source of Ophelia's dissatisfaction and sour attitude. Perhaps there had been an early affair, or an imagined one. There was never talk of divorce. The couple lived together for sixty-two years, until Alvin's death in 1986.

But Ophelia's suspiciousness had a profound impact on her impressionable daughter. Her mother communicated that it was in the nature of men to stray and the fate of women to suffer it. In fact, the message Mary got was that if a man strayed it was somehow the woman's fault. All this dug into Mary's psyche, and would later reverberate in her own life and marriage.

Mary's adolescence seemed to her like an uncharted voyage with no one at the helm. Things happened *to* her, it seemed, rather than the other way around. She didn't know where she fit in. Timid, sexually repressed, feeling unattractive, she blamed her sinful nature for leading her into trouble: not getting along at home, the occasional excessive drinking, the sex. She believed that everything that went wrong came from not being right with God. She desperately needed an anchor.

Mary's first meeting with her future husband had the makings of an Archie Andrews comic mixup. It was a double date concocted by Mary's friend Barbara. Mary was to be matched with John, Barbara's most recent ex-boyfriend. Barbara was to meet Bob Griffith, John's buddy. But Bob's impression was that he was to match up with Mary. They all converged at a bowling alley and piled into Bob's car for some illicit beer drinking in the Oakland hills. Barbara ended up in the front with Bob, Mary in the back with John.

It soon became apparent that the boys were primed for some heavy petting. Mary was not at all interested in John, and

Barbara was proving resistant up front. John persuaded his ex-love Barbara to switch, and Mary found herself in front with a passionate and persuasive Bob. She resisted him, but her lips hurt for a week from his ardent kisses.

Bob showed up at her doorstep the next night, and the night after. They began dating intensely. To Mary, Bob seemed worldly, yet kindly and considerate. She felt safe with him, in spite of his passionate advances.

. . .

If Mary's childhood had been less than idyllic, it was heaven compared with Bob's. He was the son of a blue-collar worker, Robert Sr., and Blanche, a frail, quiet young woman. At the age of nineteen, six months after giving birth to Bob, Blanche Griffith died of an internal infection caused by remnants of the after-birth, which a careless doctor had failed to remove. (For years Bob had the vague sense that he was somehow responsible for his mother's demise.) Her death left Bob at the mercy of his hot-tempered father. Robert Griffith was a lout, subject to bouts of unpredictable anger and violence. Bob learned to anticipate beatings regularly and for no logical reason. At least once his father locked him in a closet for hours. Robert Sr. had even once knocked his infant son out of a high chair in a burst of anger.

Bob feared and hated his father. Robert would disappear for long periods, leaving his son with his maternal grandparents, who treated him well but without much warmth. But Robert would turn up regularly, continuing to terrorize his young son, who anticipated these arrivals with purest dread. Miserable, with no one to confide in, Bob turned inward. He learned to think through his own problems, and to choose solutions with a minimum of communication. He read a lot, skipping school and dropping out in the tenth grade. He turned a defensive shield to the world, telegraphing a shy, taciturn nature. Inside, strong opinions and emotions boiled.

Hungry for emotional bonding, he turned to the streets of his rough neighborhood in Oakland and a mixed-race crowd of friends who lived on the edge. To overcome a legacy of physical fear Bob flung himself into street brawling and other more dangerous peer rituals. One day the gang decided to burglarize the store of a Chinese merchant who dealt numbers, hoping for a big haul. They were immediately caught, and Bob was packed off to reform school for a year.

He emerged determined never to foul his life that way again. Soon after, he met Mary. To her, Bob seemed self-confident and courageous, things she felt she wasn't. He was mature, a man of the world, not one to be manipulated by anyone. Slender, blue eyed, with rugged good looks, Bob could thank his Scottish heritage for his air of understated charm. He was not equally stricken, but he felt at ease with Mary, and she was comfortable with him. Mary's obvious neediness and lack of self-assurance appealed to his masculine, protective side. And even though Ophelia opposed the match, Bob was at first highly impressed with the Harrisons, who, at least externally, seemed to be a large, happy, normal family—something he had never enjoyed.

Before long, Bob and Mary launched into an affair. Mary graduated from Oakland High School with barely passing grades (the only book she read through to the end was *Rebecca*) and took a twenty-dollar-a-week job as an elevator operator at Capwell's department store in Oakland. She moved from home to a rented room in a hotel in Oakland, where Bob covertly spent many nights. For Mary the romance was wildly passionate yet tinged with guilt, especially after she had accepted Christ and been baptized during a brief visit to her grandparents in Florida.

Within seven weeks of their meeting, Bob proposed. "I want to hold you forever," he said. He bought, on account, an engagement-and-wedding-ring package for four hundred dollars, the bill cosigned by Mary's mother. But they delayed marrying for nearly two years while Bob worked toward his electrician's license and they saved money.

Finally, in July 1955, they drove to Reno with Mary's sister Jean and her husband, to be married by a justice of the peace. Bob was down on religion and had resisted a church wedding. Mary had borrowed a navy blue taffeta dress from her mother and had bought a new pair of shoes. Bob had purchased a jacket, slacks, and shoes.

The ceremony, in a little office space, took about five minutes. It was not very romantic; the corsage Bob had bought her was wilted by the appointed hour. Still, the occasion was magical for Mary. The judge was friendly, and Bob's kiss was lingering and passionate. For that moment everything was right with the universe.

Mary was twenty, Bob twenty-one. Each brought to the union separate images of marriage and family. With no role models in his life, Bob had not the least concept of "man and wife" or, for that matter, "parent." His pictures came exclusively from books and movies. He was winging it. Mary, her head still filled with fears and insecurities, was determined to undo the mistakes of her own upbringing. No busy social whirl for her; no career. She would be a proper wife and mother. Her children would feel loved, welcome, and nurtured; their home would be a shelter. Together, Mary and Bob embarked on a Norman Rockwell journey in the midst of the complacent 1950s, unprepared for what lay ahead.

They settled in a one-bedroom apartment in downtown Oakland. Through an uncle, Bob had obtained a four-year apprenticeship with the electrician's union. He worked as an electrician and went to Laney Trade College. Mary continued at Capwell's. A year later, Mary conceived, but she miscarried before even realizing she was pregnant. Within another year she was pregnant again, with a girl, who came to term prematurely at seven months.

Mary was rushed to Oakland's Providence Hospital in great pain and had to be anesthetized for the delivery. Bob was at her side when she awoke, and told her that everything was fine. But a day later the infant died. Young Jennifer Ambria was given a funeral and a proper burial. The loss traumatized Mary. She brooded, stunned by a mix of pain, confusion, and guilt. Again, her mind latched on to the specter of an angry and penalizing deity. She was convinced that God was punishing her and Bob for their premarital sex.

Mary sought comfort in the church, at first at Lakeside Baptist in Oakland, confessing and praying with the minister, and later at an evangelistic missionary church in their neighborhood. Mary prayed and read the Bible, trying to pull out of her depression.

The world was indeed a dangerous place. Unable to trust her own judgment, Mary turned herself over to doctrine. She began putting little Christian icons around the house and collecting Bible verses.

Her insecurity extended to her marriage. For a long time she had difficulty calling her husband by his name, usually substituting "honey" or "sweetheart." Ophelia had drilled into her, "You don't call people by their first names." She found it difficult to be openly affectionate outside the privacy of the bedroom.

For his part, Bob was attentive and caring. But Mary focused on the empty half of the cup: "What if he doesn't really care?"; "How could he truly love someone like me?" One Christmas, Bob bought her a beautiful strand of pearls and earrings. Mary asked, "Were you drunk when you bought this?" She couldn't believe his gift was sincere. Nothing he could do would erase her self-doubt.

She began to feel intensely jealous. Yet there was nothing real to fear; Mary's anxieties arose from the depths of her own tarnished self-image. She panicked and felt inadequate if Bob seemed to pay attention to other women. Gradually, the same paranoia that obsessed her mother began to possess her: "He could find someone else. One day I'll wake up and it will be over." Such thoughts filled her with terror. In her brooding fantasies she created a phantom woman, hovering, waiting to swoop her husband away forever.

Typically, Mary shared none of this with Bob. Maybe it was all wrong, a figment of her imagination. Bob would be furious. It could endanger the entire marriage. She kept quiet, kept praying, and tried to stay alert.

Thus, externally, life was smooth. Bob got his apprenticeship and began making a good living. Their first child, Joy, arrived in 1960. Fifteen months later, Ed was born in the home they had bought for thirteen thousand dollars in Danville, a suburb east of Oakland. Mary was able to quit work and devote all her time to motherhood.

She was a dedicated, loving mother. The kids had the run of the house. Granny would come and complain that she was being too lenient, but Mary persisted. She was more sensitive to the opinions of her peers—neighborhood mothers, who urged her to wean the kids from their bottles early, or to hasten potty training.

Despite her preoccupation with motherhood, Mary's secret agony over her imaginings about Bob raged on. The obsession seemed like a thorn in her gut, which she likened to the thorn in the flesh of the apostle Paul. She prayed about it, begging God to take it away. She inscribed in the margin of a page in her Bible: "If you will not remove it, Lord, ease my thorn. It is too painful. Satan digs it deeper. I sometimes feel I will die, it hurts me so."

But God was not answering. Mary began suffering anxiety attacks accompanied by depression and a loss of energy. She felt too humiliated to tell anyone—not the counselors at the church, and certainly not her family.

Her doctor had prescribed diet pills to control weight during her pregnancy with Joy. After Joy was born, Mary found it easy to keep renewing the prescription. The drugs gave her energy, lifted her self-esteem, and made her obsession about Bob more bearable. Soon, she had to increase the dosage to get the desired effect. Without realizing it, Mary was getting hooked on amphetamines and other substances, such as painkillers. She used them increasingly over the next nine years—through the birth of her third child, Bobby, and into her final pregnancy with Nancy in 1970. All this was in secret. Once, a friendly druggist even dispensed drugs to her without requiring a prescription. Mary hid her drugs in the stove, always remembering to remove them before using it for cooking.

FOUR

The Sissy

Despite the currents running beneath the surface, daily life in the Griffith family fit the "Leave It to Beaver" image with amazing accuracy. Mary was gentle, soft-spoken, self-effacing, good-humored. Bob was a kindly if taciturn father who worked hard on the job and puttered constantly around the house in his time off. Her children remember the 1960s and early 1970s with great fondness. They felt sheltered and loved, and perceived their parents as a devoted and affectionate couple. Life was a pleasant round of school, afternoon play, church activities, and summer visits to the grandparents.

In fact, within the whole Harrison clan, Mary got the votes as the preferred relative. Her brothers and sisters were experiencing tumultuous lives. Bob and Mary's was the place to go if you wanted an oasis of sanity and stability. The family would find any excuse to turn up there. Granny and grandfather Harrison, who after his retirement had settled three hours away in Sonora, in the Sierra foothills, went down a couple of times a month. Jeanette and Debbie, Jean's daughters, who lived in nearby Lafayette, loved spending time at Aunt Mary's, playing with their Griffith cousins. With the birth of three infants in rapid succession, Mary's first years in Danville were devoted to child care. Bobby arrived fourteen months after Ed, on June 24,

1963. (Nancy came much later—in January 1970.) Mary welcomed the busyness; it distracted her from her fertile imaginings.

Religion completed the circle of Mary's neatly contoured life. She joined the local Baptist church. There was prayer meeting on Wednesdays, and both morning and evening services on Sundays. Mary also taught Sunday school, which her children attended right up through high school. At home there were prayers at dinner—as the children got old enough, they would be called on to recite—and prayers before bedtime. Mary conducted a mini–Bible study session at home each day after school, complete with a small blackboard on which to list Bible verses. Mary encouraged her kids to "plant a seed," urging Joy, the eldest and the first to go to school, to "tell the kids about Jesus."

Her view of religion was eclectic, quilted from a variety of sources including the Southern Baptist roots of her earliest church experiences, her mother's fire-and-brimstone admonitions, her own later church exposure, and the ubiquitous drone of evangelists on the religious radio station she loved to listen to. She relied solely on Christian-oriented books to guide her in child raising, and read little else.

She held certain beliefs sacrosanct: all humans are born sinners; original sin may be redeemed only through the transformative acceptance of Jesus Christ as savior, usually through baptism; the Bible is the revealed word of God and as such the unquestionable authority on pious or sinful conduct; Satan is a living presence of enormous power, capable of luring the unsuspecting victim into sin; an unrepentant sinner—which includes anyone who has not accepted Jesus Christ—faces eternal damnation. Conversely, those who accept Christ and lead godly lives will reunite with their loved ones for eternal life in Paradise.

These elements, an approximation of traditional orthodox Protestant doctrine, defined the realm within which Mary could ensure both her family's safety and its immortality. Indeed, for Mary, accepting Christ was a way of finding self-acceptance. She used the Bible and its verses—one for every occasion—as sentinels against the fearsome agents of Satan, who she knew must be contriving to infiltrate her comfortable suburban bubble.

As it was for her mother before her, religion was a weapon of control, but Mary wielded it less like a general, more like a zealous shepherd.

She was comforted by the belief that God and his guardian angels would always keep her husband and children out of harm's way. Yet a contradiction was always present: she admonished her children daily with the statement "God cannot protect you from Satan if you are disobedient."

One evening a tearful Joy, then five years old, came to her mother. "I want to be saved," the child pleaded. "I'm afraid I won't go to heaven." It was 7:30, but Mary insisted that Bob drive them to the church. Somewhere she had learned that a child was not accountable for her sins until twelve years of age, but she wasn't taking any chances. At the church, Joy accepted Jesus as her savior and was baptized by the minister.

The missing link in all this was Bob, who resisted all of Mary's efforts to get him baptized. He saw religion as based on ignorance at best, and founded on intimidation and fear. Characteristically, he tolerated it as long as it didn't interfere with his life. He watched Mary's emotional involvement with a kind of detached bemusement. He could never fathom the depths of her immersion, but he never chose to argue about it. And he never interceded when his children became involved. He reasoned that they were intelligent enough to draw their own conclusions.

Mary worried that Bob would be denied the kingdom of heaven, but, after initially making a pest of herself, she settled for subtle nudgings. (But she didn't give up. When Bob suffered a painful ulcer attack in 1980 and required an operation, she accompanied him to Kaiser Hospital's surgery prep room. As he was about to be wheeled away, Mary leaned over and asked, "Bob, do you accept Jesus Christ as your savior?" Bob shot back, "Hell, no!")

Bobby Griffith came into a world that was erupting with social change. It was 1963: the South was immersed in a fury of protest, and Buddhists were self-immolating in Vietnam. By the time Bobby was five months old, the American president had been assassinated and the age of post–World War II innocence was forever gone. The deep pools of American culture and politics were being stirred up, and discontent was rising to the surface.

None of this had an immediate impact on the Griffith enclave. Bobby's infancy and childhood had all the earmarks of an idyllic time. He was loved and valued. He was a happy child who displayed a sunny disposition and gentle manner.

Mary, the nondriver, and her three kids would walk the two miles to downtown Danville to shop; or they would walk to the dentist, Bobby in the stroller, Ed riding the back support, and Joy walking alongside. The children loved to go to Merrill's Fountain for treats. As they got older, Bob and Mary would pile them in the backseat of the station wagon on Friday nights for an evening at the drive-in theater.

Bobby was a gentle spirit, almost too good and too obedient, yet endearing and lovable. He was a skinny child, with a space between his two front teeth that brightened his whole face when he smiled. This feature, together with his sheath of blond hair, gave Bobby the look of the all-American boy.

But it didn't take much further observation to see that he was different from most other boys. He was not a cut-up, not given to roughhousing. He was content to be in the house coloring or playing with stuffed animals and dolls. Outdoors, he loved nature and paid more attention to the detail of natural settings than did any of the other boys. Once, at age three or four, he said, "Mom, when I woke up this morning I said good morning to all the trees and the forest."

It was around that time that Bobby dressed up in his sister's fluffy half-slip one day and ambled next door to a neighbor's house. There, he got into a playful scramble with the neighbor boys, kissing and hugging them. The boys' mother called Mary, perturbed by the incident. Mary felt angry, humiliated, and frightened all at once. When Bobby came home, all smiles and happy, with the slip bunched up around his neck, Mary yanked it off and remonstrated, "Don't get into your sister's things ever again."

Bobby was not like Ed, who loved his tanks and soldiers and Tonka trucks and who liked to hang out in the garage with his dad as he puttered at the workbench. Ed was assertive, at times aggressive. Bobby was quiet, even timid. He wouldn't speak up for himself as the others did. Yet he was outgoing in other ways, often racing up to strangers and hugging them.

Bobby liked being in the kitchen with Mom, or rummaging through her costume-jewelry box in the bedroom, or playing with Joy's things. Mary caught herself more than once shaping the word *sissy* in her mind, then quickly suppressing the thought. The idea of Bobby's being somebody society didn't approve of scared her, not only for Bobby's sake but also for hers. It didn't help when Granny would visit and scold Bobby for smearing on his mother's lipstick or messing with Joy's things. She warned her daughter, "Mary, if you aren't careful, this boy will turn out a sissy."

Mary strove to discourage anything feminine. Once, she bought Bobby a pretend shaver so he could shave with his dad. Before Christmas in 1968, Bobby, then five, got hold of one of Mary's Christmas catalogs. He turned to a display of beautiful dolls and asked his mother if she would get him one for Christmas.

Mary said, hastily, "Well, Bobby, I don't really have the money."

"If you had the money, would you?" Bobby insisted.

Mary tried to divert the discussion. It did not seem right to her for boys to want to have dolls. "Someday, Bobby," she said, "you'll have your own wife and you can dress her up in all these beautiful things."

She had felt squeamish enough to lie to a five-year-old. She could not have said exactly why. In her heart she had wanted to buy him the doll. But knowing Bobby, he would have wanted to take it to school. It would have been embarrassing. Worse, the other boys might have teased him. A vague sense of threat to her carefully ordered existence caused her to wish this problem away.

Big brother Ed, a second grader to Bobby's first, tried to teach Bobby how to throw and catch a ball. He never got the hang of it. "You throw like a girl," Ed would yell. Indeed, through his childhood Bobby seemed to prefer playing with girls—a behavior that led Mary to feel intimidated when a teacher reported it to her at a parent-teacher conference.

Mary fretted about Bobby through most of his childhood. Even as she admired his artistic bent, his growing proficiency in drawing and writing, she reacted with embarrassment to his girlish way of swinging the bat, the flourish of his hand as he swept his long hair from his forehead, the doll he made for her one Christmas in junior high from scraps of lace borrowed from her sewing basket.

In the early days she never equated *sissy* with *homosexual*. She simply feared difference. Others can be different—fine for them. Those hippies she was seeing on television, talking about love and peace—well, nothing wrong with that. But she shuddered to think of her kids turning out that way.

Pamela [not her real name], a nearby neighbor, was different. Uninhibited, outspoken, Pamela would regale Mary with stories about her sex life with her husband, sometimes in front of the kids. She talked about wife swapping. This made Mary squirm, but their kids liked one another, and the mothers helped each other out, so it was convenient. Eventually Pamela got divorced, which played directly into Mary's darkest fears. She was already suffering the daily agony of paranoia about Bob, and now practically next door lived an available woman of no apparent morality!

Mary told Bob it was time to move; the neighborhood was going downhill. Reluctantly, Bob hunted for a new place and eventually found a two-bedroom house in Walnut Creek, a smaller and more expensive community than Danville. They moved on Halloween Day 1969, Mary six months pregnant and happy to have escaped Pamela's orbit.

They soon regretted the move. The children—Joy especially—were traumatized by being wrenched from school, neighborhood, and friends. Bob was unhappy, too, and soon Mary found herself depressed over the change. They made a lame and fruitless effort to back out of the deal, then settled in to make the best of it. Bob made plans for an additional bedroom.

Mary, pregnant with Nancy, was on diet pills again. Like all people with dependencies, she thought she had it under control. After all, there had been long gaps between pill sieges during the previous ten years, albeit imposed by lack of availability.

Now, a few months after Nancy's birth, she had run out of pills and neglected to get a refill. Within days she began feeling ill, as if she had a bad flu, minus the cold symptoms. She was vomiting and shaking. Frightened, she phoned her doctor. He prescribed a sedative, and the symptoms ended. But Mary had been scared straight; she knew she had just gone through drug withdrawal. Never again, she vowed. She made up her mind to stay away from those happy capsules—a vow she kept.

But her obsession with Bob's infidelity, potential or real, would last another two years. On one occasion, she was reduced to investigating hairs found on her husband's clothing. Only once did she dare to confront him on the subject. Bob, whose style of internalizing everything led to infrequent but powerful outbursts, responded with fury. "If I wanted to leave you I would have left you a long time ago," he shouted.

Mary's self-imposed torment ended suddenly and strangely. She was watching a television drama about an unfaithful wife who nonetheless still loved her husband. A thought struck her: "Suppose there were two things that could happen to your husband. Another woman, or a car accident that would cripple him for life. Which would you choose?" She knew the obvious answer, but the starkness of the choice cast a revelatory light. The very prospect of a choice gave Mary a sense of control that she hadn't felt since her marriage began. It was not about the phantom "other woman," and it was not about her. It was about making the choice that involved the least harm for her husband.

At once she felt a great wave of love for Bob and an enormous sense of release. Of course she could live with anything as long as Bob was alive and healthy. At age thirty-eight, seventeen years into her marriage, the dark cloud lifted. She would remember it as one of the pivotal moments of her life. The phantom was gone. It seemed to her as if God had sent the message, at last answering her prayers. It reaffirmed her faith.

. . .

Mary had enrolled in Walnut Creek Presbyterian Church, about three miles from home. St. Luke's, next door, was too far-out for her: they used handouts for services instead of the holy book itself. Walnut Creek Pres, as it was known, was founded in 1878, in the midst of a furious national debate about the merits of Darwinism and its theory that man was descended from apes. A century later, Walnut Creek Pres was still trying to cling to tradition while shepherding a flock of well-to-do urban expatriates living in semirural exclusion. But the city literally was growing around it into a minimetropolis, perhaps best symbolized by the massive Route 24/580/680 freeway interchange taking concrete form right at its doorstep. The 1970s brought the church fast growth, a membership of more than twelve hundred, and a host of issues that rattled the congregation.

Mary and the children were soon as involved with Walnut Creek Pres as they had been with the Baptist church in Danville. Mary taught Sunday school and went to a women's Bible class on Tuesdays. The church had a strong social-educational program for young people, and all four Griffith kids took part.

Walnut Creek Presbyterian is one of three major Presbyterian churches in Contra Costa County. As is true of most other Protestant denominations, Presbyterianism has been wrestling throughout the twentieth century with far-reaching issues of traditionalism versus modernism. The traditionalist view, closely associated with evangelism, which is concerned with the rescuing of souls through Christ, holds to a literalist reading of the Bible as the sacrosanct word of God. The modernist view sees the Bible as a living document, revealed by God to holy scribes, yet subject to interpretation in keeping with changing times and customs.

A survey of Contra Costa County churches by the local council of churches in the late 1960s placed the Presbyterians in the "moderate" column when measured against an index of Biblical literalism.

Walnut Creek Presbyterian tilted to the conservative end of the spectrum. It was, for example, one of the last of the San Francisco Bay–area Presbyterian churches to accept women as deacons and elders (it did so in the early 1980s), and then only after the national church voted in 1982–83 to amend the Book of Order—the Presbyterian "constitution"—to force recalcitrant congregations to act. A bitter internal struggle over the issue ensued at Walnut Creek Pres, resulting in more than 220 parishioners' splitting off and starting their own congregation.

The teachings at Walnut Creek Pres were in the evangelical, missionary tradition: The Bible was God's word. Man was born a sinner. Through God's grace, via a conversionary acceptance of the Lord Jesus, Man could enter the realm of salvation. In this construct Satan is alive and recruiting, and hell is a reality.

Walnut Creek Presbyterian was orthodox, but not fundamentalist in the aggressive or militant sense of that word—no fire and brimstone, no television ministries. It maintained a benign surface, was mildly liberal on some social issues, and accommodated a large staff that ran the gamut from progressive to doctrinaire. It tolerated individual differences as long as they were neither blatant nor disruptive. Even gay parishioners were accepted as long as they stayed closeted.

. . .

While Mary's religiosity was probably more conservative than that of Walnut Creek Pres, the church's practice was traditional enough to accommodate her.

At home, she was the architect of her own religious universe, a pastiche of her fundamentalist upbringing, radio and television evangelists, reverential doodads, and, at the heart of it all, her personal Bible, which held a place of conspicuous honor on a book stand in the shape of a cross on the kitchen table. Calendars from Norman Vincent Peale adorned the walls, and there were Bible verses pinned up in the kitchen and in the boys' room (along with a portrait of Jesus). Also in the kitchen, near the phone, was a wooden box of Bible verses, and, hung near the window, a cross with a ceramic child in blissful repose against it.

Mary encouraged her children to partake of Walnut Creek Pres's prodigious menu of activities. They plunged in and became, to varying degrees, active and committed devotees. Ed was most aggressively devout. Bobby was a close second. After he and Ed were baptized together, Bobby bought a ring with an image of Jesus on it and told everyone of his commitment to being a Christian, to living for God and not himself.

Joy, despite her early conversion, was more ambivalent, vacillating about religion but sustaining a deep faith in Jesus well into adulthood. Most resistant, except for Bob, was Nancy, who remained skeptical of organized religion from an early age.

The Griffith youngsters and their parents spent much of their time within the extended family circle. The Griffith-Harrison family constellation was rather insular. Ophelia and Alvin were always at the ready to rescue one of the children involved in a messy divorce, an illness, or financial straits.

The Griffiths knew little about outreach—how to navigate institutions outside their narrow universe. They had little need to. Bob's profession and its powerful union met their modest needs. Their suburban lives were relatively sheltered. Although Bob liked to read, dabbling in Hemingway and even Faulkner, the Griffiths retained an unworldliness that would work against them when real crisis struck.

In his prepuberty days Bobby would have been described as a happy, free spirit. He organized carnivals in his backyard for the neighborhood kids. He loved animals and longed for a pet raccoon. He liked to write, and won a prize for an essay he did on John Muir. He was shy, yet loved to laugh and had a mildly mischievous streak.

Bobby wanted and needed to feel accepted. The family unit, a tightly bound circle of love and protection, was the universe in which he defined himself. He rarely acted out, flared with anger, or did anything that would draw anger in return. He was so good that his mother once told him, "Bobby, I wish I had fifty more little boys like you." Privately, she worried that her son was fading into the woodwork, so good as to be almost invisible, ignored.

If he felt different from the others, Bobby never showed it. "When I was little, I never gave a second thought to playing house, or playing dolls or wearing my mother's jewelry," he reminisced in his diary. Yet, he records, "when I was young I was always very sensitive, and it didn't take much to make me cry."

He waxed nostalgic about the good old days: "What a good time in my life that was. I was really a beautiful little boy then, right before high school. [In] 9th grade all my troubles began."

Before the "troubles" surfaced, some warning signs appeared. At age thirteen, Bobby became fascinated with the television fitness guru Jack LaLanne, whose syndicated show enjoyed wide success in the early stages of the health boom. Bobby would rise early and sit at the tube for a couple of hours watching the muscular LaLanne go through his routines, then catch reruns after school. Mary noticed that Bobby merely watched, never joined in the routines. It annoyed her. "Bobby," she asked once, "why don't you ever do the exercises?" Bobby reacted with rare anger and walked out of the room.

Homosexuality was much in the news at the time. The gay liberation movement had begun in 1969 and surged in the 1970s with a blatant and vocal flourish. San Francisco, a mere fifteen miles from Rudgear Road, was its heartland. The Castro district, a run-down neighborhood off Market Street, blossomed as gay and lesbian America's Main Street for the thousands of homosexuals who were flocking to the tolerant city from all across the country.

Some gays celebrated their newfound sexual freedom and political clout with the intensity and excess of longtime prisoners on a weekend pass. The annual Gay Pride Parade each June presented television images of flaunting, seminude people strutting in bizarre getups and makeup, exulting in the sheer joy of visibility.

For Mary, a few miles and several light years away, the spectacle was frightening. She knew little of homosexuality, but the little she did know had overtones of a decadent and carnal secret ritual, a cabal somehow aligned with the satanic, condemned by her Bible and her church. When a group of mothers marched by the cameras in the pride parade carrying a sign that read, "We love our gay children," Mary wondered aloud, "How can they do that? How can they support their kids being gay?"

Bobby probably heard that remark. If he didn't, he certainly heard others. Granny often said of gay people, "They should line 'em up against a wall and shoot 'em."

Channel 42, the religious station that Mary watched for hours, had its share of horror stories. There was the tale of the young girl tempted by Satan into lesbianism who managed to wrest herself away and return to the family fold. God was helping her to be strong and not backslide into sin.

Then there was a girlfriend of Mary's brother Charles, who visited the Griffiths for a weekend, and when the weather turned cool one night borrowed a coat from Mary. Later, Joy stumbled on a letter to that same woman that made it clear she had experimented sexually with another woman.

Joy told her mother about it. Mary was horrified. She strode to her closet and ferreted out the coat the woman had worn. She could never bring herself to wear it again. She sent it off to Goodwill.

When Mary's niece Debbie heard about the incident, she asked her, "Mary, don't you think you should have more compassion and understanding?" Mary's answer was simple and direct: "You can't love God and be a homosexual."

Across the country the gay movement was stretching the limits in all directions. In San Francisco, George Moscone openly campaigned for the gay votes that helped put him into office as mayor in 1977. Elsewhere, states and municipalities were passing antidiscrimination laws.

In Dade County, Florida, which encompasses Miami, voters in January 1977 approved the first gay civil rights law in the South. Within weeks of the Dade County result, Southern Baptists had organized to overturn it, putting forward as their spokeswoman the lady of the orange juice commercials, the former beauty queen Anita Bryant. The story went national. Bryant appeared on TV screens to declare that gays were out to proselytize America's children. "Homosexuals cannot reproduce, so they must recruit," she said. The Ku Klux Klan endorsed her effort, which was called Save Our Children. That organization's brochures featured headlines about men molesting boys.

In Walnut Creek, Mary watched Anita Bryant with frank admiration. Her own vague fear of homosexuality was being articulated by a powerful and devout Christian, an admired public figure. So, when the Dade County gay rights ordinance was repealed by a vote of two to one in June 1977, Mary naturally approved. Bryant's victory speech was a declaration of war against homosexuals, who, she said, are "dangerous to the sanctity of the family, dangerous to our children, dangerous to our survival as one nation under God."

After Bryant's victory, the gay rights movement went into retreat. Other gay ordinances were overturned. Jerry Falwell's Moral Majority emerged on the scene. In Mary's own church, the pastor vigorously opposed ordination of gays, which had been recommended by a national Presbyterian study group. "Were avowed homosexuals to be ordained," he wrote in Walnut Creek Presbyterian's church bulletin, "they would have a role-modeling effect upon those under them, and this would not be good. . . . This is an explosive issue—but my confidence is in a great God who can disarm the bomb before it has a chance to go off. . . . Our enemy, the Devil, never sleeps." His confidence was rewarded when the national church overturned the study group's majority report and rejected its recommendation. (The ordination debate has continued into the mid-1990s.)

Meanwhile, across the bay, gays in San Francisco seemed undaunted by the rising forces of opposition. In November 1977 they flexed their political muscle to elect Harvey Milk to the city's board of supervisors, the first openly gay elected public official in a major city. The next June, 375,000 people marched in the city's Gay Freedom Day Parade, the nation's largest turnout for any cause since the antiwar movement. And the following November, California voters defeated by two to one an initiative that would have banned gays and lesbians from teaching in the state's public schools.

Three weeks later, gays were jolted into reality. Harvey Milk was shot dead in his office by Dan White, a deranged ex–city supervisor who hated gays. The city's liberal mayor, George Moscone, had fallen minutes earlier to White's bullets. Six months later a jury gave White a mere six years in prison.

. . .

Bobby undoubtedly picked up these contradictory signals and processed them in the crucible of his adolescent fears and yearnings. Puberty brought him face to face with the reality that the cravings he was experiencing now had a label, a label abhorred by his family, his church, his school, and much of his nation. Being gay, it seemed, could be lethal.

With the benefit of hindsight, Mary, Joy, and the others remember a sudden change in Bobby at adolescence—a draining of spirit, the suggestion of melancholy. In retrospect, the direct link to sexuality is clear. At the time, however, it registered as the weltschmerz of a young adolescent. The onset of adolescent acne, which would plague him to the end of his life, also took its toll on his psyche.

Bobby yielded a clue to his inner storm in an essay written for a high school English class. He wrote about a recurring dream of childhood, an exhilarating flying dream that wafted him above the trees—free, alive, and happy:

As I got older, around junior high age, the dreams ceased and I missed them. The last flying dream I had was what I think might have been a sort of warning. The dream begins outside my window, but I find myself anxious. As I fly I'm afraid. There are telephone lines, and antennae and electrical wires. How painful it would be to run into one. This causes me to be very paranoid. I wonder why I can't be happy and free like before. . . .

During the early years of my life (up to about 11 or 12), I was in fact happy and free. I liked who I was. I knew I was very individual and maybe even a little different in the eyes of my friends. But that didn't stop me from being ME. . . . But as I grew up and became more and more conscious of others and what they wanted, I think I maybe began to see the differences between myself and those around me. I had felt rejection before, but when you're younger for some reason it doesn't hurt quite as much. Now I was older and really felt a stronger need for acceptance. So, unconsciously, and slowly, I began to lose touch with who I really was. That's where the paranoid flying dream may play a part.

The teacher, obviously moved by this confessional essay, remarked in his marginal notes, "Your paper is wonderful. . . . The change you describe is pretty typical. Pure, loving and young souls soon learn negativity and insecurity by being exposed to the bombings of society."

The bombings were getting to him. He was fifteen and a half, a sophomore at Las Lomas High School. He was taking antibiotics for his acne. He was engrossed at the time in a drama workshop sponsored by the youth group at the church. Bobby began recording his feelings at the beginning of 1979, in the midst of an unusually wet and gloomy winter. His first effort, written on a piece of notebook paper on January 29, 1979, was titled "Survival."

I will survive, because God wants me to. God wants us all to survive. No, God wants us to survive and be happy. There's a big difference between surviving and surviving being happy. But surviving is the first part. How do we do it? I think that inside each one of us there is a kernal [sic], in this kernal is the power and energy to survive. But when we think that we can no longer survive a decision has to be made: between sinking and swimming. The latter is the best choice now.

By then he had purchased an 8½-by-11-inch spiral notebook and resolved to keep a diary. On January 30, he began it. On February 5, he asked,

What's next? Who knows what strange evil force lies around the corner, waiting in the shadows? I find that life is a giant challenge, a challenge I will meet.

The entries of the first three months resembled those of any adolescent going through the throes of teenhood: disliking school, struggling with grades, seeing movies like *The Outlaw Blues* and *Dawn of the Dead,* going to a weekend Christian camp, constructing the sets for a church skit.

But in the spring of 1979, near his sixteenth birthday, the tone took a drastic turn.

I can't ever let anyone find out that I'm not straight. It would be so humiliating. My friends would hate me. They might even want to beat me up. And my family? I've overheard them. They've said they hate gays, and even God hates gays, too. Gays are bad, and God sends bad people to hell. It really scares me when they talk that way because now they are talking about me.

Bobby Griffith's secret world was about to blow apart.

A Rope with No Knot

In the days and weeks after Bobby's funeral the members of the Griffith family found themselves behaving like survivors of a great natural disaster. They wandered about in a daze of grief and guilt.

Joy would cry in the car every day on the way to work. Ed decided not to sign up for the fall semester at Hayward State, where he was studying law enforcement; he took to sleeping long hours, sometimes staying in bed for two days at a time. Nancy, just thirteen, was shaken. "Can that happen to me?" she asked. "Could I turn gay?"

"No," her mother quickly assured her.

And Mary felt as if she had been sucked into a bottomless pit of pain. The loss was at once unacceptable and inevitable. That cruel, unceasing contradiction made her dizzy; it was more than her circuits could absorb.

The night after the funeral, the family, alone at last, gathered around the kitchen table: Bob and Mary, Nancy, Joy, and Ed.

They talked. They reminisced. They came to the remarkable conclusion that while they knew that Bobby was miserable, none of them had ever entertained the notion that he was in danger of taking his life. Mary said she wasn't surprised when she heard it, and yet she hadn't anticipated it. The unspoken question was, Why not? If only they had been more aware, more sensitive, maybe they could have prevented it.

Bob got up from the table, his face twisted. Joy followed and found him in his bedroom, hanging his head. Joy put a hand on his shoulder and said, "I hope you know that none of us feel like it was something you should have done, or could have done." Bob's eyes were wet. He said, "I just didn't know Bobby was in so much pain. I wasn't there when he needed me."

In the days that followed, first Mary, then Joy read the diaries. Both were stunned by the depth of Bobby's despair. They got a faint glimmer of Bobby's fatal contradiction: he knew he could not change what he knew he never could accept. Yet Mary always believed he *could* change, that God *would* change him.

When the grief counselors from Walnut Creek Pres came to the house, they found the family in shock. Assistant Pastor Cully Anderson, a compassionate man, felt helpless in the presence of such grief. Suicide is always awkward for a pastor, and when a young life is snatched from its future as in this case . . .

He and the family sat in uncomfortable silence in the small living room. A picture of a smiling Bobby sat on the buffet, next to which Mary had placed a lighted candle, vowing to keep it lit forever. Finally, Mary haltingly voiced a subject that had been forming in her mind. "There must be other Bobbys out there," she said. "As far as I know the church had no program to reach out to my son. What about other young gay people who may be thinking about taking their lives?"

"I don't know," Anderson replied, weakly. There was no such program at the church. There was nothing more to say.

Mary did not bring up the issue that gnawed at her: the state of Bobby's mortal soul. She knew the church would have her believe he was safely in heaven. There was no use arguing her personal theology, drawn from Revelation, the section of the New Testament from which fundamentalists derive the prophecy of imminent Armageddon: "And anyone whose name was not in the book of life was thrown into the lake of fire." Bobby in the lake of fire! Her child! Unthinkable, unbearable! It seemed clear to her that her church was not going to provide the answers she needed.

Still, she went to the church with Joy a few days later. They sat in the prayer room, prayed, and signed the prayer book. But they received little solace. Mary felt engulfed, beyond reach.

She did not know how to handle grief. In her family, death was something to be whispered about, a taboo subject. Other than the death of her premature child years earlier, nothing had assaulted her with such a devastating affect. Left to her own devices, she contemplated her own suicide. She found temporary comfort in imagining how she would go about it, and finally settled on a bizarre image: if she tied two or three bricks to her ankles and jumped into the deep end of the pool she would sink forever, gangland style.

Typically, she kept her thoughts to herself, brooding over the prospect for weeks. Gradually, the idea of ending her life grew more frightening than contemplating the pain of going on. She realized she wanted to live—for herself, for her other children, for Bob. The suicide scheme evaporated.

After three weeks, she returned to her job at I. Magnin, barely going through the motions. One day she was having coffee in the company cafeteria with another employee when she suddenly felt a cry rising from her gut to her throat. She knew she was going to stand up and start screaming, "My son is dead!" Somehow she stifled it, got up, and fled to the bathroom. But this incident frightened her. She had never lost control like that.

At home, her relationship with Bob was showing the strain. Their sex life had fallen to zero; Mary was in too much pain to tolerate the contact. Bob accepted it at first, not understanding it, but as weeks went by, his frustration mounted.

Adding to the tension, Mary, casting about for explanations, blamed Bob for not trying harder to reach Bobby. Perhaps, she argued, if he had spent more time with him, been a buddy, he could have cultivated in Bobby the manly qualities of strength and self-esteem. But Bob had stayed mostly on the sidelines, only reluctantly sharing some fruitless and artificial "together" events with his son.

Bob Griffith's role in the family was often unclear to his children. Inward directed and taciturn yet loving and concerned, he nonetheless harbored deep strains of anger, probably rooted in childhood, which expressed themselves in unpredictable verbal outbursts. To Nancy, her father's long silences and occasional tirades were frightening. She imagined at times that he was disappointed with her, only to learn as she grew up that his moods had nothing to do with her. Joy, as well, often felt as a young girl that her father was angry with her, for reasons she could not divine.

Now, looking back, Bob let himself believe that at some level he might have failed Bobby. But for him, reaching out to his son meant reaching across a giant moat of ignorance. He hadn't the slightest concept of what *gay* was. He had heard the jokes and snickers, but they didn't really register. He never judged *gay* as bad. But *gay* was alien, irrelevant, incomprehensible. He could have tried any number of ways to reach out to Bobby, but none of them had a chance of connecting; he and his son were on different frequencies.

As tension grew, Mary wondered if her marriage would survive. Typically, she shielded these thoughts from Bob. But one day, across a cup of coffee at the kitchen table, she discussed them with Joy. "Mom, it's one thing to talk about it, but have you thought it through?" Joy protested. "What would you do? Tell Daddy to leave? Where would he go after twenty-eight years? To some hotel? Let's be realistic."

Autumn arrived soggily, and with it the round of holidays and memories. Halloween had been Bobby's favorite, and it was Mary's custom to go to the elementary school Halloween fair the kids had attended and volunteer at one of the booths. This time, she got as far as the door, from which she could see all the youngsters in costume. She turned back and went home. They reminded her too much of Bobby.

Mary desperately wanted a sign, something from the other world to assure her that Bobby was okay. One night, she, Ed, and Joy decided to go to Bobby's room and pray for one—a ring, a feather, something. They sat for a long time in the lamplight, praying in vain. Nothing came. At Christmas, they noticed a limb of the Christmas tree beginning to wiggle. Mary said, only half-jokingly, "That must be Bobby. It would be just like him to pull a stunt like that."

But Bobby's absence was no joke. Mary could not accept that she might be eternally cut off from her son. She could not reconcile herself to the notion of acquiescing to God's judgment, which she had never before doubted. This was risky territory: challenging divine action gets you into the realm of blasphemy.

· · ·

Three unfathomable realities tormented her: (1) the prospect of never seeing Bobby again; (2) the fact that God had not cured Bobby, but instead allowed him to die—an inexplicable heavenly screw-up; and (3) her growing obsession with unearthing within the Bible some citation, a strand of proof that Bobby was part of God's creation, that his way of life was compatible with God's law, that he was not burning in hellfire.

The religious television stations confounded her with panel shows giving the testimony of people who had been cured of being gay. The shows struck a sour note: here were these guys claiming God had cured them and they were on the right path. She thought, "Then why did God pass Bobby over?" Something wasn't right.

Instinctively she knew she must make sense of all this as a path through the brambles of grief and loneliness. Through all of her life she had relied on the Bible, and God's book had had the answers, the comfort. Now she would turn to it to help her explain the greatest tragedy she was ever likely to know.

In early 1984, Mary quit her job at I. Magnin. She stopped going to church. Walnut Creek Pres held little for her now. The chief pastor, returning from a vacation in Hawaii, had sent her a form letter of solace. Someone in the pastoral ministry would call once a month to see how she was getting on, but these people's interest was in Mary's state of well-being, not her odd personal quest, which, of course, she did not share with them. Eventually someone took her off the church mailing list.

So she remained at home, paging through her old Bible, wrestling with a jumble of thoughts. The rest of the family resumed their normal routines. Mary pondered. Nancy, bemused, started referring to her mother as a recluse. Mary took to pecking on her ancient Remington or scrawling notes at a makeshift desk in a converted garage that now served as a utility room. Bob would bring her coffee from time to time. She spent hours and hours, jotting odd thoughts at first: "They say your children are really not yours, they belong to God. Well, if I thought I was going to be a surrogate mother, I would never have had children in the first place. Selfish I guess."

She began digging back into biblical passages on sodomy. She noticed for the first time that the word *homosexuality* never appears in the Bible, nor does homosexuality appear as a concept or a syndrome. Most references, she saw, related to male-male rape, or a proscription against pagan ritual.

But there was no doubting the Bible's strong language in reference to same-gender sexuality. In the Old Testament, Leviticus commands, "If a man has intercourse with a man as with a woman, they both commit an abomination. They shall be put to death; their blood shall be on their own heads."

And Paul, in the New Testament, admonishes the Corinthians: "Do not be deceived! Fornicators, idolaters, male prostitutes, sodomites, thieves, the greedy, drunkards, revilers, robbers—none of these will inherit the kingdom of God."

In Romans, Paul excoriates idol worshipers who have abandoned the monodeity and lead dissipated, decadent lives in which men and women "were consumed with passion" for those of their own gender. "Men committed shameless acts with men and received in their own persons the due penalty for their error. . . . They know God's decree, that those who practice such things deserve to die."

Mary read the passages as if for the first time. To be gay is to be no better than a thief, idolater, or robber. Punishable by death. "Their blood shall be on their own heads." The judgment and its implications held a nightmarish relevance to her son's destiny.

But the ultimate conundrum lay in the Sodom and Gomorrah story. Nowhere else in the Bible did God's judgment of sexual deviancy play out with such apocalyptic fury. For Mary, this story—along with that of the Flood—had always been the supreme affirmation of God's willingness to wreak his vengeance on a wayward mankind.

The Lord warned Abraham, anointed to found the Hebrew nation, that he was going to destroy Sodom and Gomorrah in response to the unspecified "outcry" against the cities. Abraham tries to bargain God down, finally getting him to agree to spare the cities if his angel scouts, in the guise of two men, can find ten righteous people there.

The angels come to Lot's house in Sodom and are treated well. But soon the house is surrounded by the city's entire male population, who demand that Lot give up the visitors, so that they "may know them." (Some versions say, "can have intercourse with them.") Lot offers his daughters as substitutes, but the men refuse, proceeding to charge the house.

The angels blind the raiding throng, then lead Lot and his family to safety as the Lord rains "sulfur and fire" on the cities.

To Mary the account was flatly unambiguous. The Lord unleashed his wrath when his angels confronted the prospect of being violated by the males of Sodom. Confirmed in his belief that the town was evil, God destroyed it. Thus, homosexual sex is such anathema that God is capable of resorting to genocidal fury to punish it.

What consolation was there for Bobby in that account? she wondered. Mary plunged on, burrowing deeper and deeper into the Bible with a growing sense of despair. She located a classic biblical commentary by Matthew Henry from the seventeenth century, hoping it would help her decode the book and find a glimmer of optimism. But Henry, predictably, reserved his most eloquent denunciations for those groups most biblically indicted. She dug into her collection of Christian self-help books: *A Man Called Peter; Don't Wrestle Just Nestle: How People of All Ages Can Turn to God and Enjoy Life; Warfare Against Satan;* and *God's Psychiatry.*

She turned more and more frequently to Ed as a sounding board for her lonely search. Ed was now in junior college, working toward an A.A. degree in law enforcement, but he continued at Walnut Creek Pres, volunteering as a camp counselor, teaching Sunday school, and taking Bible study classes. He was the most religiously connected of her surviving children, and Mary felt comfortable discussing these issues with him. Ed detected a change in his mother. She was no longer spouting verses as gospel. She seemed to him like a student, or a seminarian, rummaging through the Bible in a spirit of inquiry. It was strange to watch.

In August 1984, a year after Bobby's death, the scourge of AIDS had finally begun to penetrate the nation's consciousness. There were already more than seven thousand Americans dead or dying, nearly all of them gay men, and there was no telling how many more were infected. Conservative ministers were calling AIDS God's vengeance on gay people, a modern-day echo of Sodom. Shying from bad news, most Americans chose to focus on the Olympics in Los Angeles; the Republican National Convention, which nominated President Ronald Reagan to run for a second term; and the much-heralded fact that the "1984" of Orwell fame had actually arrived.

It was a year after his suicide, and Mary had found nothing to relieve the pain of Bobby's absence. She hadn't expected things to happen this way. She had thought at first that after a reasonable time she would have comfort and peace, that Jesus would take the sting out of her loss. That was what she had been taught—that you come to accept that the departed have "moved in with the Lord" and you trust the end results to a kind and loving father.

It hadn't happened. Not a day went by without the stab of memory, the aching emptiness. What's more, she found herself feeling guilty for begrudging God the presence of her son. "I experienced, through my spirit, how hurt our Lord was because I did not want Bobby to be with Him," she wrote in a letter to a friend. "It really turned me around to how Jesus felt, instead of how Mary felt."

But this complex of considerations rooting around in her brain could not suppress a growing mood of impatience, even bitterness. She could feel rumbling inside of her an unfamiliar anger, and she began venting it in a series of handwritten communiqués to God.

"Dearest Lord. I haven't really gotten a grip on life since you let Bobby leave us," she wrote.

I have no doubt Bobby is alive. I think that's what bothers me. He's alive and I'm not part of his life anymore.

I feel my relationship with you leaves a lot to be desired. Your Holy Spirit has taught me in a hundred ways, but I need something more. It seems like being Christian is somewhat one-sided. You see me every day. When do I see you? Why is everything so vague with you? It seems if I blink the wrong way I've quenched your Holy Spirit and, ooops, Mary, you're out of fellowship. Whoopee! Have I been taught wrong? My sinful nature is always busy, so how can I ever be your perfect little dawling?

I'm really glad you gave us a free will and a mind to think with. When it comes to you, I've come up with some really unique questions. But a questioning mind is quite a privilege. . . . It is an exciting quest getting to know you more, one I'm sure will be rewarding!"

Her mind was beginning to engage gears it had never used before. The questions she could not resolve came tumbling out. On October 13, her fiftieth birthday, she wrote:

*I'm sure you knew when Bobby left us, I would not take it
lying down! . . . Joy, Nancy and Ed and my husband need me. I
guess we didn't need Bobby. How can we help people feel
needed so they will not want to leave this world? Lord, how
can we ever get along without our Dear Sweet Bobby?*

*When Jesus died on the cross in our place, his mother
watched his suffering. . . . But Jesus rose from the grave and she
saw him and knew all was well with him. I didn't get to say
even good-bye to Bobby. Nothing. I think that was very rude,
impolite to say the least!*

Indeed, Mary was very annoyed. Her faith had always provided assurance: God had removed her agony of paranoia over
her husband's fidelity. But he had let Bobby slip away and now
she wanted—had to have, in her addled grief—some word that
her son was safe. Hadn't Jesus raised Lazarus from the dead?
And after the Crucifixion, Jesus had appeared to many people,
assuring them that he had risen. Take Doubting Thomas, for
example. One of the twelve disciples, he refused to believe that
Jesus had returned, and he told the others he would not believe
unless he saw "the mark of his nails in his hands" and put his
fingers "in the mark." Sure enough, a week later Jesus reap-
peared and bade Thomas touch his scars. No longer doubting,
Thomas exclaimed, "My Lord and My God!"

Others, less exalted, had received signs. Catherine Marshall,
the widow of the saintly minister Peter Marshall, wrote that she
had seen her husband in a dream in a beautiful garden, and that
he had looked up and said, "What are you doing here?"

There were records of many similar experiences where faith
had been rewarded by divine intercession. Surely, loved ones will
reveal themselves if there is an unfinished piece of their lives.

You ask for something in faith, knowing that whatever happens will be God's will. They teach you that God answers your
prayers in one of three ways: *yes, no,* or *wait.* And you are supposed to have the spiritual awareness to know which it is. Well,
in her case, Mary hadn't the slightest idea.

"I know Bobby didn't fit here from the day one, so why did you send him to us to begin with?" she demanded.

Why did you allow him to end up hating himself? You knew what had to be done for Bobby, for anyone who's hanging onto a rope with no knot on the end. You could have given Bobby something or someone to hang onto, but you didn't, and you don't for a lot of people. For a lot of people you do, and they live happily ever after. How do you make these awesome decisions? You didn't want Bobby to live happily . . . so why send someone to this earth to be miserable?

Give us something we can live with, Lord, and pass on to others whose life will never be the same because of a loved one's death, especially when loved ones are so young.

Ever since we discovered he was gay, it's like his life was over, and I didn't help make it better. . . . So, Lord, you're the only one with the answers to Bobby's life, so I would appreciate your input on this whole matter especially since there are a lot of Bobbys and Janes stumbling around down here. . . . What's the message Bobby left? I could say, Well, this life is just temporary anyway and they're better off with you, Lord. But that belief does not mend broken hearts or ease the loneliness. Is time going to make me stop hurting Lord or will you! How could you let Bobby do this! I'm really selfish. Forget it, who am I, nobody!

· · ·

Christmas 1984. The Lord's birthday, and the second Christmas without Bobby. The family celebrated with determined gaiety, avoiding any allusions to the past. Mary cooked a turkey. They exchanged gifts. Mary found herself musing about the Christ child. God had sent him to liberate man from sin, the greatest mission in the history of the world, and even he at times lost sight of why he was here. How could mere mortals with one-zillionth the amount of insight ever understand why we are placed here and why we die?

But God is about justice, she thought. Where was the justice in Bobby's death? Or the deaths of other gay kids, for that matter. For the first time, her consciousness turned to the notion of a ministry for self-despising gay children:

"Dear Lord," she wrote in her book a few days later,

I listen to KEAR and according to your Word, Bobby is in hell, or at least waiting his turn. I know better, Lord, but what about the kids that believe they are going there because they are gay?

I did not decide on hazel eyes for myself. Bobby did not decide he would be gay. . . . If you say in your Word, it's evil and wicked to have no arms, and a child is born with no arms, what is the child to think? When he or she finds he or she is going to hell for something they have had no control over, it can put a person under maximum stress, and feeling like the scum of the earth.

You already know this, but the church here is sending innocent people to hell by the droves, or [driving them] to drugs, alcohol, sex, or in Bobby's case, suicide. What can I do to undo my ignorance? I did it all wrong with Bobby, Lord, you know it and I know it!

She had made a major leap, probably without conscious recognition. If being gay is something one has no control over, like eye color, then to brand it a sin is unconscionable. Yet brand it a sin God did. It is there in the Bible. The Bible is God's word. So Bobby—and she—were tokens in some malevolent and unwinnable board game, tokens whose moves were predestined to end in disaster. She had done it all wrong, but what would have been right?

. . .

Mary obsessed over this puzzle into the mild California winter. On February 8, Bob Griffith turned fifty-one. Mary gave him an afghan she had crocheted. Things had gotten better between them as Mary had retrained her sights on the cosmos. Joy gave her dad a pair of tennis shoes. Nancy gave him a shirt, and Ed contributed peanut brittle and socks. It was a lovely day, but Mary felt exhausted and drained. She felt that she was losing both patience and hope. At what may have been her lowest point, she sat down at her notebook that evening in a fit of frustration and anger. "Lord," she wrote,

I'm still waiting for assurance beyond a doubt that all is well with our son! It's been 16 months! . . . Doesn't Bobby ever think about us anymore? I feel it's bad manners to ignore people who love and miss you. . . . We can communicate with you, so why not everyone else that's there with you? I don't think that it's very loving of you. I thought you were a loving Father. I'm not so sure anymore. I can't help it Lord, your method of communicating is just lousy!

I don't think any of you really give a hoot about us left behind! So, why should I care about you, and you, too, Bobby, you got what you wanted so the hell with the rest of us. . . . Lord I can't believe you and Bobby have left all of us out in the cold, deserted. I feel like I've been had all these years. . . . It's real B.S. and I'm sick of this one-sided deal.

It was a frustrated, last-ditch appeal. The next day she pleaded for a sign so that she could

get on with life, and stop all this begging. I would do the same for my children if they ask me. I would not shut them off forever from a brother or sister they missed, or any relative. So, I will not write anymore.

And she didn't, ever again, in the manner of that pleading, haranguing colloquy with God. She had crossed the Rubicon. She had had a glimpse of some new and frightening reality, one in which she could depend neither on the Bible nor on her faith to sustain her any longer. Jesus had said, "The kingdom of God is within you." She would have to find the answer in herself.

Coming Out

Bobby was choking on his secret. He needed desperately to confide in someone. The diary was not enough. It helped, but he longed to unburden himself to another human, someone who could help him sort out the powder keg of feelings imploding within. But who? He couldn't tell his parents, certainly not his mother. He had no friend he trusted enough. Joy? Ed?

He turned to Ed, setting off a chain of events that might have made him wish he had kept his secret to himself and his diary.

Ed Griffith turned seventeen on a rainy day in late April 1979. He was a junior in high school, an accomplished athlete with dreams of becoming a professional baseball player. Ed was a strapping, muscular young man, with sandy hair and a square, chiseled chin. He was a straight shooter free of guile or subterfuge. He believed deeply in the Gospel and the teachings of his church. For the longest time as a child he related being a Christian to being a soldier. He loved war movies, toy soldiers, playing army. Yet behind his macho aspect there was a caring, nonjudgmental person.

Perhaps it was those traits that led Bobby to choose his brother as the person to whom he would unburden himself one warm spring afternoon in May. The two lounged near the blooming apricot tree in the family's backyard. Bobby, a month away from turning sixteen, seemed very nervous. Finally, he said, "There is something awful I have to tell you. You are going to really hate me and never want to talk to me again."

Ed's heart fluttered with a rush of worry. He imagined everything from criminal activity to drugs. He responded, "Bobby, it doesn't matter what it is. I'm never going to stop loving you."

It was true. They had grown up together, sharing the same small bedroom. They had had many a long heart-to-heart through the years. They were different, true, and there were times they had been jerks to each other. But their love for one another was solid. What's more, Bobby trusted Ed.

Bobby said in a choked voice, "I'm gay."

Ed breathed a momentary sigh of relief. It could have been worse. He said, "Bobby, how do you know this?"

"I've known for a long time," Bobby answered.

"But how can you be sure?"

"I'm sure, Ed. Believe me, I'm sure." Bobby hung his head as if in pain. They talked some more, and Ed could see that Bobby considered his gayness to be a terrible defect.

Ed asked, "Are you going to tell Mom and Dad, or see a counselor?" he asked.

Bobby flared, "No! I want you to promise you won't tell anyone, especially Mom and Dad!"

Reluctantly, he said, "Okay, okay, I promise."

Nothing in life had prepared Ed for such a burden. Homosexuality. It was like something from another planet. He had seen it on television. And he'd heard different religious people say it was a choice and a sinful one at that. He preoccupied himself with other things and tried to convince himself that this crisis would work itself out. He had a new girlfriend, and it was baseball season. There was lots to distract him from such an unpleasant disclosure. Ed collaborated with nervous silence in keeping Bobby's secret.

Oddly, after the initial revelation, Bobby did not talk much about his homosexuality to Ed. He continued to pour his agony into his journal.

May 11, 1979. Sometimes I feel like I'm at the edge of a cliff, looking down at the crashing surf with nowhere to go . . . but down to the jagged rocks below. . . . I can ask myself why all this B.S. is happening to me, but would it change anything? No, I'll have to change before circumstances do. But fuck, right now I have neither the will or the energy to change my way of thinking.

May 18. Dear God: Are you there? I ask because I really don't know. . . . Sometimes I hurt so bad, and I'm scared and alone. I wonder why you or somebody doesn't help. I'm so mad and frustrated, I seem to be at the end of the road. Why do you remain silent?

May 30. Gentle springtime weather surrounds me, but a fierce unrelenting storm rages within. How much more can I take? Only time and a million tears of bitterness will tell. . . . I guess I am slowly sinking in a vast lake of quicksand; a bottomless pool of death. I wish I could crawl under a rock and sleep for the rest of time.

June 1. I'm scared of the person I could grow up to be. Oh, how I hope the changes in myself ahead of me are good ones.

He composed a poem:

I've locked myself out
and don't have the key
I blew the light out
and now I can't see. . .
Afraid of answers I don't have
and might not ever know
I wonder in which direction my life will go?

On June 24, Bobby celebrated his sixteenth birthday.

. . .

As the weeks went by, Ed became more and more alarmed at Bobby's melancholy. Bobby had taken a part-time job as a custodian in a convalescent home. He told Ed he hated the job—cleaning up after the deaths of old people. But he kept at it, he said, as a kind of penance.

The capper came one summer evening when Bobby disclosed to Ed that he had recently swallowed half a bottle of aspirin. Nothing had happened beyond a severe headache, but Ed's resolve was shaken by a cold fear. He couldn't handle this by himself any longer.

What if Bobby tried to hurt himself again? How could he ever explain to his parents that he knew something this serious and didn't tell them?

Ed agonized until, one day in early July, as he was driving his mother home from the local 7-Eleven, he said, "Mom, if you found out that Bobby or I was gay, would you not love us anymore, or would you kick us out?"

Mary felt a jolt of panic. "Well, no, of course not," she said.

Ed blurted, "Bobby told me that he's gay." He related the full story, leaving out nothing except the aspirin incident.

Something crumpled inside her. To suspect was one thing. To know. . . But she simply said, "Well, Ed, there's no doubt in my mind that God can handle this. God will help us, and he will heal Bobby."

A familiar verse came to mind and she repeated it: "All things work together for good to those who love God." She believed it. This will work out. If it's true that he's gay, God will heal him.

Mary told Bob when he returned from work. They knew they had to talk to Bobby as soon as possible, but hadn't any idea how to approach the subject. They were dumbfounded. It was as if a missile had blown through the roof.

They waited until late in the evening, when the other children were asleep or in their rooms. Mary asked Bobby to come sit at the kitchen table with her. Bob joined them. The boy must have known something was coming, since this was the traditional spot for important family discussions.

There was an awkward silence. Finally, Mary began, making a clumsy effort to draw him out. "Bobby, isn't there a problem that you need to tell us about?"

Bobby stiffened. "No," he insisted. "What kind of problem?"

Mary persisted. "Bobby, you know there's something wrong, and you need to tell us about it."

Bobby squirmed. He was starting to panic. He clammed up.

Bob chimed in. "Bobby, you know if you don't share this with us, it could blow this whole family apart."

Bobby sat speechless and horrified. He lowered his eyes and scrunched his body as if preparing to ward off a blow.

Finally, Mary spilled it. "Bobby, it's all right. We love you no matter what. Ed had a talk with me and he was very worried about you and he said that you told him you're gay."

Bobby blew up in a fit of fury and tears.

"Why couldn't you tell us?" Mary asked.

"Because I was just too humiliated!" he cried, fleeing the room.

Bob and Mary followed, trying to calm him. Mary put her arms around him. "Bobby," she said, "let's go into your room and we'll talk about it."

They began to talk. Bobby said he had felt this way as far back as he could remember. "When I dream, I dream about men," he said in despair. "Other guys dream of girls. I dream of men. And I enjoy it!"

Mary said, "Bobby, we can beat this. If we trust in God. Homosexuality is curable with God's help. We've seen it on television, remember? It's not a natural thing. God will help you weed it out. Healing through prayer. That's the good news, Bobby." She believed with total faith that a God so adamant about the abomination of homosexuality would not be so diabolical as to fail to cure her son.

They talked till four in the morning, Bobby wanting desperately to believe he could change. Bob, who didn't buy the religious rationale, had less to say, as usual. He knew nothing about gays except that they were shunned by most people, and he worried that Bobby was headed for a very rough time. He felt helpless, but suggested to Bobby that he date more girls; perhaps that would help him grow out of it.

"We'll find a counselor, Bobby," said Mary. "Maybe there are some books. I'll check with the church."

"No, I don't want anyone to know outside this house," Bobby demanded. It was bad enough that Ed had told on him. (Bobby later told his diary that Ed's disclosure had strained relations between them.)

Mary agreed readily. She was not eager for anyone to know, not the church, not Granny and Grandfather, none of the others. Bobby was right. It was humiliating. She did not want her family talked about in that way.

"Of course," she said, "I won't tell them a thing, just ask about counseling in general."

Finally, exhausted, they went off to bed, each knowing that their lives had changed forever. Bobby, ultrasensitive, his still-developing ego paper thin, must have realized that he was at the beginning of a monumental struggle. At a time when his body was generating massive doses of hormonal stimuli, he would have to stifle his sexual impulses. His pleasure impulse would be identified with the forbidden and depraved. Worst of all, the revelation had blown apart the intimate familial contract; for all his family's protestations of love, the bubble had ruptured and Bobby was on the outside looking in.

Mary felt invaded by an alien, unpredictable force. Of all the evils religion condemned, homosexuality was among the most despicable. It dwelt in her mind in the realm of Satan, associated with bestiality and other horrors. And now, this thing lived in her own son! Of all the dangers she had fought in her life—the loneliness of childhood, the fear of losing her husband, the period of pill popping—this seemed the greatest threat. She was determined to beat it.

She set to work. She sent Ed to the library and the bookstore at the church for some works on homosexuality. She culled the Bible for appropriate verses. Ed could find only three books on homosexuality in the bookstore and the small Walnut Creek library. One was by Tim LaHaye, an official of the Moral Majority, and took a frank fundamentalist line, confirming that homosexuality was a distortion of God's will for mankind. The others stressed the popular theory that homosexuality was caused by an overbearing mother and distant, indifferent father.

Mary began her search for a counselor. Her sense of urgency escalated to alarm when Ed finally disclosed that Bobby had told him he had taken an excess dose of aspirin. Mary pleaded with Bobby, "Please don't ever do that again. I'd rather have a homosexual son than a dead son!"

She called a former assistant pastor at Walnut Creek Presbyterian and asked if he knew of a Christian counselor "to deal with a family issue." Yes, there was Del Jones, a psychologist with a local practice who was religiously sensitive and had done seminars at the church. Mary called and made an appointment for Bobby.

The day came. Joy drove Mary and Bobby to Jones's office in Walnut Creek. In the waiting room, Bobby was asked to fill out an information form. There were one or two others waiting, and Mary felt their eyes burning into her with certain knowledge. The form asked, "Reason for seeking counseling," and Bobby hesitated.

"What should I write?" he asked.

Mary thought for a moment and then said, "Put down 'I'm here because I want to be the kind of person God wants me to be.'" Bobby wrote it in.

Del Jones was a round-faced, balding man of about thirty with a friendly, soft-spoken manner. Bobby saw him once a month (at fifty dollars a session) for four months but didn't provide many details at home, except that Jones felt that father and son needed to develop a firmer relationship.

Mary bought into it, and at a group session with Jones, Bob, and Bobby, she unloaded on her husband. "I've always taken the kids to church. . . . I'm the one who's taken this burden on. Sometimes I feel like a single parent."

Bob said laconically, "Yeah, maybe we could do more things together. We could try. I don't now how much it would help."

Bobby's sessions with Jones tapered off and finally ended. He told his mother he wasn't getting enough out of them to be worth the time and money. Mary did not inquire further.

But Bobby wasn't giving up. This was his intense self-help period; he was attempting to get on top of the forces that seemed to be taking over his life. He enrolled in a communications workshop at the Center for Living Skills in Walnut Creek. And after leaving Jones, he enlisted in a thirty-one-day experiment in "dynamic Christian living" through the church.

The communications workshop posed a series of problem areas and goals that Bobby painstakingly answered in a notebook. "Problem areas: 'Saying I'm sorry. Keeping my anger inside. Avoiding people I don't like. Saying what I really feel.'" The ideal parent, he wrote, understands, doesn't act like a know-it-all, is easy to talk to, and, "does not try to mold my life after anyone else's"

"I think my parents trust us kids," he wrote in an essay. "We can talk openly about things if something is bothering us. . . . I don't think of them as 'parents,' but two grown-ups who we love and who we try to work our problems out with. Sometimes we can, other times we can't."

Bobby dropped out of the workshop before it ended because of cash problems. He soon plunged into the demanding Christian living experiment devised by Walnut Creek Pres's high school ministry, then headed by Dave Daubenspeck (the minister who later presided at his funeral). This involved daily prayer and guided Bible study. Daubenspeck laid out the premise in a study guide:

> For 31 days I will seek to cultivate the mind of Christ that I may discover for myself the super-life He claims to make possible. I begin the experiment today by getting on my knees and praying this prayer:
>
> Lord God, I am so self-centered, thinking of self, dreaming of self. . . . With ME as the center of my life I cannot enjoy abundance in living. . . . The only way I can be a whole and complete person is to have YOU at the center of my life. Therefore with trust and in love I give myself to you. . . . And now, Lord Jesus, use Your Word to revolutionize my life. . . . Make me the kind of person You want me to be.

As tough as the exercise was, Bobby added on a Spartan regimen that included rising at 6:30 A.M., rigorous physical workouts, prohibition of junk foods, and a solemn promise not to pick at facial zits, which he called "adolescent casualties."

In a six-page single-spaced typewritten prep sheet that provides a rare glimpse of Bobby's whimsical side, he expanded the duration of the regimen to three months (October through December) and swore "in blood" to see it through, noting that "if for any reason I fail to successfully complete this experiment, grave consequences will follow."

"This experiment is to be kept top secret until completion," he added. "Then and only then may you exercise the right to sell the exclusive copyright to the leading publisher of your choice."

He called the quest Operation Alter Ego, and obviously spent long hours thinking about it. "It is my goal to achieve a sense of pride and worth as a human being," he wrote. "Despite the fact that perfection will never be a possession of mine or anyone else on earth, I believe that I have the right to discover the fact that I am a unique and special individual worthy of God's love and worthy of seeing my dreams come true."

He worried over perseverance, cheering himself on with such statements as "When one strays from one's routine schedule, that's when trouble starts. . . . No one likes to work. I know I don't and I'm your average American in an average small town. . . . But if the goal is important enough you can and will do it. . . . Stick with it, and don't give in to any tricks one might play on one's self. If you succeed you win the whole jackpot. If you lose, it's heartbreak hotel, baby."

In the beginning, Bobby kept a daily record, based on the biblical verse of the day assigned by Daubenspeck. Also required was an unselfish deed of the day. One assigned verse, Romans 12:1–2, urges the giving of one's body to God as a living sacrifice. "I apply this to myself by thinking that when I give my body to God he will keep it, not me," Bobby wrote. "If the Lord keeps it, he will keep it clean." His unselfish deed for that day, October 5, 1979, was to "make chocolate chip cookies for Mom."

October 6. "Psalms 119:9–11 say a person can stay pure by reading God's words and following its rules. It's not that easy. . . . If we store the words in our hearts they will hold us back from sin. But that doesn't work for me. I hold words in my heart and sin anyway." Unselfish deed: "Give chickens water for Joy."

October 8, day 7. "Don't let anyone accuse you of the following: greed, impurity, foul talk, coarse jokes, etc. The funny thing about this passage is that they don't tell you *how* not to do these things, just not to or you won't see the kingdom of God. They don't seem very reflective of God's love or forgiveness." Unselfish deed: "I can't think of any good deeds."

The Bible experiment didn't make it past week one, and Operation Alter Ego didn't make it through October. Bobby drifted to other things, like a typical adolescent. But it was part of a pattern that was to assert itself through the rest of his short life. He struggled to find the ego strength to vault the wave of negatives that threatened to overwhelm him. Again and again his resolve failed him. Again and again he struggled, literally, to survive.

. . .

Meanwhile, Mary continued on the offensive. She began pinning Bible verses targeted to Bobby's "condition" around the house, even over the bathroom mirror. "Cease straying, my child, from the words of knowledge, in order that you may hear instruction (Proverbs 19:27)." Or, "Little children, let no one deceive you. Everyone who does what is right is righteous. . . . Everyone who commits sin is a child of the devil. . . . The Son of God was revealed for this purpose, to destroy the works of the devil (1 John, Chap. 3, 7–8)."

Again and again, she drove home the dictum that homosexuals are cast out of God's kingdom.

When not scribbling verses, she was turning up the volume on the Christian radio station so that Bobby could hear it from his room. She would tiptoe at night into the room he shared with Ed and pray over him while he slept. Once she put her hand on his chest. He awoke and asked, groggily, "Do you think this will heal me?"

Ed, also jogged from sleep, muttered crankily, "Why not?" Bobby just laughed.

Bobby was not noticeably effeminate, but he had a way of flipping his longish hair back from his forehead that annoyed Mary. Once she saw him doing it while primping before the bathroom mirror. Mary said, "You know, Bobby, maybe it would help if you didn't toss your hair around like that."

She told him he had to trust God to heal him, and that Satan would try to discourage him. She urged him to be careful of the company he kept, and not to go out with gay people.

She pushed books on him: Tim LaHaye's *What Parents Should Know About Homosexuality,* Eugenia Price's *Christian* opus, *Leave Yourself Alone*. LaHaye presented the issue of homosexuality in terms of a massive battle of good and evil. He warned of Satan's fatal clutch, of how he could take on the guise of "an angel of light" and establish a mental and emotional hold on a child. The book quoted widely from clippings about the excesses of gay people. Like a progressive disease, he warned, homosexuality draws its victim ever deeper into a whirlpool of sin.

Terrified by such a prospect, Bobby battled to ward off Satan. Dutifully, he read, believed, and prayed. He immersed himself in church activities, especially the youth drama group, headed by a warm and sensitive woman named Teri Miller, a progressive Christian and a musician. Miller's view of God emphasized love and acceptance. She saw righteousness as a gift offered by the grace of God rather than a club to pummel mankind toward salvation.

Bobby was powerfully drawn to Teri Miller, like a weary traveler to a safe haven. He and another teenager, a girl named Terrie Tate, spent long hours, often into the morning, helping build sets for Miller's miniplays, which were entertainments with subtle moral messages. *The Touch of the Master's Hand*, written by Miller, was a parody on the Creation and the Fall, using several pop-culture figures to illustrate the void in mankind when separated from God.

Miller, then in her mid-twenties, saw Bobby as a teenager looking for a place to land. Gangly, with braces on his teeth, usually dressed in overalls, Bobby was a gentle soul with an artistic temperament, not one of your cookie-cutter kids. In a gesture of trust that delighted her, he invited her home to show her the notebooks of poetry he had written. He seemed hungry for affirmation.

But he revealed nothing of his inner anguish, not even to Miller. He could not blurt it out. She saw him as shy, in need of approval, but not dysfunctional or self-destructive. Certainly she never thought of him as gay, and found out only when Terrie

Tate called her more than three years later to tell her that Bobby had killed himself.

Terrie Tate was tomboyish, also shy if a bit more openly cynical, the product of a violent home environment. She felt close to Bobby as a fellow lost soul. They met during a Miller production of *The Wiz;* they both worked on the sets, and Bobby played the chief Munchkin, who presents the scroll to Dorothy.

Bobby's sensitive melancholy attracted her. They would play touch football or volleyball together, sit around and talk, or go for ice cream. He told her he was interested in becoming a nurse and even confided that he felt he did not fit in with the world— an admission that further bonded the pair. He told her that he saw his athletic brother as the success of the family. (Tate knew Ed and was best friends with his girlfriend at the time, Jeanine.) When the church sponsored a boat ride to honor graduating seniors, Tate invited Bobby to be her date. She was disappointed that during the event Bobby was uneasy, even shying away from holding hands with her. She felt inadequate, fearing he didn't like her in a male-female way. She reported that to Jeanine, who said, "Don't worry about it; he likes men."

That was a dilemma for Tate, who had yet to resolve her own sexuality (she accepted herself as a lesbian several years later, after a long bout with drugs and alcohol). She could not bring herself to mention the subject to Bobby. At the time, she was quite antigay as well as religious, and Walnut Creek Pres did not encourage that kind of discourse. Only recently she had taken a course in which a youth pastor had expounded on sexual immorality, twinning homosexuality and bestiality as prime examples.

Sexuality was the Presbyterian Church's—and most churches' —most discomfiting moral problem, more it seemed than abortion, planned parenthood, or racial discrimination. Homosexuality, in particular, sticks in the church's craw to this day. The United Presbyterian Church, the governing entity, has been haggling over the issue intensely since 1976. The church's general assembly was petitioned for major reform in 1978 and again fifteen years later, and each time it wrestled unsuccessfully with such questions as the ordination of gays and lesbians, and the full acceptance of gays and lesbians as congregants.

Bobby was probably not aware that, although it rejected the ordination of gays and lesbians in 1978, the assembly did urge its ministries to support civil rights for gays and lesbians, and to initiate courses to explore ways of allowing gays to participate in the life of the church. Being gay was still to be considered a sin, but gays could be encouraged to be celibate or, through prayer, to revert to the natural order of heterosexuality.

At Walnut Creek Pres, at the time run by a conservative minister, these were not considered live issues. When they came up—as in the case of a devoted parishioner who was unsubtly fired as the chair of an event-planning committee when it became known she was lesbian—these matters were dealt with quietly and expeditiously. There was no external demand for reform in this area, as there was for ordination of females. The real agitation for a change in attitudes toward gays and lesbians came in the urban parishes of Oakland, Berkeley, San Francisco, and Los Angeles.

Thus there was no motivation for someone like Bobby (or Terrie Tate) to come forward to seek help, nor was there an institutional framework to accommodate their needs. (In 1994 there still existed no overt pastoral mission at Walnut Creek Pres specifically for gays.) On the contrary, to be branded gay in an environment where he dearly wished nothing more than acceptance would have been the ultimate humiliation for Bobby.

And he knew that the potential for humiliation lurked in every corner of his surroundings. He certainly must have noted, for example, the big story in the local papers in 1980 when a young man almost his own age was dismissed as an assistant scoutmaster in the Berkeley Boy Scouts because he was gay. (The young man sued, and in early 1995 the case was still dragging through the appeals process.)

So he would store his anger and despair, assuming a public facade of bland neutrality, much like Ralph Ellison's invisible man. This is the face his dearest cousin, Jeanette, saw during a visit she made to the Griffiths in February 1980. The daughter of Mary's older sister, Jean, Jeanette was several years older than Bobby, yet close enough to him in age that the two of them had played together as kids. Jeanette and her sister Debbie had eventually moved north to Portland, Oregon, but Bobby and Jeanette had clicked from the start. They would maintain a rich, loving friendship to the end.

Her visit was a glorious interlude for both of them. They exchanged back rubs, took long walks, ate quiche, watched television, and talked, talked, talked. Jeanette had empathy for her unmolded, coltish cousin, appreciated his artistic bent, and understood his adolescent angst.

During the visit, Jeanette witnessed an intense discussion about her cousin's homosexuality that took place in the Griffith living room. She and Bobby were on the couch, with the rest of the family ranged around the room, her Uncle Bob watching in silence. Mary stood in the center like a teacher, her hand gesturing. "This is what the Bible says," she exhorted, launching into a recitation of Scripture.

"You won't bend, will you?" Bobby said wearily.

"Bobby, I can't erase these words from the Bible," Mary said.

Jeanette, who was questioning her own sexuality at the time, thought, "A family is supposed to be about love, and they're crucifying Bobby with their words." A person's sexuality didn't seem to her worth all the tension and rejection. She could feel an invisible wall between them and Bobby. The more he struggled, the more they would fight him. It seemed especially strange because, of all her aunts and uncles, the Griffiths were in every respect the most loving, the most giving. This was the one issue that tore everyone apart.

In May 1980, a year after coming out to Ed, Bobby—having lived through a year of intense effort, of stops and starts—made his only diary entry for 1980. Eerily prophetic, it introduced the theme of the next three years.

May 16. I write this in hopes that one day, many years from now, I will be able to go back and remember what my life was like when I was a young and confused adolescent desperately trying to understand myself and the world I live in. At the rate I'm going right now, though, I seriously wonder if I'll live to be very old, that is if I will live past being a teenager.

Another reason I write this is so that long after I die, others may have a chance to read about me and see what my life as a young person was like....

Except for the aspirin incident, Bobby would not attempt to act on his prophecy for three years. But the entry makes clear that suicide was an escape option he considered throughout his adolescence. That he did not exercise it for such a long period strongly suggests that having the option gave him permission to keep fighting against his homosexuality. And fight it he did, using his diary as a kind of safety valve, dumping his fury, despair, hate, hopes, and dreams into it with unselfconscious eloquence, profanity, and violence.

The real Bobby lived in his diaries, although even there he exercised some reserve, afraid that his family was snooping. (And they were. Mary, desperate to know what he was thinking, if he was moving in the right direction, would peek in from time to time, especially as communication between them diminished. Joy, worried about him, also took a few furtive looks.)

Bobby's gayness was a family obsession. But life did go on. Joy, herself an adolescent, was caught up in a four-year unrequited crush on a neighborhood boy named George. Her own journal of that period is overflowing with breathless references to sightings, snippets of conversation, anonymous gift offerings, tailing the boy in her white 1971 GMC truck so she could arrange "chance" meetings. Joy's girlfriends as well as her brothers and sister were enlisted in this harmless and apparently fruitless conspiracy. To celebrate George's twenty-first birthday, Joy and Bobby blew up twenty-one helium balloons and tied them to an oak tree, planning to photograph it and fashion a customized birthday card. Unfortunately, they later discovered they had inserted the roll of film backward. It made for great adolescent drama, but George's seeming indifference (aside from his polite attentions to her at a very few social meetings) was a source of pain and frustration for Joy.

She was a pretty girl with hazel eyes, an oval, contoured face, and long, straight brown hair. She laughed easily—a husky, infectious laugh that gave her face a warmth and openness that implied a lack of wariness, even a vulnerability, at her core.

She had problems with her weight. Her teenage journal is filled with frequently broken vows to go on one or another draconian diet. Joy's was a caretaker personality. She grew up with a strongly developed sense of responsibility for the well-being of others, especially her immediate family. As soon as she could drive, she became the chauffeur of choice, not only for her mother but also for her brothers, even when they had licenses and cars of their own.

As a giver, she was hurt when her gifts were unreciprocated. She had brother-sister squabbles with Ed, whose interests lay in sports and friends outside the home. Once, when the family went to a concert together, she resented the fact that as soon as they got there Ed disappeared with his friends. She wrote in a journal she kept as a teenager: "Mom called Ed over and said something to him about being rude. Then I said, 'Well, Ed, what do you care? You got your ticket.' He said something snotty, then left to go join his friends again."

. . .

Joy's concerns with Bobby were more serious. Sometime past his seventeenth birthday in June 1980, Bobby began making contacts with other gay men. His first sexual experience was with a man he met in the Walnut Creek Safeway store. As Bobby later told his friend Andrea, he went to the man's house and they had sex on the living-room floor. Then Bobby began getting calls from male friends. He'd disappear on weekends to all-night parties. Frequently, to avoid his mother's lecturing, he would lie about his whereabouts.

To Joy, Bobby's gay orientation was less worrying than the notion of gay promiscuity, which she viewed as sleazy, vaguely immoral, and, worst of all, potentially dangerous. She fretted about his safety. And, still her mother's daughter, she wrestled with religious and moral judgments.

For Mary, this new phase of Bobby's was extremely threatening. As long as Bobby was relatively home-bound, the situation could be controlled and the correct measures applied. But now he had a car—a 1950 Nash Metropolitan he called "Little Jewel," which his parents had helped him buy and which Bob had helped get in shape. And now boys were calling, and occasionally coming to the door to pick Bobby up. Mary maintained a civil demeanor toward these callers, not wanting to alienate Bobby. But she cringed underneath: this was not the way it was supposed to go. Bobby had to *want* to change for change to happen. "What is God doing?" she wondered. "Why does Bobby want to go out with gay people?" This going around with other homosexuals didn't demonstrate desire to change. It was more of Satan's work, she was convinced.

"Bobby you're not trying hard enough," she would say. "You're not praying hard enough. You need to have more faith."

"You're right, Mom," Bobby would say. "I'm just doomed to be a roasted marshmallow in the next life."

"Don't say that, Bobby."

"Well, that's what your damned Bible says!"

"Don't use profanity. And the Bible also says a person can change."

"And what if they don't want to!"

"With God nothing shall be impossible," Mary quoted. Bobby groaned.

"Bobby, you may want to *think* that what you are doing is the right way, but that's only Satan working his ways," Mary said. "I know you don't truly believe that God meant for man to be lying with other men—"

"I don't know what God meant for anybody anymore," Bobby interrupted. "And I wish people would stop watching my every move to make sure the family pervert is locked up for the night."

Joy exasperatedly pitched in, "Sure, Bobby, just so you can go out and screw your head off."

• • •

Bobby had a sympathizer in Andrea Hernandez, a school friend of Joy's who had attached herself to the Griffith family as an antidote to her own toxic family situation. Andrea spent most of her week with the Griffiths, and actually moved in for several months in 1981. A would-be artist, emotionally fragile, feeling like an outcast, she soon bonded with Bobby, two years her junior. He had confided in her about his gayness shortly before the family discovered it.

Andrea was witness to the endless debates. In retrospect, she viewed Mary and Joy as a kind of "religious tag team. They'd corral Bobby under the guise of philosophy, but what I saw was fanaticism, religious rantings and ravings, well into the night. I saw the hammering away, the chiseling of his soul."

Bobby challenged them, but Andrea could see that deep down he was succumbing, believing what they told him. He was no match for the combined power of God and family, she concluded. Underlying it all was his overwhelming sense of

failing his family and himself. Bobby was indoctrinating himself, becoming a foot soldier, and it angered her. Yet, wrestling
with her own sexuality at the time (she later accepted herself as
a lesbian), Andrea was too dependent on the goodwill of the
Griffiths to speak up on Bobby's behalf.

Bobby's own anger resounded in his diary.

*No one does understand me. No one in this house can ac-
cept my side of the story. Each person has his or her own pet
theory about me, including the solution to my "problems."*

*I really hate being damned. It's always for the same reason,
my sexuality. "Even the animals know who to do it with,"
that's my mother's logic. Well, Mother dear, you don't know the
half of it. Why am I the way that I am? If I only knew. "You
can change if you really want to," they say. "Don't underestimate the Lord's power." God damnit, how in the hell do any of
them know? What gives them the right to tell me I'm going to
burn in eternal hellfire and damnation? They account my "deviation" to an inherent sinful nature. Well, then, if God gave it to
me, I'm gonna keep it! They think I'm so blind and stupid, well
they're the ones who are wrong. I feel good about my rebellion.*

Now seventeen, a senior at Las Lomas High School, Bobby
in his rebel mode contradicted his mother, and became increasingly silent and removed. In early 1981, he gave his hair a
strawberry blond rinse ("to see if blondes really do have more
fun") and moved from the room with Ed. He fabricated a bedroom in a tiny attic space built by his father at the top of a stair-
case between Joy and Nancy's and Ed's bedrooms. There he
spent long hours alone, staying up late, emerging to watch
Marilyn Monroe movies (a wounded and ill-fated soul with
whom he could identify).

*Last night, about 2 A.M., I heard a familiar voice singing,
"That Old Black Magic." It was Marilyn. I jumped up and ran*

*into the family room and there she was as big as life in beautiful
living color. Oh, God, she is so gorgeous. The movie was* Bus
Stop. *That was a good movie. . . . I could feel exactly the frustration she was going through.*

School offered little respite. Bobby felt like an outsider at
Las Lomas as well. It was a typical sprawling suburban campus
high school in a pleasant section of Walnut Creek, with a reputation for good instruction. But Bobby made few friends there,
and kept to himself. He obviously was not interested in participating in his peers' heterosexual mating games, and was terrified of being exposed. His strategy was to remain as invisible as
possible, although even at school he would express his individuality in subtle ways, such as dress.

"I have a bittersweet relationship with Las Lomas," he
wrote in early 1981, his senior year.

*Sometimes I hate it and other times I really enjoy it. Today, I
enjoy being here. I wore my "penny-loafers" and my peg leg
jeans with my white gas station shirt—"ERNIE" the name on it.
And on top of it all I wore my new, old trench coat which looks
like the one Sherlock Holmes used to wear. I just know people
think I'm weird, weird, weird! But that's exactly how I want it.*

*Right now I'm in second period, "World Lit." Of course I'm
sitting alone in the corner. No one would dare be caught sitting
near a weirdo like me! These stupid high school kids! Sometimes I just can't figure them out. Oh well, I can always enter-
tain myself with fantasies about Marilyn.*

A motherly school secretary named Grace Lewis befriended
Bobby, offering a sympathetic ear. She saw him as a tortured
soul, deeply unhappy. Handsome, almost pretty, unathletic, and
not gregarious, Bobby fit the pattern of the oddball, a deadly
ranking in the vicious high school caste system. Although not
obviously effeminate, he was a stark contrast to his older brother,

who enjoyed all the benefits of a jock ranking. Bobby became the target for cutting remarks by some of his classmates, remarks questioning his masculinity.

Either Bobby revealed himself to Grace Lewis or she found out some other way; in any case, she was worried enough about him to refer him to a male schoolteacher who she knew was gay. There was (and still is) no formal counseling outreach to gay youngsters at Las Lomas. The teacher made an effort, even introducing Bobby to another gay student, but the tatters of Bobby's relationship to his high school were beyond repair.

His grades slipped, and he slackened his composition writing, turning more and more frequently to his journal.

The anger never erupts. . . . My timid nature would never allow a full fledged thunder storm to occur, but it is there, looming quietly on the horizon. . . . Sometimes my only refuge is sleep, and yet sometimes my sleep is invaded by nightmares which break the only quiet and solitude I have.

I can feel God's eyes looking down on me with such pity. He can't help me though, because I've chosen sin over righteousness.

His mood vacillated from depression to grandiosity. "It's very strange, but despite my gloomy outlook I still feel that one day, maybe very soon, I will be a success," he wrote in early March.

Barely a month later, just weeks short of graduation, Bobby dropped out of Las Lomas, telling his parents after the fact.

"Bobby, you don't want to be a quitter," his mother protested.

"Well, I will be, because I've gone to my last class."

His parents decided it would be useless to try to force their son to return to school.

"I won't be graduating in June," he wrote in his diary, even though he had paid for his yearbook and placed an order for his graduation gown. In fact, his picture appeared with the rest of the graduating class, with an inscription from George Bernard

Shaw that Bobby had apparently chosen himself: "Do not follow where the path may lead. Go, instead, where there is no path and leave a trail."

He told his diary, "I feel sad about this. . . . I've quit my job and pretty much withdrawn from the mainstream of suburban life. These days I can be found whiling away the hours daydreaming and progressively growing more and more lonely." (Actually he was not that inert. He had started jogging several times a week to Alamo, a town nearly five miles away. "I feel a sense of accomplishment when I jog. Like my life is worth something.") He found himself staying up till the early morning hours, raiding the icebox after everyone was long asleep. Then he'd stay in bed till ten or eleven the next day.

The usually placid Bob—classified by the experts Mary consulted as the essential male role model, and fired up by Mary's nagging—made a special effort to develop father-son rapport, with ludicrous results.

Bob went with Bobby to an art show. They attempted to develop a mutual interest in photography. They hiked together on Mount Diablo, a lovely peak not far from their home. That outing was a disaster, most of it spent in silence or stilted conversation. Bobby talked about wanting to be a writer. Bob, strong on the work ethic, tried to discuss strategic career planning. Bobby zoned out, uninterested in the long view. Bob felt he was playing at being a father. Bobby apparently did, too. They both dropped into silence, wordlessly acknowledging that the whole effort was basically phony.

After that, the rift between them widened: their interactions became polite, infrequent, awkward. To Joy, hypersensitive to family tensions, it felt horrible. "Bobby can't stand (at times) to be near my Dad," she wrote in her journal. "I'm going to fast until Bobby and my Daddy can 'show & tell' they do love one another. . . . I know I can do it because I'm doing it for the Lord, for Bobby and Daddy. I will not stop until their relationship is 'reborn,' mended, whole."

That did not seem likely. Bobby felt increasingly uncomfortable in his father's presence and in fact confided to his diary that this condition dated back many years.

This morning I was going to get out of bed and I heard my dad downstairs so I just laid there until he was gone. It reminds me of how when I was real little at the breakfast table I would always build a barrier between my dad and myself with the cereal box and milk carton and then I would pretend he wasn't there.

While searching unsuccessfully for a job, Bobby made noises about joining the air force, or even the Peace Corps. Mary discouraged these ideas, worrying secretly that he would be found out as gay. Bobby filled the hours with brooding and fantasizing.

If I could have one thing in this world, anything, I would have a beautiful man to love me. Just to have a pretty man hug me and gently kiss me. . . . I daydream that one day I'll be casually strolling through a store or a park and from out of nowhere will appear this dream man and our eyes will meet and we'll live happily ever after. It's too bad I have to be such a hopeless romantic. It will never happen that way. I'm not even sure I really want it in the first place.

Despite his longings, Bobby's romantic encounters were generally short and abortive. They flared intensely but burned out rapidly. He lost interest, or withdrew when the other party started getting serious. They were doomed either by Bobby's guilt or by his self-loathing, which he expressed as contempt for anyone who could be dumb enough to care for him.

Sunday, May 2. What happened was very innocent and yet I feel very guilty about the whole thing. I went to a party last night. I lied to everyone and said it was in Orinda, when it was really in Berkeley. I also said it was being thrown by one of my straight friends. Oh the evil webs we spin! Anyway, I met a lot of interesting people, one in particular. He's tall and his boyish features were cute. So he took me to all the San Francisco nite clubs, which in itself was an unforgettable experience. Our first stop was the "White Horse," a sleazy little bar in Berkeley. Next was the I-Beam [in San Francisco]. This was a huge steamy disco with slimy floors. . . . S. is a nice person. After we danced the night away we parked at the pier. It was very peaceful and quiet. Just the sound of crashing waves and crying seagulls. I wasn't in any mood or frame of mind to enjoy it though because it was about five in the morning. I knew I had made a mistake going out and staying so late. I'm sorry, I know how much my mom and everyone worries about me. I shouldn't do this to them. They don't deserve it.

Anyway we parked and did what most couples do in parked cars. Big deal, innocent kid stuff, but I still feel immoral. Finally I got home at 8 A.M. and surprisingly I didn't get into a lot of trouble. I suppose I should say, yet. They still might be plotting. Especially Joy. She knows my every move. She can see through my feeble lies like Saran wrap. But what I say is, why should I have to lie in the first place?

Caretaker Joy did keep a close lookout, and had strongly mixed feelings. She hated that Bobby lied and wondered equally why he felt the need to.

"You make me lie," he would say.

"That's crap," Joy would respond. "If we drive you to a party, there's no reason to lie and then go off somewhere else. It's not as if Mom or I am saying, 'Don't do this' or 'Don't do that.' Then when you don't come home we end up worrying ourselves sick over you."

Her judgments were never as severely Jehovan as her mother's, but she fretted that Bobby was doomed to unhappiness. She had trouble seeing how his lifestyle could ever fit the patterns to which she was accustomed. Sometimes she would

Prayers for Bobby

blurt out hurtful things. "I hope you find a really nice guy, Bobby," she once told him, with total sincerity. "But it's going to be a very lonely life. You won't be able to bring your boyfriend around to Christmas or Thanksgiving or anything like that. Can you imagine what Granny would say?"

Joy could get to Bobby. "I hate Joy," he wrote once, with exquisite melodrama.

I want to claw her eyes out with a sharp stick. I hope she dies fat and alone. She hurts me. I hate everyone, but mostly Joy at the moment. When she makes her fucking remarks it slashes a raw bleeding wound deep deep. It will never heal. . . . If anyone says anything to me from now on, I'll try my hardest to slash them with my voice and my choice of words.

Those moments passed, leaving the core of affection between brother and sister intact. But to Bobby, the contrast with earlier days was palpable, the days when brothers, sisters, and parents seemed joined by an unbreakable bond of togetherness. Something had irrevocably changed. Bobby was loved, but was simply not okay. To be acceptable and accepted, he would have to change. It occurred to no one at the time that it might have been the family's responsibility to change, not Bobby's.

Another irony unrecognized by anyone in the family was the contrast between the way the family embraced Joy's endless efforts to snare young George and its disapproving response to Bobby's adolescent explorations.

Mary, in fact, was ashamed of having a gay son. Once, he arrived instead of Joy to pick her up from a pizza lunch with some women friends. Mary saw him entering and practically bolted with him to the door. She was terrified that Bobby's gayness would somehow telegraph itself.

Despite Bobby's differences with Joy, they remained simpatico. With Joy he had no need to hide his gayness, and she did not constantly harangue him about it. Bobby could in fact confide in her, talk about his infatuations, and compare notes with her in her pursuit of dream boy George.

They delighted in cruising around together. Joy liked nothing better than climbing behind the wheel of her truck and hitting the road with a brother or sister along. Main Street, Walnut Creek, was the weekend cruise choice for local kids, a real-life evocation of *American Graffiti*. One weekend night, Bobby dressed Joy in some of Granny's jewelry, including several big zircons, and a period dress, and tied her hair in a turban. They piled into Bobby's fire-engine red "Little Jewel" and tooled downtown. Joy hung out the window, attracting attention and camping it up, greeting everyone with a ludicrously pompous "Good evening!" They had a ball.

Joy loved animals. The family had a menagerie of chickens, dogs, cats—and goats. She bought three goats and bred them, tending the family in the backyard: Esther, Sweepea, and Clyde, and offspring Bucky and Bud. Bobby would help feed them, or go for walks with Joy, with Esther on a leash. (Joy actually had Sweepea trained to use a cat box.)

On a typical day they might watch reruns of "The Brady Bunch," have dinner, then go downtown or watch Ed play baseball. For all his brooding, Bobby had a manic side. When with Joy, he loved quoting the camp movie stars, mimicking Crawford or Davis, reveling in their bitchy "up yours" attitude. "Fasten your seat belts, darlings. It's going to be a bumpy night." This would send him into gales of laughter, his head thrown back in momentary glee.

Bobby would sometimes accompany Joy on her motorized pursuits of George (he, too, thought George was good-looking), and she on a couple of occasions went with him on gay jaunts. Once, they combed Berkeley and parts of San Francisco looking for someone Bobby had a crush on. On San Francisco's Polk Street, a popular and somewhat sleazy strip where gays congregate, Joy for the first time saw same-sex couples touching, even kissing. The sight of openly amorous lesbians was particularly shocking for her.

Joy enjoyed the outing as another adventure, yet she felt depressed by what she viewed as a decadent slice of the gay scene. She wished her brother would find young people of similar upbringing, interested in art and other high-minded things.

She wrote in her journal in the spring of 1981:

Nancy, Wesley, and Bobby are here in my bedroom. We're listening to Kim Carnes's song "Bette Davis Eyes." Bobby's presently looking for work. He says his choice of life is on and off from day to day. He went over to Berkeley last night to watch Alice in Wonderland. *He got home around 12. He left at 6:30 to 7 wearing his Hayward Bowling shirt, a light turquoise with his name on it, Bob. He got it at the thrifty Salvation Army Store in Pleasant Hill along with his skinny, skinny black tie, his faded Levi's and Nike's.*

Bobby's life seems to be coming along fine. When I remember to say my prayers he is ALWAYS in the top 10. Bobby's a good guy, just a little confused and possibly off the Lord's path. And when he starts talking with his friends they all have him believing we're bent, narrow-minded. Bullshit.

This was a month before Bobby's eighteenth birthday. His own entries during that period make it clear that he was not coming along fine at all. They reflect the emotional state of someone without a compass. He had a keen mind; he was intelligent enough to grasp the irony of his dilemma and to assert every ounce of his will to navigate his way out. But his determination and drive were sabotaged by overwhelming feelings of guilt, sinfulness, and self-contempt. These factors combined to keep him in a depressed state far more intense than his mother or anyone else perceived. This is the way it went for Bobby shortly before his eighteenth birthday and during the first half of his nineteenth year:

May 1. You really know how to make yourself unhappy, did you know that? Half of you despises the world and the other half tries so hard to be a part of that world. . . . You must feel a need to punish yourself. Is that why you do the things you do? Ask yourself this, Do I really deserve to be punished? And the worst part of it is that you know exactly how to punish yourself. . . . What will it take to satisfy you? Why don't you just kill yourself and get it over with? That's exactly what you're doing. Only you're doing it slowly and painfully.

May 5. I have to get up at 6:30 and here I am watching some Ethel Merman movie, eating crackers and drinking Pepsi. God, what a combo. It's 1:30, always around this time of night I get very philosophic. I was just wondering if man would be better off if he had no sex drive. Babies would be grown in greenhouses as though they were tulips; some with blue eyes, some green, some hazel. Men wouldn't kill each other over women and women wouldn't kill each other over men. Oh, and vice versa, if you get my drift.

People would like each other for their inner beauty and admirable qualities such as honesty and loyalty. . . . Why couldn't God have thought up a much more simple way for man to reproduce?

July 23. I think I only write when I'm depressed. Right now I just want to die, just die. . . . I sit here groveling and wonder who in the fuck is up there watching. Is there anyone? I really doubt it. Sometimes I get so mad I feel like I could just scream loud enough for God to hear me: "What in the fuck do you think you're doing sitting on your ass just watching the damn mess you created down here?" But I guess it just echoes around, bouncing from cloud to cloud unheard by anyone.

September 27. Last nite I attended a tea party in Berkeley. Everything was going wonderfully until this little queen started making moves on me. God! I never know how to react. . . .

Anyway, as usual I couldn't say no, and the rest isn't history. . . . I guess at the time my rationale was that he really wanted me. I mean he wouldn't give up, so I figured, "Give him a piece" and maybe he'll leave you alone. Oh, God, he was gross, and the worst thing about it is that boys can't fake it quite as well as girls!

September 27. Ed is unhappy with my situation. Oh, he tries to hide it but I can tell it tears him up inside to know about my "carnal" wheeling and dealing. But what can I do? I don't know.

September 29. I didn't go to work today because of my sore throat. I read in a book that you can get gonorrhea of the throat. I hope like hell I don't have it. That would be really terrible. I'm scared, and there's no one to turn to.

October 13. Today is "Mommies" birthday. Her cake read, "Happy Birthday Mommie Dearest." A little joke. Ha ha. [The joke included an image of a hanger inscribed on the cake.]

December 14. I have the worst luck with guys. So far they've all been flakes. I shouldn't complain though, I'm pretty flaky myself. Anyway, there was Jose, who I just couldn't get all that excited about. And then Enri who I guess is the kind of guy who loves 'em and leaves 'em. He got tired of me after the third "date." I don't really care, though, because by our third date I was beginning to see what a jerk he was. God, why can't I find some cute, sensible boy? That's all I want.

December 20. It's almost Christmas. You could have fooled me though. It's more like Groundhog Day or some other holiday no one could care less about.

January 3, 1982. Sometimes at night, I get all nervous and I can't sleep. I just feel like my brain is spinning around and around in my stomach. I'm all mixed up as a result, and I can't identify my feelings. It's like they're all here but they're blindfolded. They bump into each other inside my head and just get more and more mixed up. I wish life were black and white, like old movies. Everything was crisp and in focus. Sometimes I sense that life is very fragile and that at any given moment it could be snuffed out the way a candle is by a sudden draft. I just want someone to protect me.

Often I feel very inadequate. . . . I hate that feeling. Do you ever feel like you're some stupid kind of intellectual person who has lost his glasses and is stumbling through life? I guess that's a pretty odd question. Do you love me? Do you really love me? Tell me how much. I love you.

The Healing

Mary knew she had embarked on an open-ended journey. Everything she had ever believed in lay in a jumble, like so many Pick-up Sticks waiting to be reassembled in some new order. She had no idea where she was headed, only that she was going, driven by a need to understand.

She was shaken by the realization that the Bible had nothing to say to confirm her son's place in God's creation. All her life she had taken the Bible as God's own word. Conformance to it brought safety and comfort; deviation brought penalty—a truth as certain as the cycle of days. More than a year after her son's death it was clear to her that if Bobby's life and death were to have meaning, she would have to look beyond.

She turned, nervously, to a book Bobby had given her to read, *Loving Someone Gay*, by a California psychologist named Don Clark. When Bobby offered it she had picked it up briefly and then dropped it like a hot coal. It seemed repulsive, a satanic apologia for a deadly sin.

Now she sat with it. What she read hit home.

Once upon a time, people selected the most beautiful and talented youths of the community and ceremoniously threw them into boiling volcanoes as an offering to appease the angry gods. . . . Some parents are still willing to sacrifice their beautiful gay offspring to appease the god of conformity. . . . I feel compassion for the parent who breaks the sacred bond and turns away from the outstretched arms of a son or a daughter. . . .

Some youngsters immerse themselves in religion, devote themselves to being good 24 hours a day and/or have inexplicable emotional breakdowns. . . . More than a few commit suicide. Having cut deeply into an already injured self-esteem with the hurtful self-confrontation in which ugly labels are self-assigned, a part of the previously valued self is murdered. . . . The rage turns inward. The misdirected rage provides the energy for the emotionally drained person to finally pull the trigger or tie the noose. Their act of self-murder is a shame that we who represent their society must bear.

To survive, a gay person must see that she or he cannot afford to accept unchallenged any prepackaged set of assumptions even if they were given by such exalted authorities as parents, Church, government or revolutionary political group. . . . For a gay person to trust any culturally given set of values is suicide—often literally.

From this perspective Mary's and Bobby's roles were reversed: if Clark was correct, then her Bible-thumping self-righteousness might have been totally, tragically wrong, and Bobby's efforts to assert his gay persona—including his offering her this very book—might have been desperately right. The implications sent a chill down her spine. She wondered as well whether the book had helped Bobby. Perhaps it was too little too late. *He had wanted her to read it.*

Soon after, she had a dream about Bobby. He was at the extreme left of the dream's frame, in a state of torment. Bobby kept pointing to a book, which was old and tattered. He beckoned her to find a page, which she did after a long search. All it said was "God is all goodness." Mary woke to the thought that if God is all goodness he could not do all the terrible things the Bible says he does. He could not be a God of wrath and vengeance. He could not turn against Bobby. In the dream Bobby could not understand how God could want to inflict such pain.

She pondered, and scrutinized the holy book with newly critical eyes. She reread Deuteronomy 22:18: "If someone has a stubborn and rebellious son who will not obey his father and mother [then he or she] shall take him out to the elders of the town. . . . They shall say to the elders, 'This son of ours is stubborn and rebellious. He will not obey us.' Then all the men of the town shall stone him to death. So you shall purge the evil from your midst."

Stone a rebellious child to death? Mary struggled with this notion, remembering that Moses had gone to the mount, conversed with God, and returned to the people with the Law, which included this directive. But if God had spoken directly to Moses, he would have given him the full benefit of his infinite wisdom and knowledge. The prophet would certainly have known more about human nature than is displayed in this verse. Kids have a will, and they're going to raise that will toward their parents. To think that God commanded that such a child be put to death! Mary heard herself intoning, "I don't believe that."

In her new, analytic mode, Mary began to notice other portions of the Bible that seemed barbaric and inhumane. In the story of Elisha, the Bible recounts how some boys taunted the prophet about his bald head. Elisha summoned two she-bears to devour forty-two of the children. Such acts, it now occurred to her, were the doings of a sociopath. Yet Matthew Henry, in his annotation to the Bible, condoned Elisha, calling his act the result of "divine impulse."

She felt as if a ledge were crumbling from under her feet, as if she were risking heresy. She yearned for the comfort of unconditional belief, but could not turn back. It frightened her.

The Sodom and Gomorrah story especially haunted her with its straight-out condemnation and savage vengefulness. This was the God with whom she had grown up. This was the God who killed sodomites. The God without mercy. The God who could have allowed and did allow Bobby to die.

Mary realized she had gone as far as she could go alone. She needed some expert theological help. But where to turn? The traditional church was no longer an option. It was a twist of irony: Just a few years ago she was desperate to change Bobby to conform to a rigid standard. Now, still as driven, she sought a context in which to validate him as he had actually been.

She remembered the Metropolitan Community Church, the gay church. There was one in Concord, the next town to the north. Bobby had actually gone there a couple of times, which disconcerted her. The notion of so-called ministers using God's name to justify homosexuality had made her shudder: it was the devil's work.

Now she needed help, and MCC was, after all, a church. If gay people had found a way to reconcile sexuality with religion, she wanted to know how they had done so. She thumbed through the phone book to get the number. She punched it, hand trembling, and hung up after the first ring. She called a second time, panicked, and hung up again. Then a third try.

"MCC. May I help you?"

"I'm . . . I'd like to talk to your minister."

"One moment please. Reverend Whitsell will be right with you."

When Larry Whitsell got on the line, Mary said, "I'm the mother of a gay son." She hesitated. "He killed himself."

"I'm truly sorry to hear that," Whitsell answered. "There unfortunately are so many like him."

"Yes. I . . . was wondering, could I come and talk to you? I've had to do a lot of thinking and . . . "

"By all means," he jumped in. They made an appointment, and Mary breathed a sigh of relief.

Larry Whitsell had been a gay activist for eighteen years, twelve of them with MCC, and seven as pastor. He presided over a congregation of mostly closeted gay and lesbian professionals who lived quietly in the suburban setting in and around Concord. That peace was in the process of being shattered.

At the time Mary phoned Whitsell he was embroiled in controversy over the suicide of a young black gay man in the parking lot of the Concord mass-transit station. Concord was soon to become an unlikely battleground between far-right religious conservatives and the moderate center over the issue of gay civil liberties—a struggle that would expand across the nation over the next decade.

Ed drove Mary to the Metropolitan Community Church, which was housed in an old one-story wood-frame cottage on Concord Avenue. It consisted of a living room that served as the sanctuary and two or three small offices in the back. She entered with trepidation. She expected Whitsell to look and act different from "ordinary" people, and that made her uneasy. But when Whitsell came forward to greet her, he looked quite ordinary: slender, of medium size, with brown hair and a beard, dressed casually. His appearance put her at ease. They sat in his office drinking coffee. He mostly listened as Mary told her story.

They talked for three hours. She had done something wrong, she acknowledged. But what was right?

She had had no guidance. Her church offered nothing on the subject. She was going strictly on her limited knowledge. "I did something wrong," she said, weeping, "and look what happened to my boy!"

Whitsell tried to comfort her, but Mary was looking for information rather than sympathy. She wanted to know about Sodom and Gomorrah. How could he as a minister justify homosexuality in light of what happened there? How could she make peace with her son's memory, with such condemnation hanging over it?

Whitsell proceeded to explain the modernist view of the story of Sodom and Gomorrah, a story that, he noted, had been handed down as an oral account before it was codified in Genesis. Progressive biblical scholars interpret the sin of the cities to be inhospitality rather than sodomy. In biblical times, the refusal to grant hospitality was an extreme breach of the social contract. The act of the townspeople in threatening the angels— whether it had been rape, murder, or some other form of violence—was in this view the essential sin of Sodom, the kicker that assured God's action. In that era, when consensual homosexual activity did not exist as a known "condition," rape of

any kind would have been seen as a society-threatening deviation—an abomination, the most extreme act of inhospitality.

It was not until the Christian era that the sin of Sodom became connected with homosexuality as a practice, Whitsell explained. The Roman historians Philo and Josephus, writing in
the first century A.D.—a period of great moral turmoil—were
responsible for linking the Sodom story (which had occurred
two thousand years earlier) to some of the Dionysian excesses
of the era in which they lived. This interpretation was adapted
by the fathers of the Christian church, and the tradition became
fixed for all time.

Mary was stunned. The possibility of an alternative view of
the Bible was, in itself, a major revelation. Why then had the
existence of such a view not been made known to her and her
fellow parishioners? Yes, it was unacceptable to traditionalists,
but why suppress it? She felt cheated, felt that the church
should be called to task for that. What else was out there that
she didn't know about?

She made a second appointment with Whitsell, and a third.
Then she agreed to come to a service.

The experience animated her, giving her permission to question
the infallibility of Scripture. Consider this, she thought: these men,
these prophets, Moses and the rest of them quoted in the Bible,
were intermediaries. The prophets were not God; they were ordinary people who merely lived in a different time and place.

For example, she thought, nobody takes Deuteronomy
22:18 seriously today. No one in his right mind would condone
stoning a rebellious child to death. There were other biblical admonitions honored totally in the breach these days: that lepers
wear torn clothing and cry out, "Unclean, unclean!"; that adul-
tery with a neighbor's wife be punished by death; that having
intercourse with a menstruating woman be a capital offense;
that no clothing of mixed fibers be worn; that bastards not be
allowed in the synagogue; that a brother marry the wife of his
dead sibling.

So the church no longer recognized many things as being sinful or worthy of death. Why, then, wouldn't her son's homosexuality be among them? True, the Bible declares the death penalty for "men lying with men." But she could see Moses instituting such a law in the name of procreation—to get the Jewish nation to grow. If one were to examine the Bible in the context of the period in which it was written, as a document authored by humans *interpreting* God's will, that left room for error. How much did Moses really know about human sexuality?

This was exciting—and scary. She was moving very fast. One Sunday, Joy drove Mary to MCC services and waited for her outside. A gay church held no interest for her, and besides, weren't they going to interpret things in their favor just as other churches did? Joy herself was beginning to question any organized approach to spirituality. One good thing was happening, though: her mother's spirits were picking up.

In the sanctuary, Mary noticed immediately how "normal" most of the people there looked. About forty men and women crowded into the tiny living room. They were well dressed, probably professionals. The mixed congregation of men and women would have passed for that of any traditional church were it not for some same-sex couples holding hands or with arm over shoulder. The church used the King James version of the Bible, and Whitsell offered Holy Communion. Mary moved to the small altar to receive the wafer and wine.

Mary felt a quality of camaraderie in the small space, a sense of oneness with the spirit of God that surprised and moved her. It took a few visits for her to realize that these people were elated because they were able to bring their spiritual and gay natures together here without fear or embarrassment.

She remarked to Larry Whitsell during one of their talks, "You know, I never felt such a sense of the spirit of love in church before."

"I've had many people say that," he replied. "People who come here are hungry for the spirit, to connect with the Divine. They had to be very determined to keep that connection considering the hostility and rejection most of them had to go through in their native churches. So what happens here is a mix of joy and gratitude, a rediscovery that they are worthy of God's love, just like anyone else."

Mary confided, "You know, Bobby came here a couple of times. I discouraged it. But I think now the reason he stopped is he never could allow himself to feel worthy of God's love. And we didn't help."

As the discussions accumulated, Whitsell could see that Mary needed ongoing help to ride out the turbulent change she was experiencing. "Have you heard of P-FLAG?" he asked.

She had not. "This is a national group," he explained, "literally 'Parents and Friends of Lesbians and Gays,' that has been very successful in reconciling parents to their gay kids and vice versa. There's a local chapter trying to form. I think you would learn a lot. There's a Concord woman involved named Betty Lambert."

Whitsell arranged for Mary and Betty to meet in mid-1985. Betty Lambert was in her mid-sixties, a talkative, knowledgeable widow, short and chubby, with fingers gnarled by arthritis. She had a forty-year-old gay son named Mike who was sick with AIDS. "He was fourteen years old when he came out to us," she told Mary. "I knew this before then. We as mothers always know, don't we? I knew there was something different about this very special child. In those days, the sixties, there was no one to talk to about homosexuality. His father didn't even want to hear about this. Mike finally found me a book, *A Family Matter: A Parent's Guide to Homosexuality.*

"He and my sister and I went to see this M.D. He looked at me and said, 'Yes, your son does have an emotional problem, and should see a psychiatrist.' Mike went into a fit of rage. What did he need a psychiatrist for?"

Mary felt a wave of envy. Betty's son was ill with AIDS, but he was alive. "She totally accepts him, in fact seemed proud of him," she thought. "Where was I for Bobby when I had the chance?"

Betty asked Mary if she wanted to attend a P-FLAG meeting. Mary said yes. They drove to Saint Francis Lutheran Church in San Francisco. ("They meet in a church!" Mary marveled to herself.) On the way, Betty told her, "It's okay to be nervous. You should have seen me my first time. I looked at those stairs and I thought, 'I can't!' I walked out, got in my car, and drove off. Then I turned around and came back. I went up and there were these wonderful people."

There were more than twenty people at this meeting, parents and offspring. Most of the children were in their teens or twenties. The parents were mostly mothers, with a smaller scattering of fathers. For the first time, Mary found herself among a group of parents who accepted, loved, even honored their gay and lesbian children. She heard family after family tell stories of coming out, the shock of first knowledge, initial rejection, a subsequent compulsion to learn, and, ultimately, reconciliation.

"I finally realized that Sam was the same person *after* he told me that he was before—a wonderful, talented, loving child," a parent remarked.

Another said, through tears, "My biggest regret is that she felt she had to hide such an important part of her life from me for so many years. And she was right! I was not ready to hear it."

A young man in his twenties described in a choked voice the thrill of marching with his family in the gay pride parade. "I never in my wildest dreams thought I would see that day— strutting down Market Street with me and my parents and my lover, holding hands and waving."

Mary took it all in with a mix of awe, excitement, and regret. These were people with the same life experience as she, people she could talk to. And yet, they still had their children; they had found a way to overcome their fear and hostility and unite with their kids. For her, it was too late.

She told her story, shyly and briefly. "For me there was no doubt. It was an open-and-shut case. I didn't have to deal with 'This is the end of my world; I don't have a son anymore.' All I had to do was trust in God. He was going to come to Bobby's rescue. It didn't work out. Now I'm trying to figure out why."

The P-FLAG experience opened another door. Soon, with Betty at the wheel of her blue Ford, she and Mary were making the circuit of local P-FLAG gatherings—Oakland, San Jose, the northern California regional meeting in Marin County. Mary read the P-FLAG pamphlets. She learned that the organization had originated in 1972 as a tiny support group created by a New York couple, Jules and Jeanne Manford, who had been outraged when their gay son, Morty, was assaulted by antigay rowdies. Four years later a group formed in Los Angeles under the aegis of Adele and Larry Starr, and soon other cities followed suit. Following the 1979 March on Washington for Gay Rights, twenty-six parents met and later formed a national federation under the present name; it held its first national convention in Los Angeles in 1982.

P-FLAG, which today stands for Parents, Family, and Friends of Lesbians and Gays, maintains a national office in Washington, D.C., and has a membership of thirty-five thousand. It has evolved from a family support group to a strong lobbying organization for equal rights for gay people. There are now more than three hundred chapters, a huge jump from the forty or so that existed when Mary first got involved in 1985.

Educating herself about the organization, she listened to tale after tale of mothers whose children seemed different when growing up. She heard from the children themselves about how they had felt. She witnessed heart-wrenching scenes in which parents, new to the knowledge, pleaded for help in accepting their kids and no longer blaming themselves.

"I'm learning," said a mother. "I've read every book in the library on the subject. But I can't escape the terrible feeling that if only I had done something different. . . . I know it's not rational. I know Tony is a perfectly happy, well-adjusted young man. I'm beginning to think that I'm the abnormal one."

Each time, Mary went home and processed what she had seen and heard. She held frequent discussions with Ed, who was beginning to test his own orthodoxy. He had been shaken deeply by his brother's death. His mother's explorations took seed in fertile soil. Her new ideas made sense, but when he discussed them with people at church, they were dismissed as manifestations of grief or guilt. A minister theorized that Mary was reinterpreting Scripture as a way of finding peace or diminishing the guilt that comes whenever a family member takes his or her own life.

Ed felt increasingly that the arguments he got at church were legalistic interpretations of the Bible, frequently linked to the ego of the interpreter. On the other hand, he felt that the things his mother was saying had the ring of truth.

Ed's life was changing. His lifelong hopes of a professional baseball career dissipated after a disastrous tryout with the Lodi Dodgers (a Los Angeles Dodgers farm team). He came to realize that he had had an inflated picture of his athletic ability. It was time for some realism. He finished his police studies at Los Medanos College and went on to intern with the Concord Police Department. He drifted away from Walnut Creek Pres.

For Mary, the exposure to P-FLAG had crystallized a truth she could no longer resist. The repeated testimony of parents and children portrayed gay kids as being different at an early stage of life, maybe from birth.

This triggered a memory of another dream she had had shortly after Bobby's death, which made little sense at the time. In the dream, Mary heard Bobby laughing happily. "Bobby, is that you?" she asked, incredulous. "Why shouldn't it be?" his voice replied. She was exhilarated. Bobby alive! When she turned to look, she saw Bobby as an infant, back in the kitchen of their Danville home, as real as life. Her attention focused on the child's head. He looked beautiful to her, and yet there was something different about his head. It was not deformed, just different. She couldn't figure it out.

Now, nearly three years later, she finally understood. The dream was saying that Bobby was born with the seed of his sexuality. He was different. Not sinful or evil or sick, just different.

If that was indeed the case, she had, at last, an answer to her question of why God had not healed Bobby. He had not healed Bobby *because there was nothing wrong with him.*

The Leper

Joy went to work as an office manager at California Frame Company in Walnut Creek in mid-1981 and soon afterward got Bobby a job assembling frames at $3.50 an hour. He would stay there off and on for eighteen months, even though he found the work dull and repetitive. "It's not really hard work," he wrote in his diary, "but it's so redundant that it exhausts you. My fingernails are darkened from staining the wood. It's hard to get it all off."

Partly as a result of the tedious routine, the factory crew were a boisterous lot. They did their jobs, but broke the monotony by engaging in rubber-band fights, staple-gun battles, and other high jinks. One worker swallowed an earthworm on a five-dollar bet.

Bobby soon discovered to his delight that there were several lesbians among the thirteen or so assembly-line workers. Once they had come out to one another, Bobby and the women formed a tight little clique, chatting in code, bopping to the latest rock hits on the radio, and occasionally sneaking in booze during the night shift.

Bobby bonded with Alice Hamilton, Alice's lover, Diane Haines, and two others at the worktable. Their presence, he wrote, "is the only reason I stay. I don't feel so alone in the world."

There was an underground feeling to the gay circle. Cal-Frame was Mormon owned, and many of the employees were Mormon, especially the print-division workers across the driveway—mainly male jock types driving forklifts. Though it was tacitly known that Alice and Diane were a pair, the gay group kept a sub-rosa buzz going while discreetly avoiding obvious provocations.

Their secret phrase for *gay* was "on a bike." When a good-looking man came through, Alice, twenty-one and nearly six feet tall, plump and brassy, would ask in an audible stage whisper, "Hey, Bobby, is he on a bike?"

Bobby would reply, "I don't know, but I'd love to find out!"

The radio blared throughout each shift, cycling with numbing repetition the hot groups of the early 1980s: Blondie and "Eat to the Beat," the all-girl Go-Go's, the Human League, the Cars (Bobby's favorite group, with its hit "Shake It Up").

They played Name That Tune, giving points for the first one to guess a song. They especially loved Devo's "Whip It." When it came on, their group would drop to the floor and writhe to the music; they'd twitch and roll about, "doing the bacon" and laughing.

They contrived to beat the system. They'd occasionally take long lunches, or sneak out early. One night they conspired to smuggle in a bottle of liquor for the night crew. Bobby took part enthusiastically.

He had his antic side. But it seemed to the women that while Bobby yearned to break loose, he didn't know how to fully enjoy himself. Alice noticed the sad eyes behind the laughter, the need to be the "good boy." Part of Bobby was always observing, watching to see others' reactions. She thought of him as a tap dancer, always on his toes.

Once, returning from the lunch truck that showed up daily on the premises, Bobby asked Diane, "Did they say something about me?" "Of course not," she replied. It may not have been all paranoia. The Mormon crew was capable of muttering slurs when Bobby or one of the lesbian group came by.

Typically, Bobby suffered in silence, venting his fury in his journal:

I hate the assholes across the street. . . . They can all burn in hell for all I care. . . . They're cruel and insensitive. One of these days I'll give them a piece of my mind when they catch me not caring about what in the fuck anyone else thinks.

The burden of differentness weighed on him. Alice and the blond, shapely Diane, also twenty-one, were two years older, self-accepting, and ages more worldly than Bobby. They could assume the role of guru. He said to Alice during one of their long talks about gay life over the assembly line, "If I could only know that it gets easier afterward. But it's just so hard."

Alice assured him, "It takes a while, but it does get better." Yet she and Diane were not so sure the message would sink in. Bobby's self-image seemed frayed. He dreamed of being a model, but worried constantly over chronic facial acne. He never confided much about his family, but he did let it be known that they did not approve of his activities.

That impression was confirmed for Alice and Diane by Joy, who seemed to them both to love her brother deeply while looking askance at his lifestyle. (Joy's journal for that summer records, "Bobby is such a sweet person. Everyone loves him dearly. His talents, depth, understanding. I know he'd love to love, take care, be taken care of, loved by some girl of the same wonderful characteristics, but his true doubt and fear puts him where he's at now. Aggravated dislike for himself—lost. He wants a loving friendship with Christ but is so impatient. He wants Christ but he doesn't want to give anything up in the process. He wants to have his cake and eat it too.")

Diane felt that Bobby needed friends, a group to hang out with. He went night crawling with her and Alice once—to a

gay bar in Sacramento called Bojangles. But their social life off
the job never jelled. He wanted community, yet he seemed to
hold back.

Still, they fell for Bobby's sweet nature. Diane found him
lovable—a very soft, warm man. Alice felt both love and compassion. Bobby was at a turning point, she believed. He was
struggling with the decision to go with his sexual leanings and
risk losing the acceptance of those he loved. For her, Bobby
wanted to be good and was genuinely good, yet faced a life that
would go against everything he was raised to be.

For Bobby it was going to be a hard road ahead, Alice
thought.

* * *

Meanwhile, Bobby and Joy were toying with a wild new
idea. Joy, who loved nothing better than driving, saw an ad for
truck-driver training and convinced Bobby to sign up with her
for the three-month course. Think of it! They'd have a truck
driver's license—a passport to anywhere in the country. Freedom! Flexibility! Money!

So they traveled, nightly, the twenty-five miles to the truck-
driving "academy" in Hayward. At first, Bobby was incredulous. He noted in his diary,

> *Sometimes when I'm sitting behind the wheel of one of those
> big rigs, I think to myself, "What in the fuck am I doing here?"
> God, I must be insane. The very last thing I see myself as is
> some big butch truck driver.*

But he started enjoying himself: "I had a lot of fun driving
last night. I got a C-plus, which I suppose isn't bad for me."
The final test fell on Christmas Eve. Joy watched nervously as
Bobby executed the difficult back-up maneuvers, steering the
truck effortlessly but incorrectly off the blacktop and onto the
grass. But he got a chance to try again. Joy held her breath. "He
needs to pass this," she thought. "He needs the confidence."

Bobby did it. "Joy got a 93 and I squeaked by with a 75. . . . If I hadn't passed I probably would have killed myself."

The two newly licensed truckers started scanning the want ads. But the available jobs required senior drivers and involved rigorous schedules to remote cities. Joy and Bobby dropped the idea as fast as they had embraced it—an expensive fling. Bobby had taken out a fifteen-hundred-dollar loan to pay for the lessons.

Around that time he revisited his old campus at Las Lomas, where his gay teacher friend walked him over to the tennis court to introduce him to Mark Guyere, a senior. Mark, a year behind Bobby in school, remembered him, but had never spoken to him. His impression upon meeting Bobby was of someone timid, soft-spoken, "like a lamb," he later recalled. Mark asked Bobby for his phone number and soon afterward called him. They planned a date.

They went to a matinee showing of *On Golden Pond*, a four-Kleenex film starring Henry Fonda and Katharine Hepburn as an aging married couple. Bobby was near tears throughout. He made a private wish that he, too, would have someone with whom to share his life when he got old.

Afterward, they drove to Heather Farms Park in Bobby's red Nash and walked around the lake. It was a foggy afternoon. They played on the swings and slide and rode on the merry-go-round and talked. Mark, slender and short, with brown hair and sharp features, stood in strong physical contrast to Bobby, with his gangly blondness. Mark talked about his home life, about his fanatic, survivalist parents, their rejection of his gayness, and his struggle to assert his independence.

Something in the moment—Mark's candor, the emotional impact of the film, the misty beauty of the day—prompted Bobby to lift the curtain and reveal himself. He told Mark about his religious dilemma, about his mother's Bible-pounding moralism, and, as Mark remembers it, about a time when Mary had told Bobby to burn his Bible.

To Mark, an agnostic, Bobby's tale seemed unbearably sad and incomprehensible. He could not remember ever seeing anyone hurting so badly. It was in Bobby's face, in the way he talked. It was clear that the most important thing to Bobby was that God love him. Yet God was turning away his face, and his mother was telling him he was headed for hell if he didn't change. To make matters worse, Bobby seemed to want to please his mother as desperately as he wanted to please God.

Mark felt anger building. Here was this gentle, shy, self-conscious, beautiful person who couldn't hurt a fly. And somebody was telling him he was going to hell because of what he felt in his heart. It didn't make sense.

They went on a second date, this time sitting in the car in the parking lot at the Emporium Capwell department store and talking so long that the windows fogged up. Mark, who was searching for someone to become involved with, found Bobby highly attractive. He had never met anyone so gentle, so free of hate.

But they merely sat, each hunched against his door, neither touching nor caressing. Bobby seemed distant despite their verbal intimacy, unreachable, absorbed by his unsolvable problem. And it didn't appear to matter to him that he had someone to talk to about it. To Mark, it seemed that Bobby wasn't taking in what he was saying. Worse, Bobby seemed to lack the tools to make use of any advice that came his way. Bobby, Mark concluded regretfully, was a lost cause.

Bobby wasn't interested in Mark "that way," in any case. In his diary he refers to him as a friend, and they did continue to see each other on occasion. Bobby, going on nineteen in early 1982, was not disposed to settle down, no matter how much he expressed the longing to do so. He was caught up in the erotic swirl of San Francisco nightlife. It was in this period that he began working out diligently to pump the muscles he felt he needed to improve his sexual currency. Before long, he looked the part of the quintessential California beach boy.

. . .

San Francisco gay life in this period was a carnal circus in its final spasm of excess before the dramatic changes wrought by the AIDS epidemic. In late 1981 *Time* and *Newsweek* had written the first stories about a strange and fatal disease affecting gay men. In March 1982, doctors at the Centers for Disease Control reported 285 cases nationally of what they called Gay-Related Immune Deficiency disease, or GRID; 70 of the cases were in California. Few people took notice.

The city offered something for every appetite. Its streets, back rooms, bars, bathhouses, parks, restrooms, and dance palaces were the backdrop for a bacchanal of epic proportions. Tens of thousands of repressed gays and lesbians had moved to San Francisco from small-town America to engage in the most defiant, clamorous, public, and unabashed expression of sexual freedom since the Roman Empire.

For Bobby, it was a banquet table laden with tainted food. He indulged, propelled by sexual hunger and loneliness, then turned ill with guilt and self-recrimination. "I feel these cravings and I feed them despite their dirty origins," he told his diary. "I think I'm capable of twisting anything into something wicked. . . . I feel guilt pangs whenever I do something that gives me real pleasure."

Soon he knew his way around the streets, the bars, the bathhouses, and the glory holes like a veteran. (He described "glory holes"—adjacent, person-sized compartments with circular openings carved in the walls to accommodate anonymous genital sex—to a disbelieving Diane at work one day. "Really," said Bobby, "I could show them to you. Wanna come?" "Aaaargh!" was all she could manage in reply.)

One night, borrowing Joy's car to drive to the I-Beam, a Haight Street dance club, he parked at McDonald's without noticing the tow-away sign. Later, when he emerged, the car had been towed.

I tried to call the number [of the towing company] but I kept getting the wrong number so I thought I'd go to the police station. I hopped in a cab and said, "To the police station." The driver had other plans, though, and I ended up sucking his dick in exchange for fare, which wasn't so bad except for the fact that the police station was practically around the corner. I guess you could say I was suckered. Ha ha.

What little pleasure he got from these events was subverted by self-contempt. If he was doomed to decadence, Bobby seemed to be saying, he would embrace it with a fury. But at the core of his personality he was not good at debauchery. He was too much the innocent, the naïf. Some could immerse themselves in the life with self-affirming intensity. For Bobby, inoculated with the serum of abhorrence and disgust, there was no joy to be had.

He wrote:

Dear Lord. I wish making you happy was the only thing that I lived for. Unfortunately, it's not, as you well know. Sometimes it seems like you've given up on me and all these rotten things that happen to me, and then I don't care what I do, because it doesn't matter.

Other times I get the feeling that you love me so much that I can't even see it when it's right in my face. Like your love for me is so big that there's nothing else to see, but I'm too ignorant to see it.

I'm sorry for being so inadequate. You are so good to me and then I get like this. I could be good and obedient if I wanted to, but I don't. I want things my way. I wonder if you'll send me to Hell for this.

His sexual nature expressed itself as lust, for which he felt ashamed. Feeling unlovable, he could not perceive how love might transcend lust, how sexuality could be gay and also healthy. He was adrift, incapable of expressing his longings for love and affection beyond a series of minicrushes.

At home, there was little respite. The deeper Bobby's gloom, the closer Mary believed him to being cured. After all, didn't the church teach that misery is the surest sign that God is "convicting" the sinner of his sin? Like a boil ripening to its bursting point, the unhappy sinner demonstrated symptoms that clearly indicated he was experiencing God's cleansing pain. If he could maintain, be diligent in prayer, release would be imminent.

In this way, Mary misread Bobby's deepening depression. Convincing herself that success was within range, yet increasingly uneasy about his secretive night and weekend outings, she kept up a nagging mantra: "Bobby, are you praying enough?"; "Bobby, don't underestimate God's power to change lives. Just when things seem darkest and most despairing, he works his glorious ways"; "Don't give up on God. He is constantly testing our faith. Look at Job. God knows who are the faithful and who are not. But, without faith, we are lost."

Joy, who was just beginning to question the total validity of delivered doctrine, would challenge her mother: "Mom, you're not God. Speak for yourself."

But Bobby's journal echoed his mother's litany.

Why did you do this to me, God? Am I going to Hell? That's the gnawing question that's always drilling little holes in the back of my mind. I'm really not that bad, am I? . . . Lord I really hate myself for being so weak. . . . Lord I want to be good. I want to amount to something. I need your seal of approval. If I had that I would be happy. . . . Where's my faith? I need to know that this world isn't spinning around and around for the hell of it. I need to know that you did make it and everything for a good reason. . . . I don't want anyone to ever read this. They would hate me. I'm rotten inside, and then everyone would know. . . . I make myself sick. I'm a joke.

Not untypically, he rebounded from those depths, telling his diary the next day: "Today I feel better. Last nite I was just clearing some bad thoughts." As he himself noted often, he turned to his diary when most depressed. But this began to happen more and more often.

. . .

Bobby sought relief in the company of a band of new friends, a group of self-identified outcasts from Walnut Creek and Concord who took defiant pleasure in dressing and acting outrageously. They formed, cultlike, around the weekend midnight showings of *The Rocky Horror Picture Show* at the El Rey Theater on Main Street in Walnut Creek.

Dora Arnold, Justin Nagy, the ringleader Starr Pauley (a pseudonym), and a changing cast of others operated as a loose-knit fraternity of jesters, affecting in their dress and various capers the attitude of exaggerated and campy excess that lay at the heart of *Rocky Horror.* It was innocent and antic, yet the aggregation provided a sense of belonging for these teenagers who could not or would not fit the suburban cookie-cutter mold. They were fat or scrawny, dorky, unathletic nonscholars, and they had zits. "These were the first people I found to whom it didn't matter what you looked like. They'd still hug you," recollected Dora recently. At the time she was pudgy and unflatteringly plain.

Rather than live stifled undercover lives, they chose the reverse strategy. They would do anything to get attention. Justin would dye his hair green or red, make it big on top, with a duck's ass in back. They'd wear rhinestones on their clothes, most of them period pieces bought at Goodwill or thrift shops. They favored funky ties from the 1960s and hideous houndstooth jackets. At other times they'd choose to dress like the B-52's, a hot rock band of the period.

They competed to come up with the wildest ideas: go cruise and chat with the prostitutes in Oakland, dress up as Laverne and Shirley, chase old men in supermarkets, drive backward through Jack in the Box, or simply go to San Francisco and try to sneak into the bars without ID.

And on weekends there was the main event, *Rocky Horror.* The midnight showing in Walnut Creek (and simultaneously around the country) of this musical send-up of old horror films had become a national cult event. The group would make a grand entrance decked out in the *Rocky* costume of the week, to the standing applause of the audience. Here they enjoyed a kind of freak celebrity that compensated for things like never making the cheerleading squad at school. Any regrets they may have had about those times were submerged in their efforts to be cool, to consider themselves an elite clique that only the deserving and lucky got to join.

Starr, who had an unreciprocated crush on Bobby, introduced him to the group. Bobby glommed on to the band of zanies like a voyeur, a fascinated observer who admired their abandon but couldn't bring himself to fully participate. He traveled with them, dipping cautiously into their adventures like a wader in an icy lake.

They found Bobby shy and charming. With his newly sculpted physique and angelic face he was easily the most physically imposing member of the group. Justin, himself tall and blond and not at all bad looking, fell silently in love with Bobby (though fearful of stirring Starr's enmity). Bobby in turn seemed fascinated by his new friends' chutzpah. They sauntered audaciously down the street virtually daring anyone to object to their strange looks and behavior. (Some did object; several of the group were bashed by local rednecks over a period of time.)

Like a kid at Christmastime, Bobby delighted in their spontaneity and theatricality. "This is rad, this is mischief," he would exult. "This is what I heard about." He longed to let go. Once, at Starr's house, they opened a chest of doodads and baubles and somebody put a string of pearls around Bobby's neck and a pearl earring on one ear.

"Oh, I hate you," said Starr, himself a chubby. "You look good in pearls, too!" Everyone laughed, and Bobby strutted, incongruous in a formfitting Izod shirt and Gap jeans, looking great. It was a luminous moment.

Such moments were few. Dora noticed that much of the time Bobby was terribly concerned about what others thought. He would be shaken if someone gave him a snide look or a sideways glance. She tried to inspire Bobby to adopt an attitude. "If somebody doesn't like you," she lectured, "fuck these people. If they don't have good taste, who cares what they think? Just move on."

It was a radical concept. If Bobby had bought it, he might have found a pathway out. He longed to be liberated from the tyranny of external approval.

In moments of grandiosity, he didn't care: "When I feel like I do at the present moment, I don't care what anybody thinks, and I feel like shocking people somehow. Usually by the way I dress or how I wear my hair."

But he rarely felt that way. Usually he felt his life rocketing out of control. He preserved a measure of sanity by attempting to minimize exposure, to conceal his real self. He compartmentalized his world. For example, Dora and Justin knew nothing of his home life, except that it was off-limits to them. Nor did they know of his friendship with Diane and Alice at work, and vice versa. At home as well he grew ever more secretive. No one was told details of the seediest part of his routine.

Thus he moved from milieu to milieu—from work to home to *Rocky Horror* to the gym to gay night at a roller rink in Hayward to the flesh palaces of San Francisco to, in the fall of 1982, Diablo Valley College as a part-time student—rarely connecting them, maintaining a fractured identity as a form of self-protection.

For the most part I'm a pretty invisible entity on this planet. I like being able to walk around and sort of blend into the wallpaper. People tend to leave you alone, which is nice most of the

*time. . . . Being introverted has its rewards. People sort of re-
gard you as mysterious somehow when you don't go around
opening your mouth all the time.*

On June 24, his nineteenth birthday, he wrote:

*Nineteen and nowhere. That's not true. It's just that I'm not
where I think I should be, which is not very clear in my mind at
the moment. . . . This washed out faded sort of feeling has been
following me forever. When will it leave me alone?*

Two days later he informed his diary without explanation
that he had left the job at CalFrame.

The next day was Gay Pride and Freedom Day. Tens of
thousands marched in San Francisco. Bobby made no mention
of it in his diary, and there is no reason to believe he attended.
He drew little pride from his gay status.

A week later he enjoyed an idyllic Fourth of July weekend at
his Aunt Jean's house in Chico, northeast of Sacramento. His
favorite cousin, Jeanette, was down from Oregon, and it is evident from Bobby's diary that Jeanette had at some point revealed to Bobby that she was a lesbian: "Jeanette and I
entertained ourselves by reading filthy magazines at various
liquor stores. (Dikes [*sic*] in particular.) We also jogged to Bid-
well Park. I love Jeanette. It was hard to say good-bye."
(Jeanette wrote him immediately expressing her great affection:
"Would I surprise you if I told you I love you? You've become
very special for me and I care about you. . . . Be happy my
peach blossom, my daffodil, my geranium, my ice plant.")

The same week, Bobby disclosed to his journal a new and
shadowy moneymaking scheme: "Tomorrow I have an appointment for a modeling job in San Francisco. It's the kind of modeling where you do more than stand in front of the camera, if
you get my drift."

Six days later he gave a further hint:

I'm realizing that the only people who appreciate decent young boys are old ladies and that only gets me $3.50 an hour to dust the crystal and polish the silver [casual labor he did for a woman acquaintance]. So, I've got to try something new and a little more indecent if you'll pardon the implications.

On Wednesday, July 15:

I got that modeling job I told you about.... I'm terrified because I have no idea what I'm getting into. I'll be making a lot of money though. I'm really scared.

On Sunday, he laid it all out.

In 3 days I made $200—the easy way. Being a prostitute (whore, call-boy, whatever you want to use) is hard to describe in a few lines. I could write a whole book and it's only been 3 days.

First of all, I don't feel any different really, than I did a week ago. Just richer. It's very flattering, because first of all you're getting paid and you're constantly being told how beautiful, gorgeous, pretty, fantastic, etc. etc. you are. I pretend I'm playing a whore in an old movie and that makes it a lot easier, because then it's really not happening to me.... What I like most is being told how pretty I am.... I'm not going to let this job ruin me. I'm going to make it pay off in every way possible. It's not worth it to let it ruin my health.... I must think and make good decisions from now on. I've got to. I'm very excited about the possibilities.... I want to travel, see and do things in other places, meet famous and interesting people, and become famous myself, for what I don't know.

Further along, Bobby's humanity asserted itself, and he wrote one of his most eloquent passages:

The fat old men with glasses and false teeth. The taste of efferdent; sleazy apartment building with creaky old stairs. Always a smile and caressing hands that tremble. Spitting on the sidewalk after to get rid of the horrible taste that lingers in

ory. Always pushing the guilt deep inside where it can
grow into a parasite to feed on healthy brain tissue. Pretending
to be an actor playing a part in some forgotten movie. Never realizing the impact of what's really taking place. This isn't happening. Hating my parents and my family. Hating. Always
hating. Counting the money and wanting more. Afraid right before. Afraid of the door as it opens. Pounding heart. Afraid but
smiling and pretending. . . .*

*I look at myself and I can't believe I'm actually doing this.
Can it be? Is this a dream? Or is it real? Most important, why?
Now I have something to hide, like a jagged scar. I'm an out-
cast, unclean. Leper. How sick.*

Despite his revulsion, he continued for several months, earn-
ing money and giving part of it to his mother. "I think she's
going to catch on before long. That will be very sticky when it
happens. I wish they would leave me alone and stop asking so
many questions." Over the next month he made enough to pay
off the loan for truck-driving school several months before it
was due.

· · ·

During one of his trips to San Francisco, Bobby saw a familiar face on the subway train. Blaine Andrews was a boy about
his age whom he had noticed with admiration a year earlier in
a downtown Walnut Creek restaurant where Bobby had been a
counterman. Now Bobby shyly began a conversation that would
quickly lead to a hot romance.

Bobby found Blaine to be

*a perfect little doll. On the outside he's a boy but on the inside
he's very grown up. . . . He's so intelligent and sophisticated
that next to him I feel like one of the Beverly Hillbillies. . . .
Blaine's the most wonderful cook in the world. This morning
he cooked steak and eggs and hashbrowns. He's so sweet and
good to me.*

131

Blaine, slender and handsome, with dusty, dirty-blond hair and hazel-green eyes, was precocious and sophisticated for his age. An only child of a broken home, he had been brought up in Los Angeles by his mother, a high-ranking corporate executive with connections to the Hollywood elite. Accustomed to the good life, Blaine took affluence for granted and dressed the part. At sixteen he moved in with his father in Walnut Creek and completed his final two years of high school at Accalanes, where he unapologetically came out as gay.

To Blaine, Bobby was a turn-on. He especially loved his smile, which he found enormous, sweet, almost impish, an "I know something you don't know" smile. Sexually, Bobby was traditional but versatile and seemed to Blaine to enjoy the act thoroughly. In youthful ardor, Blaine whispered, "I love you" to Bobby, who records in his diary:

> *It always scares me when he says, "I love you." I've never been able to say that to anyone without feeling a little bit like a liar. That's a horrible thing to say, but it's true. Whenever I say, "I love you" to anyone, a little piece of me inside says, "No, you don't, you don't love anyone, not even yourself."*

Inevitably, it was not to become a love match. Within two weeks Bobby was telling his diary that the relationship was downgrading to friendship. Nonetheless, the two continued to enjoy periodic sex and socialized for many months. They went to movies and galleries, hung out in Walnut Creek and Berkeley, dressed up and went to the clubs (Bobby snuck Blaine into the I-Beam and introduced him to his first bathhouse). Blaine would throw frequent parties at his apartment, with the full support of his tolerant father. In fact, Bobby often stayed overnight.

It is not surprising that throughout their friendship Blaine never had the faintest inkling of Bobby's inner turmoil. Bobby talked little about his home life, and the subject of religion apparently never came up. Blaine visited Bobby in his tiny loft on

Rudgear, but he never met Mary, although he did meet Joy, Ed, and Nancy. Bobby confided to him that he had "hustled" a couple of times, but Blaine basically knew only one of Bobby's many guises. That seemed to be enough for both of them.

As the summer waned, communication virtually ceased between Bobby and his family. Bobby felt that his "illicit" activities somehow betrayed his loyalty to the family, but at the same time he felt betrayed and resentful of the family's assumptions about him. Mary kept trying, but Bobby closeted himself in his loft, coming down only for meals. In his tiny space the size of a small vestibule he managed to keep a bed, a dresser, a stereo, a television, and a trunk full of treasures: GQ magazines, antiques he loved collecting, cut-out pictures of Marilyn Monroe, movie books. After work he would retreat up the short flight of stairs, watch old movies on the TV, or scribble feverishly in his diary. He was having trouble sleeping.

There was tension between Bobby and his siblings as well. Bobby's growing edginess and aggressive teasing sometimes scared Nancy, just twelve. To Joy and Ed he seemed increasingly withdrawn and sullen. He was curt, and could be cutting. Mary and Bob did not know what to do. They tended to indulge Bobby's moods, and he learned that by playing the disturbed problem case to the hilt, he could do and get most anything he wanted.

He even rankled at the presence of his grandparents. In his diary he wrote:

Granny and Grandfather are here and I wish they'd be on their way. Granny makes me sick. She insinuates that I'm a homosexual, and of course it's behind my back. I hate her at the moment.

I feel like running away. I can't stand my parents or my family. . . . I don't like these people I'm living with. They really bug me. . . . I sound like a lunatic, don't I? . . . Even though I don't like these people I don't want to hurt them, and if I just run away they'll be hurt.

In late summer the simmering tensions exploded.

Ed fretted over his brother. He made no moral judgments but worried that Bobby might be destined to burn in hell, that his soul was in jeopardy. At one point he caught himself thinking, "Maybe it's not a choice. Maybe Mom's constant nagging is a waste of time." But he backed off fast when he suspected that his thoughts might be Satan planting the idea just to lead him astray. "That can happen, you know," he warned himself.

But he didn't have a lot of time to devote to the question. Between school, church, baseball, and girls, Ed wasn't around the house much. He had his own problems. He was already twenty, and his future seemed uncertain. He longed to be a professional ballplayer yet wondered whether he was good enough. Despite his jock image and popularity, he had his doubts about his abilities and his looks. Bobby had troubles, sure, but so did everybody at this age.

That late summer day, Ed, Nancy, and Bobby were in the kitchen. Bobby was drinking wine and teasing Nancy.

"Bobby, knock it off," Ed said. They both liked to tease Nancy, but Ed felt that Bobby, slightly sloshed, was stepping over the line.

Bobby kept it up. "I said knock it off!" Ed repeated. Bobby said something sarcastic. They began yelling at each other. Suddenly there was scuffling. The sparring moved from the kitchen to the living room to the hallway, then to the bathroom, getting more and more serious. Bobby punched Ed in the mouth. Ed punched back. Bobby reeled backward and tumbled into the bathtub.

They tussled their way to Nancy and Joy's bedroom. Bobby, red faced and furious, stood inches from his brother, pointed to his own nose, and shouted, "Go on, hit me!" But Ed could not bring himself to do it. Bobby reached for his brother and raised him up bodily. Ed barely had time to note how powerful Bobby had become when he found himself sailing over the bed and almost through the window.

Before Ed could get to his feet, Bobby turned and rushed into the bathroom, sobbing. Ed followed.

"Bobby, I'm sorry," he began. Bobby brushed past him and rushed back into the girls' bedroom. He smashed his fist into a mirror on the bedroom door, breaking the glass. Ed hurried to help. Bobby pulled away, his hand miraculously unscathed. In a voice choked with anguish, he cried, "All I ever wanted was to be like you!"

Ed surprised himself with his response: "That's funny. I've wanted to be like you! You've got the good looks, the height, and all the girls think you're really neat." It was true: he envied Bobby's physical stature and pretty-boy looks.

Bobby listened, probably in amazement, as all the energy of battle drained from them both. Bobby strode from the house. It was over.

Bobby had totally lost it, Ed observed. He was out of his head during the fight. Still, at the time Ed didn't view their scuffle as particularly serious. Later he would realize that it had had nothing to do with them, that the volcano inside Bobby had been bubbling to the surface. He would understand, too, that when Bobby had said, "I want to be like you," he had meant, "I want to be ordinary, not some freak." When Bobby drove his fist into the mirror he was lashing out at the freak he saw reflected there.

In his most rational moments, Bobby knew he was tampering with a suicidal impulse. He spent hours analyzing his every mood swing and recording it in prose that vacillated between paranoid fantasy and exquisite clarity. In a stunning entry in October 1982, he articulated the Jekyll and Hyde logic that saw self-destruction as a way—perhaps the only way—to stamp out his evil (read *gay)* impulses:

> *I've got to be strong. It's either that or I die, really die. . . .*
> *I'm really scared because I think I will die. I'm so weak. I don't*
> *know what to do. No, I won't die. I'll live and try to learn from*
> *past mistakes. That's all I can do. I've got to love myself. I've*

got to stop the self-destructive side of my brain. Half of me tries to destroy myself and the other half, which is stronger, tries to do something constructive with myself.

The evil force compels me to do self-destructive things to myself and those around me. . . . I'm determined to win over the evil. . . . I'll kill the evil force within me. I will kill the evil force within me. I will stop you. You won't win. Good will win. Evil will die. I will kill it. I will starve it to a painful death. I will cause it to suffer as it has caused me to suffer.

. . .

Through the fall of 1982, Bobby plotted to find a way to leave home. A wonderful summer visit with Jeanette in Portland had strengthened his determination. Jeanette had invited Bobby to come live with her and her partner, Tina [not her real name], who was about to purchase a house. But the thought of leaving the nest for the first time was frightening to Bobby despite his growing alienation.

He tried to sustain a tolerable existence. In October he re-sumed working at CalFrame. In addition, he was taking drama, swimming, and weight training at Diablo Valley, and hanging out with the *Rocky Horror* crowd and a new set of friends he had met through Blaine.

At a gender-bending party at Blaine's home, which Bobby depicted in a guilt-ridden account as a wild orgy, Bobby experienced his first heterosexual kiss:

Kendall was supposed to be going with Alethia and vice versa. But he was busy with Michael, and I was busy with Alethia! We were just making out, but still! I've never been that bad before, and the worst part is that I knew exactly what I was doing. The whole night was soooo weird! . . . I feel especially wicked. Please God, forgive me. Why do I do it?

For Alethia, recalling the event years later, the party and, es-pecially, the incident with Bobby were anything but wild, and far from a make-out session. The two of them were sitting on the couch, Bobby looking gorgeous in a white cashmere cable-knit sweater. To Alethia, a heterosexual, he seemed like a baby, so innocent. He put his arm around her. They kissed—a single, sweet, uncarnal kiss.

Bobby said, "That wasn't so bad," then added, "I've never kissed a girl before." He was delighted with the achievement. Alethia, who knew Bobby was gay, was just seventeen and sexually unsophisticated. She chalked it up to experience. He and Alethia went out several times. Bobby enjoyed her company, but worried that she might be falling in love with him. "I like her a lot, but I'm not in love," he told his diary.

Bobby was increasingly obsessed with his looks and got a momentary rush from being admired. His striking appearance got compliments everywhere. A Diablo Valley College classmate, Robin, a woman who went roller-skating with Bobby on the Hayward rink's gay night, found him "real cute, model cute."

Feeling empty inside, Bobby saw his externals as a ticket to validation:

I'm becoming incredibly vain. I love it when people compliment me, and it happens a lot. I love love love it. Is that wrong? I deserve it. I work hard to be pretty for everyone. I like being an ornament. See, the thing is that I'm ugly sometimes, so when I'm pretty I take complete advantage.

He agonized over his physical appearance. He thought his hairline was receding, he detected the beginnings of wrinkles around his eyes, and, most irritating, he detested the barnaclelike acne that dug noticeable ridges into his face. Bobby tried to adhere to a health-food diet and devoted hours each week to a bathroom ritual of applying creams, lotions, and antibiotics. (His preoccupation with facial makeover prompted his lesbian friends at CalFrame to begin calling him Cher.) Nothing seemed to work. Like gayness, zits seemed to cling to him with perverse tenacity.

Finally, in November, he opted for a medieval-sounding medical procedure called "dermabrasion," which promised to sand away unwanted blemishes.

This morning my face was dermabraded. I hated it. The sound of the brush as it scraped into my skin was awful. . . . The bandages are on my face now and I look absolutely hideous. My cheeks look as though someone threw acid on them.

When the bandages came off, Bobby found that his face didn't appear any different than before, only redder. His friend Robin noted that his handsome visage was marred with what looked like giant scabs.

Thus Bobby faced Christmas feeling like the Phantom of the Opera. To make matters worse, he was once again out of work, having quit or been laid off at CalFrame.

He felt as if he had hit bottom.

Here it is Christmas. The only things I've been feeling are hatred and loneliness. I'm a mess. I feel like a piece of shit. . . . Fuck you. FUCK FUCK FUCK FUCK. I hate it here. I hate everyone. . . .

I look like shit. Goddamn it all. That's the only thing that matters to me. How I look in the mirror. . . . I WANT TO TAKE A FUCKIN ICE PICK TO MY FACE AND STAB IT TIL THERE'S NOTHIN LEFT. . . . I wish I could take a knife and cut my throat. I've gotta get the hell outa here.

His grim mood extended into January. He longed to escape but was terrified of pulling away from his family, despite repeated inducements from Oregon (including a Christmas gift that included a leather carrying bag, socks, and two jockstraps tie-dyed purple by Tina). Unemployed except for a brief stint as a legitimate model for a mail-order catalog, he squirmed through days and nights of boredom, interrupted only by long monologues with his diary.

January 4, 1983. At times my feeling is that my behavior and thoughts are regarded as grossly unacceptable. Everyone around here is under the impression that all I have to do is surrender my life to Jesus Christ. It's that simple. But they can't see that it's not.... It's an awful feeling to believe that one is headed straight to fires of hell. What makes everything worse is having all these people around you telling you how simple the solution is when it doesn't really seem to be at all. They will never know what it is to be in my shoes and I don't think I'll ever know what theirs are like.

January 6. I love Jeanette a lot. I don't love her the way I do anyone else. I love Joy and Ed and Nancy and my mom and dad the way a person loves their family, but I love Jeanette in a different way.... I guess my relationship with my family is love-hate and with Jeanette it's just love.

On Saturday, January 22, he ventured out for a meeting with his old friend Andrea in Berkeley. Andrea had been estranged from the Griffith family, and she and Bobby hadn't met for a year. It was a nice reunion. They laughed and joked. To Andrea, Bobby seemed in good spirits. She gave Bobby a gold chain and said, "Next time you see me, give it back." They parted with Bobby saying, "I'll call you."

January 24. Today I went to Dr. Price for more surgery.... First they injected my face with novocain or something and then they took these hole punchers and cut out the pock marks and stitched up the hole.

January 26. I better not be ugly when these bandages come off. I've had to be ugly too long and I'm sick of it. I'm going to make myself into the prettiest thing you ever saw.

How have I survived my wicked life without catching a venereal disease? I really wonder about that sometimes. Has my guardian angel been taking care of me or what? It's either that or maybe I'm not as much of a whore as I think. That's a laugh.

I couldn't count the number of men I've slept with in the last year on both hands. Maybe on my feet. I don't really know. I try to forget.

He felt useless hanging around, told himself he must find a job, and looked forward to resuming school when intersession ended. He rarely left the house now, embarrassed to show his bandaged face. He stopped going to the gym. He limited his conversations with the members of his family. Mary, ever hopeful that profound change was imminent, began to wonder whether her son indeed needed a change of scene.

One day, arriving home from work at I. Magnin, Mary found Bobby struggling to get his car started. It wouldn't respond. In a fit of frustration and fury, Bobby began kicking the old Nash, cursing and crying.

"Bobby, can I do something? Can I help?" she asked.

"No," he said, storming into the house.

Later, Mary approached him. "Bobby, it's clear you're not happy here. Do you want to go to Portland?" she asked.

He hesitated. "I don't have the money," he said finally.

"We could give you the bus fare," she said. "We could loan you some money until you get settled and get a job." It was not as if she were eager for him to go. None of her children had yet left home. And Bobby was so vulnerable. He would be out of her orbit.

"I'll think about it," he told her.

By the end of the month, he was in a state of high agitation, a mix of ennui, self-blame, and indecision.

I made it through the weekend. How? It was the slowest, most boring weekend I've ever lived through. I'm so restless I could scream! . . . I'm getting madder and madder. I try so goddamned hard and what do I get?

Finally, Bobby made the decision to move north. The very act of being decisive lifted his spirits, and soon he was planning the transition with excitement. Things moved swiftly. Bobby was scheduled to catch a bus on Sunday night, February 7. That night a winter rainstorm swept through the area. Joy packed Bobby some cookies. Mary contributed shoe polish and brush and an alarm clock. She was crying, and so was Bobby.

Rain pelted the windows. Mary said, "Bobby, why don't you put off going until tomorrow?" The next day would be his father's forty-ninth birthday.

"No," Bobby insisted. "I'll lose my courage."

He hugged his father. He hugged his mom, while both wept. Joy and Ed were to accompany him to the station in Oakland in her truck. It was good-bye. Bobby leaned his head out the window and yelled through the rain, "I love you!" Mary turned to Bob and said, "I don't think I can go through this with three more kids."

Outside, a chill wind had gathered up the rain and was driving it in gusts. Joy cried all the way to Oakland. She was frightened for him. How was he going to make it up there? At least when he was around she had some idea of what he was doing.

She told him, "Bobby, if you ever want to come back in a hurry, I can drive up and be there in eleven hours. Remember that."

"Thanks, Joy," he said. They pulled into the Greyhound terminal, a lonely patch of light in a deserted part of downtown, at around 11 P.M. They hugged and held on to each other. Ed and Bobby embraced. Then Bobby boarded and the bus pulled out through deep oily puddles of rain.

The Second Coming Out

Mary's self-discovery that her son had had nothing to repent, that he had been untainted by sin from the start, was at once a huge relief and a terrible indictment. It enabled her to believe, at last, that Bobby was not eternally damned but was instead a happy and free spirit enjoying the benefits of a blissful afterlife somewhere in the firmament.

On the other hand, Mary for the first time grasped the full implication of what had transpired during those final years. There was no getting away from it: her well-meaning campaign to save her son had merely helped drive him to his death. Bobby had believed the verdict pronounced by the people he most trusted and cared about: his own family. *And it was wrong!*

The enormity of this revelation was almost harder to bear than the three years of doubt and grief that preceded it. She had been deaf to the agony of her own child, unresponsive to his caring, creative nature. All Bobby had needed was to be told he was perfectly all right just as he was. How blind, how stupid could she have been? she demanded of herself. What a monumental mistake!

Mary now could look back and see the roots of her fatal error. Insecure and unquestioning from early childhood, she had evolved a pastiche of religious superstition and dogma that provided an illusory cocoon of safety. She had trapped herself within that shell, totally closed to either fresh ideas or independent thought, and gathered her children within its boundaries. No wonder Bobby's feeble protestations could not penetrate.

Now she could also see how she had deprived herself of the full pleasure of her son from the earliest years. His individuality had always provoked fear and embarrassment in her. Intimidated by the opinions of her mother, her neighbors, her church, she had foisted onto Bobby the subtle judgments of social rejection that she herself feared.

By the time his secret got out, he knew his sexual identity would be a mortifying and forbidden burden to his family. Everything else about Bobby had been forgotten, Mary now saw, in her persistent focus on eradicating his gayness. Every effort Bobby made, every protest, every attempt to better himself had been sabotaged by his overwhelming sense of failing his family and himself. It was a wonder, she thought, that he had held on as long as he did.

Mary could now trace the inevitability of events. She saw her own role as the flawed parent who had sacrificed her child in the name of rigid tradition. It took her son's death to blast her free, to force her to think about beliefs she'd held all her life, like coded commands in a computer.

Guilt-ridden, she turned once again to Rev. Larry Whitsell.

"I look now at what I said and did," she told him, "and I'm horrified. Can Bobby ever forgive me? Can God forgive me?"

"Mary, God's already done the forgiving," Whitsell said. "We have to forgive ourselves." He felt compassion for Mary and was moved to confide that he, too, had lost someone he loved to suicide. A lover nearly two decades back had killed himself because of alcohol and drug problems. "I went through the guilt. I asked myself, 'Why didn't I know? Why didn't I see?' I didn't want to see it, to acknowledge that something like that could happen to me.

"Mary, you can't go back and erase what happened. But you've got a story to tell. It's got the power of ultimate truth. Share it with others. Maybe you can touch a life early on, before a tragedy happens."

She pondered this. She was a private woman, painfully shy in public. She felt poorly educated, underread. Where would she begin?

"In the schools, in the churches, in the community," he said. "It doesn't matter. Just tell about your journey."

She went home to think his suggestion through and talk about it with Bob and the family. Could Larry be right? Could she move beyond her own tragic mistake to be a living example for others? Gay kids, their parents, straight people? Could she tell them "Don't make the mistake I made. Cherish your children just as they are."?

In the summer of 1986, three years after her son's death, her thoughts took her once again to the typewriter. Bobby would have been twenty-three. Before she shared her story elsewhere she would have to square things with him. Over several weeks she composed a letter to Bobby from which she would shape the message she would take to the world.

Dearest Bobby,

It's been almost three years since you moved in with God. As a religious hard-nosed Bible thumper for 21 years, I almost rested on the cliche "God's will be done." We were thoroughly indoctrinated to believe that as a homosexual person your way of life would be corrupt and sinful. As a result of these beliefs, a terrible injustice was done to you.

Since the Christian church came into being, it has continued to remain in its ignorance, homophobia, prejudice, and pride. I am sorry your family went along in blind agreement with the church's views concerning the gay and lesbian community. I am happy to see a few churches are opening their hearts to God's gay and lesbian children. It's a start in the right direction. I have since learned the correct interpretations in the Bible where the issue of homosexuality is mentioned. It is obvious to me now that we have all been tragically misinformed. We have been listening to man's interpretations of the Bible and not God's!

I remember you said to me, "You just won't bend, will you? You won't listen to my side of the story." You were right, Bobby. Like many parents I thought I knew it all. As this letter will testify, I am listening now, and I like what God is teaching me.

What I am about to say to you, Bobby, will be considered blatant heresy. However, as the late Thomas Huxley said, "It is the customary fate of new truths to begin as heresies." I believe the writer of the Old Testament (Moses) misinterpreted same-gender relationships, and in doing so excluded homosexuals from God's plan of creation. Moses failed to interpret same-gender relationships as an indigenous part of God's creation.

God's gay and lesbian children have been robbed of their human decency, integrity, and dignity.

Well, Bobby, I am a firm believer it is never too late to make things right with you or anyone else I may have wronged unknowingly. I am trying to bind the wounds of God's gay and lesbian children, hopefully strengthening them with the oil and wine of God's love. I thank you, Bobby, and God, for bringing this family out of the dark ages.

We were not aware (at first) of the conflict that was slowly breaking your spirit and that this conflict would continue to torment you for the next seven years. So much so that living would become a daily victory. It is fact that there are an alarm-

ing number of teenage suicides happening, and no one knows why the teenager is choosing death instead of life. Could some of them be Bobbys and Janes? Our Church and society do not give the young person a realistic answer, much less a humane solution to their discovery of being a gay person.

You were the apple of God's eye just as you were. If we had only known.

Out of the many discussions we had, the one phrase that comes back to me is the age-old chant, "You can change if you want to." How that must have angered and hurt you. You began to feel you did not fit into your family anymore. You wanted to believe that you were not the person the Bible had interpreted you to be. You were at the mercy, as we all are, of the false interpretations in the Bible concerning homosexuality. The social stigma and the stereotypes presented you as a menace to society.

I have done a lot of heart searching with God. I could not rely on the Bible as I had done in the past. I knew that God would reveal his truths concerning our gay son. God's truth heals despair and hopelessness in the spirit.

In and of itself, divinely inspired love is neither male nor female, and follows only one rule as it searches for another lonely heart. Love must be true to its God-given nature, be it homosexual or heterosexual.

When God views a loving and caring heart he is pleased and all is well with him. He is not concerned with our sexuality, but with the vast numbers of humanity who are not being loved and cared for; those living in physical poverty, poverty of the soul and spirit. I feel what the Apostle Paul must have felt on the road to Damascus when God pierced his conscience. Paul's life was flooded with God's Holy Light, causing him to be blinded for three days so that his error in persecuting the Christians might be revealed to him. The scales fell from Paul's eyes and he was converted to Christ.

*My soul was flooded with darkness so that my error might
be revealed to me. I believed I was doing right in the name of
Christ. I did not know my soul; my conscience was in bondage
to the people and ministers who stand in God's stead. I went
along in blind allegiance, unwittingly persecuting, oppressing
gay and lesbian people—my own son. The scales of ignorance
and fear that kept my soul in darkness have fallen from the eyes
of my soul, my conscience. I have been set free to have faith in,
trust in the dictates of my conscience.*

*I no longer believe that an entity called Satan has the power
to guide my conscience. This belief was very, very intimidating
to you. There are those who will claim that I have been listening to Satan, that I have become a heretic. I would rather be
branded a heretic while helping a child of God out of the gut-
ters of this world, where the church and I have thrown them,
than to pass by on the other side muttering under our breath,
"The wages of sin is death." Rather this than to look away
from the pain and humiliation of a child lying helpless.*

*The heart that hungers and thirsts for God's love will find it
in the Bible. It has been said the eyes are the mirror of one's
soul. When we look into God's mirror [the Bible] will we see
God's reflection of love gazing back? Or will we see an evil reflection of man's inhumanity?*

Reviewing what she had written, Mary was a little taken
aback at the intensity with which she had passed sentence on the
church. Yet there was no denying that Mary felt, as Joy would
say, "ripped off" by the church. It should be held accountable,
Mary believed, first for its tunnel vision about the human condition, and second for imposing that vision on people like herself
who lacked the tools to resist biblical brainwashing.

She soon had the opportunity to make her first public statement on the subject. The local newspaper, the *Contra Costa
Times*, ran a story in June 1986 about a group of Christians

that specialized in helping homosexuals go straight. Mary fired off a letter, which the paper printed:

God did not cure our son Bobby, who was born a homosexual. The few that may have been "cured" by God were not born homosexuals. Due to the false propaganda, psychological abuse, and false interpretations of biblical passages concerning homosexuality, our son took his life at the early age of twenty. . . . Like many of his brothers and sisters in the gay community, our son gave up on love and the hope of ever receiving the validation he so rightly deserved. . . . There are gay children sitting in our congregations across America. They are tragedies waiting to happen, all due to homophobia and, worst of all, ignorance. Please pray about this.

The letter prompted a personal note from a lesbian deacon at the local MCC church thanking Mary, and noting that "the affirmation of myself as a valuable human being and child of God means so much when it comes from a parent. . . . Letters like yours, Mary, are another tool that helps to . . . affirm us."

Shortly after that, Mary, her P-FLAG friend Betty Lambert, and a third woman, Jackie Costa, called a meeting at the home of a gay rights supporter for the purpose of re-forming a local chapter of P-FLAG. (An earlier effort by Lambert had not succeeded.) Notices were posted at the MCC church, and some twenty-five people showed up. The Diablo Valley chapter of P-FLAG resulted, with Costa as its chair.

Jackie was a high-energy mother of three, one of whom is gay. Barely five feet tall, stocky, graying at age fifty-five, Jackie turned to P-FLAG out of anger at the bigotry she witnessed toward gay people. Unlike Mary, she had had no problems in accepting her son's homosexuality; in fact, she had guessed his orientation correctly before he acknowledged it to her as a teenager nearly a decade before.

Under Jackie's leadership, Diablo Valley P-FLAG began holding monthly meetings at MCC in Concord, across the northern boundary of Walnut Creek, and delicately initiated outreach to a few local schools. The environment in conservative Contra Costa County was not generally hospitable to the public advocacy of gay tolerance. Most gays and lesbians in the county were deeply in the closet. Meetings at MCC remained small since people—even straight parents—were reluctant to be seen entering there, or even parking close by.

Concord was a peculiar mix of blue-collar suburbanites who had fled urban stress back in the 1960s and a newer breed of office workers who had followed the new transit line and consequent business development along a rapidly spreading industrial corridor. Others—including an increasing number of quiet gay couples—commuted to jobs in San Francisco. One of the oldest cities in the county, Concord combined convenience and affordability. (Today it is the largest city in Contra Costa County, with 116,000 residents.)

Mary became an active member of Diablo Valley P-FLAG and was in fact listed as its vice president. She put together an account of her "story" for use at meetings and visits to other chapters. Still a reluctant speaker, she occasionally asked Jackie to read the account for her. The simple eloquence of the statement, not to mention its there-but-for-the grace-of-God pain, was mesmerizing to parents newly aware of their children's sexual identity.

Soon her name got around the local P-FLAG circuit. She was also interviewed for the first time, for a story about gay suicide that ran in July in the *San Jose Mercury-News*.

In November, Mary's father, Alvin, died of a heart attack at age eighty-six. Alvin Harrison had been the gentle, soft-spoken mediator of the family, who suffered the barbs of his wife but also knew when to step in if the rapier thrusts began to draw blood. His wife, children, and grandchildren adored him for his great kindness. Chosen to give the eulogy, Mary used the text of the Parable of the Good Samaritan to express some of those sentiments, alluding to her own struggle in the process: "You were with us when we had fallen by the roadside of life. For some of us, we had been beaten and robbed by our own humanity. . . . Perhaps, we used poor judgment as we walked the road of life. Perhaps we didn't listen to your kind wisdom given to us upon request. You, dearest Daddy, nonetheless came to our rescue. You never passed by on the other side."

. . .

In early 1987, a seemingly innocuous incident blew apart the tacit anonymity of Contra Costa's gay community.

Rev. Larry Whitsell, who held a seat on Concord's Human Relations Commission, introduced a resolution to the city council in January that the city's June calendar include an item designating "Gay Freedom Week," to coincide with the annual nationwide celebration of gay pride. It passed without a hitch.

Press accounts of the decision, however, stirred a hornet's nest. Protest letters flooded the city council. "We moved to this area because of the family-oriented communities, and we want the moral character of our communities to remain intact," wrote one citizen.

By the time the commission reconvened on February 19, the debate had reached a pitch of hysteria. The commission's meeting room was overflowing with 450 people. Another 300 had been turned away. Those who testified on behalf of gay tolerance were greeted with negative epithets by fundamentalists. Mary attended in support of Jackie Costa, who testified, "Homosexuality is not a choice, it is a fact of life. As a parent of a gay son who goes back three generations in this county, he has as much right to be here as anyone else." As she stepped down, people in the audience shook their fists in her face and shouted, "Your son is an abomination to God!"

The commission bowed to the pressure to excise the Gay Freedom Week reference, but went on record as supporting "gay civil rights," further inflaming opponents. The commission then kicked the whole debate over to the city council.

The emotions stirred by the controversy brought elements of both the gay community and the religious right into the public spotlight. A group known as the Traditional Values Coalition, led locally by a minister named Lloyd Mashore, spoke for the antigay side. Larry Whitsell led a growing nucleus of previously closeted gays and lesbians who felt forced to go public in response to the ferocity of the assault taking place in their once comfortable little community.

The issue was to be addressed five days later by the city council. The gay proponents mobilized forces. Diablo Valley P-FLAG was asked to participate. Larry urged Mary to speak; her story would touch the heart of the most avid gay-hater. Mary was terrified. She had never in her life addressed so large a public audience.

On Monday, February 23, an overflow crowd spilled out of the council chamber and into the courtyard, where loudspeakers had been set up. A crush of 300 people inside and out struggled for seats or a view. Mary and Jackie waited in the courtyard for the proceedings to begin, drawing stares with their P-FLAG buttons that read: "We Love Our Gay and Lesbian Children."

Mary was jumpy. "I'm really nervous," she said. "I'm scared. I don't know if I can do this."

Jackie tried to reassure her, but wondered if she would again have to be Mary's surrogate reader.

Next to them a minister was relating an anecdote to a companion in a voice loud enough to be easily heard. "I tried to run for office on the Human Relations Commission, but they named that faggot instead. I wrote him a letter saying, 'We sing hymns at our church, what do you do with the hims at your church?'"

The two women were at once startled and steamed. Jackie could see Mary straighten her back, anger rising in her cheeks. When Mary's turn came to speak, she moved to the dais with a sureness fueled by fury. Jackie thought, "God works in mysterious ways."

"May I assure you, the council, and the residents of Concord," Mary began, "that you have nothing to fear should Concord's calendar of events include the word *gay*. What the people of Concord do have to fear is their lack of knowledge concerning gay and lesbian people.

"Because of my own lack of knowledge, I became dependent upon people in the clergy. When the clergy condemns a homosexual person to hell and eternal damnation, we the congregation echo 'Amen.' I deeply regret my lack of knowledge concerning gay and lesbian people. Had I allowed myself to investigate what I now see as Bible bigotry and diabolical dehumanizing slander against our fellow human beings, I would not be looking back with regret for having relinquished my ability to think and reason with other people—people I trust for truth and guidance in my life."

Her voice low but firm, she turned to the subject of the loss of Bobby. The audience listened in rapt silence.

"God did not heal or cure Bobby as he, our family, and clergy believed he should. It is obvious to us now why he did not. God has never been encumbered by his child's genetically determined sexuality. God is pleased that Bobby had a kind and loving heart. In God's eyes kindness and love are what life is all about. I did not know that each time I echoed 'Amen' to eternal damnation, each time I referred to Bobby as sick, perverted, and a danger to our children, his self-esteem and personal worth were being destroyed. Finally, his spirit broke beyond repair. He could no longer rise above the injustice of it all. Bobby ended his life at twenty.

"It was not God's will that Bobby jumped over the side of a freeway overpass into the path of an eighteen-wheel truck, which killed him instantly. Bobby's death was the direct result of his parents' ignorance and fear of the word *gay*. An injustice has been done not only to Bobby but to his family as well. God knows it isn't right that Bobby is not here with his loved ones."

Several in the audience wept as she continued. "Correct education about homosexuality would have prevented this tragedy. There are no words to express the pain and emptiness remaining in our hearts. We miss Bobby's kind and gentle ways, his fun-loving spirit, his laughter. Bobby's hopes and dreams should not have been taken from him, but they were. We can't have Bobby back.

"There are children like Bobby sitting in your congregations. Unknown to you, they will be listening to your 'Amen's as they silently cry out to God in their hearts. Their cries will go unnoticed for they cannot be heard above your 'Amen's. Your fear and ignorance of the word *gay* will soon silence their cries. Before you echo 'Amen' in your home and place of worship, think and remember. A child is listening."

There was a moment of silence, then a burst of wild applause. The opposition, which had booed other speakers, was silent. Mary stepped from the podium and walked steadily to the rear of the chamber. Inside, she was shaking. This public moment had been her own coming out.

The city council, after listening to dozens of speakers, took refuge in a decision that ultimately pleased no one. It dropped the word *gay* from the Human Relations Commission's statement in favor of a reference to "civil rights for all individuals." The action only temporarily mollified the disputing parties, setting the stage for a bruising battle over gay rights in Concord and the county over the next three years.

But Mary Griffith's course was set. She had discovered she could move a large body of people. She had seen that her story was a potent morality tale. Her testimony had been reported in the *Oakland Tribune*. She was now an activist, involved in a cause from which she would never retreat.

TEN

Portland

Tuesday, February 16. You won't believe it. I know you won't because I don't. I've moved to Portland. . . . At first I was really scared, but now I know I'm going to be all right. The hardest part of all was leaving. Saying good-bye to my family was hard because I love them a lot. My family has really been good to me. They sent me Valentine's Day cards and soap and towels and underwear and my books and money. I think I'll be happy here.

It was a fresh start. Literally. Portland in winter had the bracing smell of rain-soaked pine trees and burning firewood. Where Walnut Creek had seemed congested and suburban, Portland had open air and open space and what seemed to Bobby to be friendly people.

I'm glad to be away from that town. Nothing but bad memories. This is my new life, a new day, and I'm going to be a success in every way I can. I'm very excited about being here.

In a way it was like being at summer camp. Everybody sent cards and letters from home, with news and gossip. Care packages, too. Ed's Valentine card said, "I love you and am thinking of you often! Blessings to the MAX!" and added that he had made second-string third baseman in junior college and was "collecting many a splinter on the bench!"

His mother sent a long letter filled with Bible references, in which she asked whether to give Bobby's new address and phone number to inquiring "friends."

"I know you want to turn over a new leaf, so to speak, but Bobby, I don't know who you want to keep as friends and who you don't," she wrote. She told him she was trying not to think about the emptiness left by his departure. "I was trying very hard one day and the Lord broke into my thoughts and said, 'Let them stay and don't fight them. You are supposed to feel sad when one you love and have lived with for almost 20 years is not around. A deep void is to be expected.'"

Jeanette was thrilled to have Bobby in Portland at last. Her lover, Tina, liked Bobby a lot, and the three of them became a tight trio, occasionally augmented by Jeanette's sisters, Debbie and Stephanie, who also lived in Portland.

Bobby had his own room on the second floor of Tina's house in northeast Portland, an older, tree-lined neighborhood of well-kept, venerable homes. He got jobs in quick succession as a server at a Dairy Queen and as an orderly at Crestview Convalescent Home, and worked both of them, trying to accumulate some cash. He signed up with a local gym and resumed a rigid schedule of weight training.

He and Jeanette would jog together, running and talking in the same rhythm. They seemed to have endless things to discuss. They felt natural together, connected. On weekends they'd go dancing, sometimes just the two of them. Sweating, exhilarated, Bobby would remove his shirt, even though he was shy.

Bobby made a major effort to curtail his sex drive. He wanted to break out of the California pattern of sex for sex's sake. One Saturday night in late February he went alone for the first time to the Family Zoo, one of the bars on Stark Street. He felt stared at, felt he was being rated by "all those old men." "I haven't been so nervous in my life," he confided to his diary. "I had to press my water bottle against my stomach to keep my hand from shaking."

Finally he ran into someone he knew, and together they planned to go to the Continental Baths.

But we didn't have the money, so he just dropped me off home. I'm so glad. My virtue is saved. I can't let myself get desperate. Desperate people do crazy things. I can't let anything ruin my new life, especially something as dumb as sex.

Refracted through Bobby's prism, sex was exciting but dangerous at best, sinful at worst. He couldn't imagine it as the expression of loving intimacy, despite the fact that he was exposed daily to Jeanette and Tina's solid partnership.

He told Jeanette he had never had sex with anyone he cared deeply about. "What is it like to have sex with someone you love?" he once asked.

"It's wonderful," she replied. "It's a lot different. You just can't compare it. Eventually you'll get tired of running around, Bobby, and want to settle down," she reassured him.

March turned unseasonably warm. Bobby wrote a cheery letter home, telling his family about how he enjoyed dressing the elderly women at Crestview: "They look so much prettier in a flowered dress and a pink sweater than in a pair of pants and a shirt. That's the most fun—dressing them and picking out pretty dresses and sweaters and jewelry for them, and fixing their hair and putting make-up on them."

He especially liked a charming woman in her nineties who tended to speak exclusively in rhyme: "My head is on the bed."

He admitted to being homesick, but insisted he was going to stick it out in Portland. "I'm not a quitter. A lot of people have it a lot worse than me and if they can do it, so can I. I think I'm a much more disciplined person than before."

Bobby soon found, however, that the furies had pursued him to Oregon. His facial acne returned. He again fixated on thinning hair and lines around his eyes.

As each day passes I get uglier and uglier. I think someone put a hex on me.

He resumed his active nightlife. One weekend he stayed away for two days, frightening Jeanette, who had asked that he inform her when he would be sleeping out. The situation was exacerbated when Bobby's weekend partner showed up at the house demanding back some cash he claimed Bobby had lifted from his wallet. Jeanette was irritated that the dispute had found its way to her door, as well as disturbed at the accusation. (Bobby later admitted to her that he had taken the money, saying he felt he "deserved" it.)

After that incident, it was agreed that Bobby would move in with Debbie across town, ostensibly because where she lived was much closer to Crestview Convalescent and Bobby could walk to work from there. In reality, the money incident had put a strain on Bobby's relationship with his favorite cousin.

"I thought my life was going to be perfect up here, but I've become disillusioned pretty fast," he wrote in early April, two months after his arrival.

I seem to have ruined my relationship with Jeanette. . . . I don't even know how it really happened. . . . I just woke up and found I had made a small but fatal mistake, the kind you don't even know about until it's far too late. I was mortified. I couldn't say a word.

Despite that setback, his mood once again turned hopeful later in the spring.

*I won't give up. I really don't know who or what is supply-
ing me with this courage and strength. It must be the Lord
Jesus. Thank you. Thank you for the will to live and survive.
Now just give me a little bit of fighting spirit and then no one
will get in my way. I will survive.*

In early June, he wrote:

*Tomorrow I'll have been in Oregon 4 months. Overall I'd
say my life is better off. . . . The pen I'm writing with says,
"For with God nothing shall be impossible." Luke 1:37. I
think it's true.*

And, two weeks before his twentieth birthday:

*It just occurred to me how happy I am that I no longer live
at home. I am my own person now and that's worth a million
dollars to me. I always feel like a failure at home. It was a constant, awful feeling and now it's gone. I'm not always happy of
course, because I do become depressed occasionally, but that's
normal. I'm very proud of the fact that I've saved $500 in my
savings account.*

On his birthday, June 24, cards flowed from home. Joy and
Ed sent different Snoopy cards. Joy wrote, "I get terribly depressed whenever I look at your picture. I miss you a lot and
love you even more." Ed said, "Hang in there and God bless
you. Don't you give up on anything. . . . I love you! I always
will!"

Mary's card said, "With God's love and ours" and included
the inevitable Scripture reference, this time Romans 8:28: "We
know that all things work together for good for those who love
God, who are called according to his purpose."

By July, however, from Bobby's perspective, God was doling
out penitence. He imagined that the premature lines in his face
were part of some kind of punishment. He also developed a

case of genital warts, and was convinced that the pain of having them removed was a retribution. "As usual I end up suffering for my sins," he told his diary.

He sensed that he was swimming upstream in a flow that engulfed optimism and determination. No matter how much he strove, a force was gripping him, pulling him down.

By mid-July, he was again in the depths of despair.

My life is over as far as I'm concerned. Isn't that awful? I thought I'd last at least until twenty-five, but I guess not. I shouldn't be writing this sort of thing; too bad because it's what I feel. I hate living on this earth and I resent it quite a lot sometimes.

My hair is falling out and I'm getting wrinkles. Fuck you God! If it's not one damn thing it's something else and a person can only take so much. I think God must get a certain amount of self-satisfaction by watching people deal with the obstacles he throws in their path. "Ha! let's see what Bobby does if his beautiful hair starts to go!" is what He must be saying to himself.

Well, I hate God for this and my shitty existence.

It didn't help that Mary was still firing off missives on a regular basis. The latest one was

an awful letter . . . full of correction and guidance designed to steer me to the path of righteousness. I thought she knew most of the reason I left was because of her preaching, but I guess she'll never quit.

Bobby would read these letters to Jeanette, and they would laugh and joke about them, which then made Bobby feel guilty.

Sometime over the next week, Mom was on the phone, driving home a new worry: AIDS.

"I know this is none of my business, but are you . . . are you protecting yourself?" she asked.

"Mom, please!" Bobby pleaded.

"Bobby, if you've got to play around, be careful. This AIDS is like Russian roulette. You might as well put a gun to your head."

Bobby sounded resigned. The truth was he had been worried about AIDS, one more danger lurking out there. "I'm being careful," he said. "Anyway, AIDS is probably God's punishment to gay people."

Mary was shocked. Even she wouldn't go that far. "Oh, no, Bobby. I don't believe that."

Bobby paused, then said, "Well, I might be better off dead anyway."

Mary took that as a provocation. Lately their discussions always seemed to end in arguments. She had a fleeting, exasperated thought she would come to regret for the rest of her days: "Maybe he would."

But she said only, "Well, maybe when you're twenty-one I'll stop being a mother."

"I doubt it," Bobby replied.

Bobby's cavalier response to Mary's mention of AIDS hid a real concern. By late June 1983, the numbers were threatening to hit epidemic proportions: 1,675 Americans infected; nearly 750 dead. Demonstrations and speeches were getting more frequent and beginning to be covered in the media. Still, the Reagan administration's response was minimal. And many gays were still in denial. Bobby never mentioned AIDS in his diaries, but Jeanette remembers him talking about it. The epidemic undoubtedly weighed on him as yet another land mine in his vaguely charted future.

Around that time he wrote to Dora Arnold, his *Rocky Horror* pal, saying that "things are getting real depressing around here. Send me a little bottle of California sunshine." She responded by mailing him a tiny crate of gum balls made to look like California oranges.

Actually, he was scheduled to go home to California for a five-day vacation. He looked forward to seeing the family, but resented paying two hundred dollars for an airline ticket "just to hear a damn sermon."

He went anyway, leaving behind an entry in his diary on July 25:

I must deserve everything that happens to me. The funny thing is that I didn't realize until now how bad a person I must really be.

Bob drove Mary to the Oakland Airport to meet Bobby. Mary was shocked at how down her son looked. He moved as if just breathing were an effort. "All those cheery letters, and he seems no better than the night he left," she thought. They exchanged pleasantries and hugged, but Bobby's heart was not in it. Throughout the stay he was hair-trigger sensitive with his mother and would go off at the most minor provocation. Clearly, he was not going to tolerate any "damn sermons," even though Mary had left a copy of *Newsweek* on the kitchen table, opened to an article on AIDS.

She tried to make small talk. Seeing that Oregon obviously had not made the changes he had hoped for, she asked if he wanted to return to California.

"No," he answered. "You wouldn't want me around. I'm too obnoxious."

"That's not true, Bobby," she protested.

They talked about his job future, and Mary, trying to be helpful, suggested he might want to become a paramedic.

Bobby snapped, "What's the hurry? Why are you pushing me?"

Mostly, Bobby seemed to want to hang out and perfect a California tan. He spent hours at the backyard pool. Then he'd join Nancy and Joy (Ed was busy with football summer camp), and the three of them would trip around town, once going to

Berkeley and on another occasion spending a day in Santa Cruz, a beachfront town about a hundred miles south. He had little contact with his father, with whom relations remained awkward.

Nancy, thirteen at the time, and Joy enjoyed Bobby's company, but they were conscious of a kind of glaze around his spirits. Nothing excited him. The three of them went to see *Risky Business,* the Tom Cruise movie, which both Joy and Nancy thought was pretty depressing. They felt even more depressed when they noticed that it seemed to have lowered their brother's already sunken spirits.

Once, walking on Main Street in downtown Walnut Creek, Nancy asked Bobby, "How would you feel if you found out I was gay?"

Bobby replied, "I'd be devastated."

"That's funny you'd say that," she responded, "'cause I don't feel devastated about your being gay."

Bobby said, simply, "Thanks."

He showed up with some friends at gay night at the skating rink in Hayward. Mark Guyer, the Las Lomas High School student he had dated more than eighteen months before, happened to be there. Bobby was wearing a tank top that accentuated a highly developed physique—no more the timid, conservatively dressed Bobby that Mark had known. Even his face had a chiseled look. He was traveling with an intimidatingly good-looking group of young men.

They exchanged "hi"s but not much more. Mark got the impression that Bobby was hanging now with a material crowd for whom looking good was important. He was happy that Bobby seemed to have come to terms with his sexuality. But it struck him as strange that someone with Bobby's gentle personality would look the way he did and travel in that kind of company.

. . .

In no time, it seemed, the vacation was over. Bobby said the obligatory good-byes, but without the emotion of his first departure. He gave Ed a pair of sand-colored paratrooper pants of his that Ed had admired, then shook hands in farewell. Ed was thrilled with the gift, but offended that his brother did not give him the customary parting embrace.

Joy took Bobby to the airport. "Will you be coming back?" she asked on the way. "I mean, to stay?"

"I don't know," he murmured. "I want to stick it out at least till December, to show that I gave it a real try."

At the airport, she walked him to the gate and, feeling vaguely troubled, gave him a hug. She would not see Bobby again.

. . .

Back in Portland, Bobby resumed his routine. Cousin Debbie, who also worked at Crestview Convalescent, as a nurse, noticed how glum Bobby seemed most of the time. She'd sometimes watch him leaving work and heading for the bus stop, looking weary and down. Debbie was thirty, ten years Bobby's senior. A stout woman with brown eyes and brown hair, Debbie had little in common with her younger cousin. They got along cordially as roommates, although Bobby had his complaints. ("Debbie grates my nerves sometimes," he wrote. "I could wring her neck and shout 'Shut the hell up!' Of course I restrain myself.")

But unlike her sister, Debbie was not equipped to reach out to Bobby. She felt sympathetic and knew about his struggles as a gay person, but she was predisposed by upbringing and nature to be stoic, to believe that life is hard and you simply take it and go on. She was not someone in whom Bobby would find a confidant. Relations between Bobby and Jeanette had improved, and were in fact almost back to normal, but they lived at opposite ends of town and Bobby had no car.

"It occurred to me how idiotic it is to be keeping a journal like this," he told his diary on Wednesday, August 10.

I write down my deepest innermost feelings and if anyone read them, I'd be at their mercy. Sometimes I just have to write things down if I don't happen to have someone to talk to.

Two days later, on Friday, he reported to his journal that he had gone downtown on a "small-scale shopping spree" and bought two jockstraps, a pair of sweats, and a few other items. "I was going to mow the lawn, but the lawn mower is having difficulties."

The following Wednesday, August 17, still in a housekeeping mode, he took the bus to the Saint Vincent de Paul store and purchased a mattress and box spring for seventy-nine dollars. Delivery was set for the following Tuesday.

Toward the end of the week, Jeanette called: "Let's go dancing Friday night, just you and me." Bobby joyously accepted. She could tell he was feeling lonely. She had missed him, too. The love they had for one another was intact.

It was a great night. They both loved to dance, and they both were tireless. The Embers Club, a hot dance spot, had a driving disco sound with giant amps and ear-piercing speakers. Bobby swigged bottled water (he could down the booze, but it was never a big attraction for him) and sweated it out almost instantly. They had individual styles, but when they boogied together it looked almost choreographed. This was something Bobby felt he could do well, and in concert with his beloved cousin, bodies pulsing in harmony, the moment was sheer pleasure.

They stayed till 4 A.M. Finally exhausted, Jeanette drove Bobby home in her '65 Rambler, which was still chugging away in 1983. It was a warm and damp Oregon summer night. She watched him enter the house on 54th Avenue Southwest. As she drove off, Bobby waved from the kitchen window and mouthed the words "I love you." At some point, maybe that night, he pasted Jeanette's picture in his diary and wrote the inscription, "This is a picture of my very best friend."

It was the last entry Bobby made.

. . .

A week later—Friday morning, August 26—Portlanders awoke to the news that President Reagan might have to send marines to Beirut to keep the peace. Merle Haggard was to play the state fair that night. The weatherman promised warm but cloudy weather.

When Bobby got home from work that day, Debbie could see he was in a blue mood. But that was not unusual. (In the past she had suggested he get counseling, and Bobby had agreed he needed it but said he couldn't afford it.) They walked together to the corner grocery store to buy something for dinner. Bobby, under legal age, asked Debbie to buy him a bottle of liquor. That struck her as odd, since Bobby was not a habitual drinker. Debbie refused. They cooked up a meal—ground turkey for him and frozen tamales for her. She could sense he wanted to talk, but all that transpired between them that evening was the usual chitchat.

Debbie planned to go downtown to shop later on and invited him to come along. But Bobby joked about not setting foot in her '73 jalopy; it was too dangerous. He said he would take a bus downtown later, maybe go dancing.

He was still at home when Debbie got back, but left at about 10 P.M., dressed in a light plaid shirt and green fatigue pants, headed for the gay strip on Stark Street.

At some point before midnight he made his way five blocks west and five blocks north through downtown. Jeanette later speculated he might have been headed for a leather bar called the Cell. No one knows for sure why he chose that route, in the opposite direction of home.

At 12:30 a driver and his passenger were stopped at a red light at the Everett Street overpass to the Interstate 405 freeway. They saw a figure alone, walking across the overpass. They watched him pause, looking south over the railing.

Within seconds, Bobby was up and over the railing, plunging to his death, liberated at last.

. . .

Why then? Why at that particular moment? Just three days earlier his new bed had been delivered to the house. Two weeks earlier he had purchased new sweats and a couple of jockstraps. These events implied a future. Thus, the leap was not premeditated in the traditional sense. But neither was it sheer impulse. As is evident throughout his diaries, Bobby had been contemplating a drastic solution for years. In those final months—and the preceding years—he was fighting a colossal battle between his strong will to survive and his even stronger drive to be clear of intense emotional pain. It was a courageous battle, fought against high odds and in almost total isolation.

He was seen as unhappy, but no one knew the dark, subterranean depths of his self-loathing and depression. He wore a mask for much of the world, a mask that showed a shy, uncommunicative boy with a wonderful smile and agreeable disposition. Hidden beneath was not just the pathology of self-hatred and fear related to his homosexuality, but the funny, intelligent, and articulate person that Bobby was and might have lived to be.

As with all humans, he had the capacity to be cruel, which showed up in his diaries and in some of his relations with family. But he was at heart the gentlest of souls, unusually fragile and vulnerable, susceptible to external judgment, with an underdeveloped ego. He was an adolescent, typical in most ways, unformed and insecure. The judgment of his mother, his father, and his siblings, no matter how blatant or subtle, had special power, the power to demolish his concept of self-worth. He heard these judgments—at church and at school, from his peers, from the media—and internalized them.

In common with his adolescent peers, Bobby experienced the chaotic surge of sexual energy, only to find that what ought to have been awesome and exciting was by some hand beyond his power rendered despicable. The imprimatur of religion on that judgment—personified by his mother, his church, and his own convictions—was the most deadly blow. Bobby felt bushwhacked.

Still, he battled for five years. He fought back at home, gamely standing up for what at some gut level he knew was the real Bobby. He at first went the religious route, trying to exorcise his demons by a kind of hair-shirt spiritual penance. He went to counseling. He grazed through gay society, attaching himself temporarily to different groups of friends; he flirted with a few gay organizations (MCC, the community college's gay club) and experimented ultimately with every variety of sexual expression in a loveless search for sensory release.

Obsessed with this singular struggle, knowing that his family was equally obsessed, Bobby found himself handicapped in every other aspect of his life—school, career, simple day-to-day living. He drifted through a series of menial jobs. He saw no future other than what took shape in unrealistic fantasies.

The one constant was his diary. There he could say the things he chose not to or dared not to say as part of the perfect-little-boy mask he showed the world. The diary was a map of Bobby's inner landscape: the excesses of libido; the violent extremes of anger, hate, cynicism, superiority, and condescension;

the uncharted depths of fear and pain. Here he could say, again and again, "I want to die," "Let me crawl under some rock and just waste away," "My life is over." Here he could rail at God, his mother, the world. Here he could rail against himself, mirroring the world's verdict he had come to accept. Having written all of it down, he could struggle on. It was as if he found in the use of words a talisman that gave him permission to keep fighting—words as agents to the heavens.

It may be that Bobby was doomed from the beginning. But he did not go gently. His impulse to live coursed through his every word—even in his deepest doldrums and moments of self-pity. He took to the pen, urging himself on, crying his misfortunes to the heavens like an angry Job. He had a vision of what his life could be, a glimpse of what self-acceptance would mean. Yet in the environment he occupied, dominated by his mother's nagging presence, it remained beyond his reach. The circuits could not connect.

By the time he fled to Oregon, Bobby may have been beyond salvaging. Old patterns of depression and hopelessness rapidly reasserted themselves. His mother's remonstrations followed him to Oregon by letter and telephone. The appearance of the AIDS epidemic may have seemed the ultimate condemnation. The final judgment.

Most of all, Bobby was exhausted. The struggle had been unrelenting, his persona totally battered by the effort. He could pump it up no longer. Gasping for psychic oxygen, Bobby decided on that summer night to exercise the ultimate option. That he chose a peculiarly brutal death, one that would shatter his body, is emblematic of how he felt about himself.

. . .

Jeanette would wrestle with thoughts like these for months and years to come. She was in the shower that Saturday morning when Debbie called. She grabbed a towel and picked up the receiver in the hallway. Debbie told her that Bobby was dead, that he had jumped from a freeway bridge in front of a truck. Jeanette burst into hysterical tears and shouted for Tina. When Tina heard, she could only repeat, numbly, "I don't believe it. I don't believe it."

Neither of them could. Jeanette, devastated, had thought she knew Bobby as well as anyone. And yet, along with everyone else in the family, she had underestimated the power of Bobby's misery. Suicide was the last thing she ever would have thought of.

Later, after having read the diaries and been astonished by the depths of despair in those pages, she would spend hours turning her cousin's life over and over in her mind. A jumble of thoughts ping-ponged in her head: Bobby was a raw heart with no defense walls. He simply never accepted himself. He had come to Portland to start a new life with family around him in an environment where being gay was more acceptable. Here, Bobby had seen both women and men living productive gay lives. Why had he not been able to take that in? Jeanette felt she had tried to be there for him, even when he began slipping back and resuming his old promiscuous ways. She speculated that the belief that he was doomed to burn for his sins was too deeply ingrained. Bobby's judgment of his own life was as fierce as that of the most fanatic right-winger. She was gripped by a feeling of helplessness that compounded her grief.

She and Tina packed Bobby's few belongings, including the four volumes of his diaries, and Jeanette began the long sad drive to Walnut Creek.

. . .

Andrea Hernandez was the young woman who had lived at the Griffith home in 1981 and had befriended Joy and Bobby. She had subsequently broken with Joy and drifted away. But she retained her warm affection for Bobby, and they had kept in touch. She saw him right before he left for Oregon just six months ago. On August 27, she was driving in Walnut Creek when she spotted her brother Nick at a bus stop and gave him a lift. Nick had a grave look on his face. "Andrea, I've got something to tell you." Andrea immediately had a premonition. "It's Bobby, isn't it?"

"Yes," he said. "Bobby is dead."

Andrea's throat constricted and she began to hyperventilate. She felt as if she were moving through a dream. She dropped Nick off and drove aimlessly. Having been cut off from the Griffith family, she didn't know whom to call or what to do. She decided she would go to the funeral.

At CalFrame, Diane Haines's boss gathered all the warehouse workers in the office and announced that Bobby Griffith had killed himself. Diane was stunned and saddened. She could not understand why he would do such a thing. She made it a point to find out when the funeral was.

Dora Arnold doesn't remember how she heard, only that it shocked her to the core. She and another of the *Rocky Horror* crowd, a boy named Vern, who also had had a crush on Bobby, decided to go to the funeral. Dora wanted to be there for Bobby.

Mark Guyer, Bobby's friend from Las Lomas High School, got a call from a mutual acquaintance. "Mark, you need to know that Bobby Griffith killed himself and the funeral's today."

"Oh my God!" said Mark. He felt sick to his stomach. Instinctively he thought, "Another one of us has died that way."

"But why Bobby?" he asked himself, even though he was sure he knew the answer. He flared with resentment at Bobby's mother for all the things he imagined she had done to hurt her son. He was angered, too, that he had learned of Bobby's death so late, and attributed this perceived slight to the family's rejection of everything gay in Bobby's life, including his friends.

"The hell with it," he thought. Impulsively, he jumped in his car and headed for Walnut Creek Presbyterian Church.

. . .

In that way, they converged—some of the people in Bobby's *other* life, unknown to one another, most unknown to his family. Most of them sat way in the back, feeling almost like intruders. In the atrium sat Bobby's closed casket, a photo of him resting on top. His startling smile beamed at the gathering of a hundred people.

Assistant Pastor Daubenspeck, a friend of Ed Griffith's, gave the eulogy. Its message, to Bobby's friends in the rear, to Jeanette, and even subliminally to Mary, was that Bobby had killed himself *because* he was a homosexual.

Diane Haines sat in disbelief. "Who in the hell is he to say this?" she thought, getting furious. "The reason Bobby killed himself was because he wasn't accepted by his family. Here it is, Bobby's final send-off, his final memory, and all these people are being subjected to an untruth."

Andrea Hernandez was having a similar reaction. She thought, "Even after he's dead, they're still killing him. They're saying, 'All you people here, this is what happens when you're gay and go against God: you die and isn't that too bad.'" She reflected angrily that this kind of treatment was a sacrilege, that it was disrespectful of Bobby's memory. Andrea resisted the impulse to run up and slug the minister.

Mark Guyer's race to the church was too late. The service was over by the time he got there. But the next day, Saturday, he drove to Oakmont Memorial Cemetery and located Bobby's grave up on the hill. The sod was still freshly cut where they had put him in the ground. Mark knelt, thinking, "If only we had talked more. If only we had become closer friends maybe some of my strength, if I had any, would have worn off on him. If only he had had someone to support him, he wouldn't have had to die."

In tears, Mark placed a bouquet of flowers on the site. He would return many times after that to talk to Bobby or play him songs from a tape deck. One song in particular, actually one line in one song, felt especially appropriate. It was from "Vincent," by Don McLean. Mark played it again and again.

"This world was never meant for one as beautiful as you."

ELEVEN

The Golden Thread

MARY, 1987

Nearly four years after Bobby's death, Mary was emerging from the shroud of grief and guilt. She would never be fully free of the emptiness left by the loss of her son. A fragment of her soul had gone with him.

But she was beginning to feel as if she could live a meaningful life again. In Larry Whitsell and P-FLAG she had found both a mission and a support group. Her appearance at the Concord City Council had emboldened her and allowed her to think she indeed might be able to make a difference.

People seemed to respond to her story. She didn't try to analyze why, but to others it was clear: her words had irresistible elements of emotional power—the horrible and unnecessary death of a child, the acceptance of responsibility by the parent, the incredible conversion, and the implicit warning: Don't let this happen to your child.

The account actually drew added strength from Mary's flat and unsophisticated delivery. She was shy and tentative. She spoke softly and with little intonation. Her appearance was pleasant, but not imposing. When she smiled or laughed she tended to put a hand self-consciously to her mouth, as if to conceal a slightly bucked overbite. She favored simple but neat blouses and flower-print skirts in muted hues.

The overall effect was of a person who wasn't trying to stand out. Thus, it was clear when she spoke that she was doing so only because she believed she must. Behind the tentativeness lay the passion of a missionary whose story stood on the strength of the narrative. There was no pretense, nothing hidden. Mary spoke with the authority of a tragedy lived, conveyed with a directness and immediacy that bore the imprint of truth. Often she would break down in the telling, brushing away tears and forcing herself to continue. Her heartbreak was palpable.

Her story's other strength lay in its uniqueness. Other parents could speak of estrangement from their gay children, of the agony of denial, of the journey back to reconciliation. But only Mary could make the link between repudiation and death. Through her, parents—actually anyone, whether dealing with gays as family members or as friends—could glimpse the horror of allowing a child to slip away beyond recall as the result of blind misunderstanding. Privately, Mary still struggled with the consequences of that loss. All the self-examination of the past few years had been driven by her need to find a place of peace for her son's spirit—and, by extension, for her own. Now she could imagine Bobby's spirit at rest. In the spring of 1987 she composed a communication from her son, a fantasy of afterlife in which Bobby enjoyed the pleasures and creativity denied him in life. She called it "The Golden Thread."

There are so many things to do. So much of life to catch up with. Time to write adventurous stories, time to write poems of hope and love. Time to paint the beauty that surrounds me. Time to make toys and dolls. Best of all I am free to enjoy the beauty of my creations.

There are forests to visit ... the birds are still singing as beautifully as ever, only now they sing for me too. ... The flowers are so beautiful and fragrant. You know how I love flowers. ... There are clothes to design and clothes to mend, but never a broken heart. We have culinary arts to perform and new recipes to try—fat free, of course. I wrote a song and played it on my xylophone.

I almost forgot Cozette [a family dog]. She was so happy to see me. She barked and barked. Grandfather is busy as usual at his favorite fishing spot. If you saw it you would understand why he goes there so often.

I'm really glad you caught the golden thread that will keep us united in this time and place that really is not as far away as it may seem, nor as mysterious as others claim. For when you venture into your heart, I'm not as far away as you thought. Just remember, Mom, a part of me will always be there with you and a part of you always here with me. And when everything comes around full circle, we will all be together again as before ... I promise. So please, stop worrying, Mom. I'm fine. I love you all and I understand. I really do.

It ended with one of Bobby's signature phrases, "See you later."

Reinvigorated, Mary went back to work for the first time since Bobby died, taking a job at a boutique in Walnut Creek.

On the second Tuesday evening of each month, Betty Lambert or one of the family would drive her to the MCC church in Concord for the monthly meeting of the Diablo Valley chapter of P-FLAG. There, a small cluster of parents and youngsters exchanged tales of revelation, pain, and adjustment.

At the meetings there was always a table with a pile of pamphlets and a list of books in the growing literature aimed at parents of gays and their children. Curiously, she learned, one of the things many parents do once they discover they have a gay or lesbian child is to retreat to the closet. Even in cases where the youngster has overcome the shame and fear connected with being gay, some parents' first instinct is to go into hiding.

Mary understood this, remembering how Bobby's gayness had become a dark family secret. "I now can imagine," she said at one meeting, "how humiliating it must have been for Bobby to have his social life talked about in whispers or just plainly discouraged, while that of his brother and sister were celebrated. We never welcomed his friends into our home. This only made what should have been normal dating seem illicit."

Another frequent topic was the almost total absence of support services for gay youngsters in the schools. In fact, kids would tell horror stories of rejection by teachers and students, name-calling, and even violence. Mary wished there were a vehicle to bring pressure on the education system to acknowledge the presence and needs of gay and lesbian youngsters. She would soon find one.

The sharing of experiences at these meetings served to confirm the delicate process of acceptance for the parents. They were in various stages. Some were still in shock, desperately seeking information and reassurance. Others, much further along, seemed personally transformed by the act of accepting their children's orientation. They expanded their social circles to include gay people, discovering with surprised delight how interesting and "ordinary" most of them were. Eventually, these parents became activists, marching in parades, lobbying and campaigning for gay rights.

In May, a progressive teacher invited the chapter to address his psychology classes at Ygnacio Valley High School. It was the first such opportunity in Contra Costa County schools, and the chapter jumped at it, sending a delegation that included Mary. Six P-FLAG members, gay and straight, lined up in chairs at the front of a classroom. Each told his or her story and then engaged in dialogue with four consecutive classes, most of whom were getting a bird's-eye view of homosexuality for the first time.

Mary, speaking in characteristic flat tones, was nonetheless eloquent as she invoked the Pledge of Allegiance. "Many wars have been fought and lives sacrificed to protect and maintain individual freedom and the pursuit of happiness. Therefore as a nation under God, indivisible, with liberty and justice for all, we cannot exclude our gay and lesbian children.

"Bobby believed, as his family did, the erroneous theory still being taught today that parents, environment, friends, relatives are the cause of a child becoming a homosexual person. . . . We believed with all our hearts that God would cure Bobby. I have since learned there is no cure for homosexuality any more than there is a cure for heterosexuality.

"Our gay and lesbian youth should find love and acceptance in this world. Hopefully, when you leave this class today, you will take with you knowledge about the diversities of human sexuality, and . . . a broader understanding of people."

Mary relished this chance to engage youngsters and teachers directly. The students seemed genuinely curious and without hostility. They asked basic questions about gay lifestyles and practices, the experience of coming out, and gay stereotypes they had seen on television. She of course assumed that among the 120 who attended, several were gay or lesbian. The experience strengthened her growing conviction that the schools held the key to reforming homophobic attitudes and creating support for young people growing up gay.

It was June 1987, and the chapter was laying plans to march in the annual gay pride parade in San Francisco at the end of the month. Mary wrestled with the difficult decision of whether to participate. She would feel like an imposter, she told herself, marching with all those people who had had the courage to accept their children. "If I had been one of them, Bobby would be alive today. What's the point now?" she asked herself.

But she also listened to the other parents relate how good their kids felt about their involvement in the parade. "We're representing the parents who can't be there or won't be there," Jackie Costa told her.

Mary talked it over with Bob and her children. They were of mixed minds. Ed did not like the idea of his mother exposing herself to unpredictable counterdemonstrators. Then Mary got a bright idea. She would have buttons made up with Bobby's photo on them. That way, he would be marching with her, at least symbolically. She decided to go.

On Sunday morning, June 28, Mary, Betty Lambert, Jackie Costa, and two other P-FLAG mothers, Gail Solt and Lydia Madson, boarded the rapid-transit train for the twenty-five-minute journey through Oakland and under the bay to San Francisco. Each of them wore a pin bearing a photo of Bobby's smiling face. The air was festive. At each stop parade-goers clambered aboard. Soon every car was filled to overflowing with chattering men and women. People hailed friends or made new friends on the spot. Most wore typical Sunday-outing garb—shorts, T-shirt, and cap—albeit more colorful than average, and in some cases downright creative.

They tumbled out onto Market Street, which was already teeming with people, many toting the rainbow-striped gay signature flags. Mary was amused to see men in women's drag, clicking along in high heels. They made their way through the crowd to the P-FLAG staging area. Mary was stunned to see how large the P-FLAG delegation was. It seemed to stretch for blocks, a thousand or more people.

She remembered with a sense of irony how a decade earlier she had watched with distaste as television cameras showed parents parading publicly with their gay and lesbian children. Now she felt a surge of frustration at the thought of how many like herself *should* be here today and were not. Times sure had changed.

Indeed they had—for everyone. Gay Pride 1987 carried the imprint of the plague that had reached full bore in the gay community. For every brightly bedecked float there was a contingent with a mission related to AIDS: the Shanti project, Project Open Hand, the San Francisco AIDS Foundation. The recently formed group ACT-UP demanded more money for research and prevention. Everywhere, signs condemned the Reagan administration's indifference. (The president had mentioned AIDS for the first time in seven years in a speech a month earlier.)

At one time the parade had exuberantly celebrated the healthy, muscular, and randy entitlements of gay freedom. Now among the hale were to be seen prematurely aged young men limping by or being pushed in wheelchairs. At this point, more than twenty-one thousand Americans had died from the disease (a tenfold increase in the four years since the time of Bobby's suicide). Tens of thousands of San Franciscans were HIV-positive.

The P-FLAG contingent kicked off and the crowd cheered. It cheered louder and longer for them than for any other contingent. Mary was astonished at the reception. She had no idea the presence of parents would mean this much.

Yet with each burst of applause, Mary felt more uneasy. The old familiar pattern of guilt and sadness came rushing back. All around her, parents marched with their children. There were sisters, brothers, aunts, uncles, even pets. The glow of love and pride shone in their eyes.

She could have been there with Bobby. She imagined him beside her, tall and grinning, proud and confident. How could she have been so wrong? "I don't deserve to be here," she thought. "I'm not what they think I am."

On the sidelines, tens of thousands of spectators shouted their encouragement as the P-FLAG contingent passed. In contrast to the dark subtext of much of that year's parade, the parents' presence radiated hope and optimism. Mary took in the vast procession of faces in the crowd, of all ages and hues, eager and smiling, almost childlike. Some were openly crying! It occurred to her that every gay person must see in the P-FLAG contingent the reflection of his or her own parents. Projected on these marchers were tens of thousands of child-parent dramas: love, pain, rejection, joy, denial, fear, remorse—the entire palette of emotions. The marchers were parent surrogates upon whom each observer could project the longing for reconciliation, the yearning to relive the experience of unconditional acceptance.

Mary spotted a man in his late thirties standing on the sidewalk at the edge of the curb. As she approached, she could see that he was quietly crying. Something impelled her toward him. She came near and embraced him. He hugged her back. They held each other tight, saying nothing. But Mary felt as if, in that moment, years of misunderstanding had been bridged.

She returned to the line of march, greatly moved. That was the embrace she wished she had been able to give her own son. But there were tens of thousands still living who longed for such acknowledgment, many of them in suicidal despair. She now understood why she was there. She was there for all the Bobbys still living. There was no longer time to indulge feelings of guilt and remorse. There was work to be done.

She quickened her step to catch up with her Diablo chapter as it made the descent down Market Street just before the parade reached the civic center. From this vantage point Mary could see virtually the full length of the parade, both ahead and behind. Her heart leapt as she felt herself in concert with this great wave of humanity winding its way in the direction of San Francisco Bay as it turned onto Van Ness Avenue for the final leg. Mary noticed that the sun had pierced the morning fog to reveal its midday brilliance.

On the Road

The next months and years were to be exciting ones. Shedding the protective shackles that had kept her spirit in check for fifty years, Mary was poised to experience the world with the newness and wonder of a person for whom everything is possible. She would make new relationships and modify old ones. She would challenge habits of fear and inferiority, passivity and hopelessness. It would take courage.

Mary had come to understand her mission. A wrong had been done and a life lost as a result. She was determined to right the injustice and save lives. She wanted to buy some time for other youngsters so they could survive the shaky adolescent years—hard enough without being lesbian or gay—and make it to adulthood. If she could affect just one person's life, it would be worth it. It was to be her own emergence, as an individual, an adult, and a woman. And because of her special situation, she would bring Bobby with her. Together they would have an impact on thousands of people.

Interestingly, she was neither an organizer nor a natural leader. She was ingenuous about how the world works in general and about politics in particular. But she was a fast learner and would move by instinct, often reacting to situations around her, yet ever alert to opportunity and intensely focused on goals.

She had the ability to recognize leadership in others and ally herself with them.

Hank Wilson was one of those. He was the kind of person whose inner engine is constantly revving. He had been an advocate all his adult life, mostly for gay causes. In person he conveyed high energy and commitment with an undercurrent of impatience. His alert eyes behind thin-rimmed spectacles seemed to be darting in all directions. As a VISTA volunteer, as a teacher, and most recently as manager of a hotel in San Francisco's Tenderloin district whose clientele consisted of HIV-positive drifters, Wilson, in his forties, had developed a sophisticated understanding of politics and power.

He helped the legendary Harvey Milk get elected a San Francisco supervisor. He helped voters defeat the Briggs Initiative in 1978, which would have banned gay teachers in California schools. But for the last ten years his special passion had been the cause of gay and lesbian youth. As far back as 1977 he had formed a gay teachers' coalition in San Francisco with Tom Ammiano, a stand-up comic and activist who went on to become president of the San Francisco School Board and a city supervisor. In those days coming out as a gay teacher, even in San Francisco, took unusual courage. (It still does.)

In the mid-1980s he crashed the first federally sponsored conference on youth suicide and challenged it to confront the issue of gay teen suicide, which, astonishingly, was not on its agenda. The large number of gay suicides among the national teen suicide statistics was still an unspoken reality. (In 1989 the Health and Human Services Department published a study that included the now-famous chapter on gay suicide, suppressed by the Bush administration under pressure from the right.)

Wilson met Mary Griffith in 1987 at a P-FLAG statewide retreat in Marin County, just across the Golden Gate Bridge from San Francisco. Mary told her story as part of a discussion group. The presentation electrified Wilson. Here was a woman whose personal tragedy transcended political rhetoric. She was not a radical activist with a predetermined agenda. She was speaking from her own personal experience. Wilson found this far more effective than any politically correct analysis. He thought it had great potential to humanize the issues for which he had been fighting for years.

At another point he heard her speaking again, this time to a state commission. "You could hear a pin drop," he later recalled. "Everyone was very moved. She touched hearts, not just minds." An inveterate networker, he hoped to find a way to help channel this asset.

The opportunity came at a dinner sponsored by Gay and Lesbian Awareness and Development, an organization that had grown out of the fight over the proposed Gay Freedom Week in Concord. It attracted most of the local Contra Costa County activists, among them Rob Birle, a young art teacher who was organizing other teachers in the county to pressure schools to include programs for gay students.

Birle and Wilson had gotten to know each other in 1984 when Rob, then a candidate for a teaching credential at San Francisco State University, had the idea of forming a regional organization of gay and lesbian educators. Wilson had already created the local gay teachers' coalition, and had become a mentor for the younger man. Birle called his organization the Bay Area Network of Gay and Lesbian Educators (BANGLE). It was an audacious concept at the time, because few teachers dared go public and face the career consequences stemming from lurid stereotypes of gays as predators of children.

BANGLE came on the scene in late 1984, during a time of renewed gay activism growing out of the AIDS emergency. Within three years the organization had 250 members (albeit most of them closeted). Rob, then twenty-nine, got a job teaching art to high school students in Antioch, a small town in the northeast corner of Contra Costa County. He moved there with his partner, Andy Bowlds, a social worker, and in 1988 started a local chapter of BANGLE.

At the Concord dinner, Wilson and Birle had coffee together and caught up on things. "By the way," Wilson asked, "have you met Mary Griffith?"

Rob, new to the area, said he had not. Wilson said, "You ought to meet her. She's here. The woman is remarkable, and what she's doing fits in perfectly with your agenda." Hank filled Rob in briefly and then brought him over to meet Mary.

Rob and Mary chatted. He listened with growing interest as she recounted her tale of tragedy and transformation. He told her of his plans for BANGLE, his interest in educating school administrators throughout the county about gay concerns, with an eye toward having them include sexual orientation as a legitimate issue in classroom instruction and counseling. At the time the subject was virtually invisible throughout the generally conservative county school system. Rob hoped at least to help demystify gayness and make it seem less threatening.

Mary listened with similar interest. She sensed from the start of her public activism that she had to find a way to speak directly with teachers, administrators, and students. But she was not an organizational type; in fact, determined as she was, she could be quite scattered. This slender, handsome young man with dark hair and beard and penetrating eyes not only had good ideas but appeared to know how to execute them.

What Mary had, reckoned Rob, was an incredible and compelling story. He was impressed that in an extremely short time she had made the journey from committed religious homophobe to fervent gay rights advocate. He could imagine what an impact this motherly straight woman's dramatic tale could have on a school superintendent.

They both appreciated the synergy of the moment. Their paths—and needs—had crossed at the right time and place. It was the beginning of a four-year working partnership that evolved into a mother-son friendship and helped propel Mary Griffith from local advocate to national figure.

Mary began attending BANGLE meetings every month, in addition to her P-FLAG meetings and other growing responsibilities. In fact by late 1988, upon the resignation of Jackie Costa, she had taken over as president of the Diablo P-FLAG chapter and moved the meetings from the MCC church in Concord to her Walnut Creek home. At fifty-three, she was gaining confidence. She became more vocal, speaking out, going to demonstrations and firing off letters to newspapers, such as a stern attack on "dishonest and deceitful" fundamentalists for opposing a self-esteem program for the county.

Rob Birle mapped a plan to visit nine school districts in Contra Costa County. It would be the first time anyone had approached these institutions with a mission specific to gay issues. Rob's plans were buoyed by successive votes in July 1988 by the nation's two largest teachers' unions—the National Education Association and the American Federation of Teachers—supporting rights for gay and lesbian students. The NEA's resolution read, in part: "Every school district should provide counseling for students who are struggling with their sexual/gender orientation."

• • • • •

In late fall 1988, Mary and Rob began their road show as a joint BANGLE/P-FLAG project, traversing the county in a series of day trips over the next few months. Rob would pick her up in Walnut Creek and they'd take off, Mary carrying an everpresent cup of coffee and stopping periodically to feed her cigarette habit. They logged enough driving hours together to learn a lot about one another.

Rob was born in the mid-1950s to an itinerant textile salesman and his wife. They moved eighteen times in Rob's young life before settling in Charlotte, North Carolina, around 1968. The boy could have handled the dislocation, but he also was living with the nightmare of alcoholism. Soon Rob himself was drinking. As a teenager, mortified by his growing attraction to males and terrified that his parents would find out, he got drunk one night and threw himself in the path of a tractor-trailer on a downtown Charlotte street. Fortunately, the driver swerved in time.

The parallel with Bobby was not exact, but it was close enough to be impressive. Rob, too, had been estranged from his parents, and in fact still was. He told Mary how he went on to art college in Atlanta, still unresolved about his homosexuality. He started popping pills and on one bleary, self-pitying night tried again to do himself in. "Being gay and hating myself combined with alcohol and pills was a deadly combination. Then I met someone, my first partner. He gave me an ultimatum to stop drinking. With my low self-esteem I didn't think I could do it. But I did, and I suddenly realized I wanted to live. I really wanted to live! We ended up staying together three years, and I never went back to my old ways."

It occurred to Rob that if Bobby had given himself more time, he, too, might have made it through. He wondered how some of us make it and others do not. He himself had come so close to dying; if Bobby had only held on, he might have discovered that it is possible to live a life of dignity and promise as a gay person.

He shared the thought with Mary. A shadow passed across her face. Then she said, "That's why we're out here, Rob. We need to buy time for these kids so they can see that they have as much right to life as anyone."

Mary was right, Rob thought. He took one arm from the wheel and placed it warmly around her shoulder. In a way they had assumed surrogate roles for one another; she the loving mother he longed for and he the gay son she could not keep.

. . .

Buying time for gay kids in the schools would not be easy. Gay and lesbian issues had never been raised at all in most of the schools of the county. Administrators knew they would be asking for trouble with suburban and rural parents if the incendiary issue of same-gender sexuality were to surface in their schools. Gay and lesbian students remained invisible and fearful. Those who could not hide were often brutally harassed.

In one district they visited, Mary made her case to the district superintendent. "I truly believe my son would be alive today if his school had let him know that it was okay to be gay," she told him. "Whether it be through counseling or books in the library. Whatever. There are other Bobbys in your schools right this moment. They are silently crying out for help."

The superintendent leaned back in his chair and asked, "What would you suggest I tell parents who ask, 'What is your justification for teaching about this'—in their words—'perverted behavior?'"

Rob wondered whether this man might have asked the same question if the subject had been racial minority studies. Fifteen years ago, probably so. Rob replied, "I would tell them that even though they may disagree with the issue, all kids, gay and straight, need this orientation. First of all, because lives may be at stake. Second of all, because gay baiting and harassment are epidemic in our schools, and they're based on ignorance and misinformation. Educators have an obligation to fight ignorance; at least that's what they told us when I was a student. That's what I'd suggest you say." They rose to leave.

They received more cordial receptions in other districts. By early 1989 they could report back to BANGLE that they had met with superintendents in nearly half the county's eighteen school districts. One district had agreed to reevaluate its nondiscrimination policies and revise its contract language to refer to sexual orientation. Another assured them that it would include homosexuality in its revised curriculum. Only one district flatly refused to meet with them.

Encouraged, Rob and BANGLE sent letters to all eighteen districts urging them to pass resolutions banning antigay slurs on campuses, to establish counseling specifically for gay students, and to prohibit discrimination in the hiring and promotion of gay personnel.

Though Mary and Rob could not know it at the time, their efforts coincided with the first stirrings of a new national debate over sex education and, more specifically, over the focus on gay and lesbian youth. It would escalate over the next several years to one of the most contentious fights in the struggle between gay rights advocates and the religious right.

Already, Contra Costa BANGLE's modest campaign was drawing fire from the local chapter of the Traditional Values Coalition (TVC), a southern California–based antigay group headed by an Orange County minister named Lou Sheldon. The national organization was at the moment going after larger game—namely, Project 10 in Los Angeles.

The brainchild of a science teacher, Virginia Uribe, Project 10 was inspired by the example of an effeminate student who had been harassed mercilessly and finally forced out of Uribe's school, Fairfax High. Uribe began Project 10 modestly in 1984 at Fairfax. Unique in the country, it caught on and enjoyed such success that it soon expanded to include teacher training and counseling services throughout the Los Angeles Unified School District. (It would become the prototype of efforts in other California districts.) In effect, what Project 10 did was precisely what Rob and Mary were seeking: it provided an in-school place where youngsters who were gay or thought they might be gay could go for counseling, referral, and reassurance.

Sheldon, who tirelessly and zealously pursued any project that threatened to "promote" homosexuality, now was lobbying for legislation that would cut off all aid to the Los Angeles school district unless it scuttled Project 10. "We've fired the first round in a total involvement effort which brings us in open warfare with the gay and lesbian community's agenda for the country," he told his supporters in a fund-raising letter. "And

California is the beachhead. We must stop it here before it spreads throughout the nation like cancer."

Project 10, he argued, drew teenagers into homosexuality— "one of the most pernicious evils of our society." With Sheldon's urging, a sympathetic legislator filed a bill in the state legislature that would outlaw the "advocacy" of homosexuality in public education.

The bill was a direct threat not only to Project 10 but to BANGLE's hopes of introducing a modicum of reform in Contra Costa schools. In response, Rob organized a demonstration. He, Mary, and one hundred other Bay Area activists picketed loudly one rainy evening in November 1988 outside a Walnut Creek church where the local TVC was meeting. The event made all the local papers.

"This is a warning," Rob told a reporter. "This is an indication that we're not going to sit by idly while we're being attacked." (As it turned out, the bill got nowhere.)

They carried candles and shouted slogans. This was Mary's first full-fledged demonstration, and for a moment she had to marvel at how far she'd come. Here she was toting a sign, standing in the rain outside the Evangelical Free Church, and shouting "Shame!" at a group of people whom four years earlier she would have considered ideological brethren.

. . .

On the home front, her family tracked Mary's activities with somewhat bemused support. Generally, they approved. Joy, Nancy, Ed, and Bob had come a long way from the earlier days, although they were left in the wake of Mary's high-velocity changes. Whatever their previous attitudes or doubts, they had been converted by the corroding pain of loss. This should not happen to a family. And if homophobia caused it, then homophobia must be opposed. And if Mary was prepared to take the lead on this, they were happy to have her represent the rest of them. They cheered her on. Thank God, thought Nancy, ironically; at least Mom was not spouting Bible verses anymore. They would drive her to events, even attend award dinners on occasion, but were disinclined to get more involved. They had their own lives to build. None of them were in evidence at Mary's P-FLAG chapter meetings, for example.

Bob consistently stayed in the background, quietly monitoring Mary's activities. He felt that what she was doing was right and was good therapy as well, but he was wary that her intensity might set her up to be hurt again. He tried to rein her in from time to time.

Joy was advancing in her job with the successor firm to Cal-Frame. She, too, had rejected organized religion and was seeking new ways to channel her spirituality. She was not an activist, but sought through meditation and other inner-directed ways to resolve an intense case of survivor guilt. Like her mother, she was unsure where Bobby's spirit was. He appeared to her in recurring dreams, and at first she greeted him excitedly. But each time, in an unsettling close-up, she would notice deep unhappiness in his eyes. Those dreams haunted her. Were they saying that Bobby held her responsible for not doing more to help him, for not being more sensitive?

Joy eventually visited a hypnotherapist and in a long hypnotic session satisfied herself that Bobby was safely in the spirit realm. She divined that everything was fine between her and her brother, that he knew she loved him dearly, and that he in turn loved her. Everything was okay; the bad dreams disappeared.

Ed was now a sheriff's deputy and dating wife-to-be Linda, whose five-year-old son, Ernesto, he would take under his wing. Ed had traveled the path with his mother away from fundamentalist thinking, and shared her new conviction that his brother's gayness was a natural occurrence. His concerns were about her security as she became more and more visible.

That visibility was to jump several notches in 1989 with the convergence of three events: the establishment of the Bobby

Griffith Memorial Scholarship; the publication of a three-week series on gays in America in the *San Francisco Examiner,* with Mary and Bobby Griffith's story serving as a major anchor; and the U.S. government's publication and almost immediate suppression of a study that concluded that suicide among gay and lesbian teenagers was nearly epidemic.

Rob Birle had a brainstorm. It happened in spring 1989, while he was reading to his class the annual list of scholarships that would be handed out to students upon graduation. There were at least one hundred different money grants awarded annually at Antioch High, including several to blacks, to Hispanics, to Italian Americans; there were awards from insurance brokers and realtors, from Rotary and Kiwanis. Why not, Rob thought, a gay scholarship?

Yes, a competitive scholarship countywide—maybe areawide—honoring college-bound seniors whose essays demonstrated sensitivity to gay and lesbian issues and a commitment to gay and lesbian rights. The ace in his game plan involved Mary Griffith.

"This would be the first such scholarship of its kind in the country, as far as I know," he told her. "With the precedent of all those other special-interest scholarships there is no way the schools could refuse it. Just think: they would have to announce it, administer it, put it in their graduation program. It's a way to get the subject discussed.

"And Mary," Rob added with appropriate import, "we'd name it for Bobby. The Bobby Griffith Memorial Scholarship!"

Mary was immediately enthusiastic. Bobby's name and memory would be immortalized. A competitive scholarship could only get people talking about the issues. And for some gay kid feeling isolated, the existence of a scholarship would reassure him or her that there are adults who care. She could see no downside.

"Okay" said Rob, "but you've got to be ready for a change in your life. The family, too. Up to now you've been operating in a small arena. I'm convinced that this scholarship is going to get a lot of attention, throughout the state, maybe the country. You'll be in the media spotlight."

Mary was not the kind of person who relished attention. She had practiced being unobtrusive since childhood. What excited her was the possibility of having a larger environment in which to get her message out. It was a single-minded and uncomplicated message: find ways to let gay and lesbian kids know they are as valued and valuable as their straight counterparts; outlaw harassment against gay children and make the penalties strong enough to enforce the ban; require schools, churches, and other institutions to provide intelligent and undistorted information about gays and lesbians to both straights and nonstraights. Education was the key.

She was media-wise enough to know that press attention could amplify this message a millionfold.

"I can handle it," she assured Rob.

They decided to announce the scholarship in June, launch a fund-raising campaign over the following months to finance it, and award the first scholarships at the end of the 1990 school year. Rob composed a letter of appeal that stressed just how often "the existence of gay and lesbian youth is denied by educators and parents. . . . We want to say to these forgotten youth, 'You are not alone. There are adults who care.'"

Independently and almost simultaneously, a *San Francisco Examiner* reporter was zeroing in on this Walnut Creek housewife who apparently had an amazing story to tell.

Lily Eng was a recently hired freshman reporter at the *Examiner* assigned to a huge team preparing one of the most ambitious projects in the newspaper's history. The year 1989 was to be the twentieth anniversary of the dawning of the modern gay civil rights movement outside a nondescript Greenwich Village bar called the Stonewall Inn. The *Examiner*, fabled as the flagship paper that launched the career of tycoon William Randolph Hearst, would commemorate Stonewall by producing a sixteen-day series encompassing every aspect of gay and lesbian life in the country. More than sixty staff members were working on the four-month project, to be titled "Gay in America," whose appearance would coincide with Gay Pride Month in June. Eng was assigned to interview young people. While digging for sources, she spoke with Rob Birle, who told her about Mary's speech before the Concord City Council.

"What made Mary so passionate about the issue?" Eng asked.

"Her gay son killed himself," Rob answered. Eng's reporter antennae jumped to full alert. She and photographer Liz Mangelsdorf sped to Walnut Creek to interview Mary. What started as a short interview destined for a sidebar ended up lasting three hours. Mary entrusted the reporter with some of Bobby's diaries. Eng and Mangelsdorf left knowing they had something special.

Back at the office the decision was quickly made to upgrade the story and allow it to stand alone on two full pages in the Sunday edition of June 18, a week before the official Stonewall celebration. (The Sunday edition shares circulation with the city's powerful other daily newspaper, the *Chronicle*, with a combined readership of close to 1 million.)

That Sunday, readers opened their newspapers to the headline "Bobby's Legacy: After Her Son's Death, Mary Griffith Learns to Understand His Gayness and Vows to Help Other Young People."

Just below was a large blowup of a sad-eyed Mary beside a portrait of her son. In addition to the story and diary excerpts, the paper gave Mary a platform from which to make a powerful statement to gay youngsters:

To all the Bobbys and Janes out there, I say these words to you as I would to my own precious children: Please don't give up hope on life or yourselves. You are very special to me and I am working very hard to make this life a better and safer place for you to live in.

I firmly believe—though I did not back then—that my son Bobby's suicide is the end result of homophobia and ignorance within most Protestant and Catholic churches, and consequently within society, our public schools, our own family.

What a travesty of God's love for children to grow up believing themselves to be evil, with only a slight inclination toward goodness. . . . Is it any wonder our young people give up on love, as Bobby did, and the hope of ever receiving the validation they deserve as beautiful human beings?

But as a result of my son's death, I have joined other caring people to try to make a pathway with knowledge and understanding within our public school system, a pathway that in time may be traveled with dignity and freedom from fear, for gay and lesbian students, and any student who is subjected to discrimination.

Promise me you will keep trying.

Bobby gave up on love. I hope you won't. You are always in my thoughts.

With love, Mary Griffith.

The combined impact of Bobby's saga and Mary's turnaround touched a public nerve. Readers jammed phone lines at the paper. Letters poured in. The reporter, Lily Eng, herself a lesbian in her mid-twenties just beginning to deal with her own coming out, basked in her colleagues' praise. She declared that this was the most emotionally exhilarating story of her career (an assessment that held up five years later). An item about the Bobby Griffith Memorial Scholarship, which had run with the package, drew thousands of dollars in contributions.

Ed Griffith was reading the article at work Sunday morning when a fellow policeman came by. "That's my mom," Ed said. The policeman glanced at the article and asked, "What do you think about what she is doing?"

"I think it's great," Ed said. "I'm really proud of her."

The policeman hesitated for a moment, then blurted, "Did you know that I'm gay?" Ed looked at his bulky, football-player-sized colleague and said, "No, of course not. But I'm glad you trusted me enough to tell me." The policeman went on to become a family friend and, in fact, participated in classroom talks with Mary, as the ultimate role model: an out gay cop.

Mary was excited by the *Examiner* package and the reactions it was getting. (Even mother Ophelia told her, "Mary, you are really doing a good thing for people.") She noticed again the power of words to move people. She hoped that parents as well as children would take the message to heart. She let her mind play with these thoughts, and it struck her that a parent's words to a child can kill the child's spirit or give it wings. In that way parents have the power of life and death over their kids. The things we say to our children in the name of love, she thought, can be lethal. She remembered the quote from psychiatrist Erik Erikson that Project 10 used in its literature: "Someday, maybe, there will exist a well-informed . . . public conviction that the most deadly of all possible sins is the mutilation of a child's spirit."

In that connection, one letter in particular tore at her heart. It was signed, merely, "Corey," and was dated the same Sunday on which the *Examiner* story had appeared.

"I felt as if I were reading about myself," Corey wrote.

Everything that Bobby believed is what I believe. I have never told my family or friends the truth, and I never, ever will. I want to fit into this society so badly and I never will be able to as gay. All I want to do is to be able to function as a normal straight man. But I cannot and I hate myself for it. I do not fit in anywhere.

I was brought up in a semi-religious household. I was told that God thinks homosexuals are bad. . . . Why the hell did he create them then?! Every single day I pray about ten times for God to make me straight.

*I sit here and think, "Why couldn't Bobby and my paths
have crossed?" We could have shared our fears with each other,
shared our dreams. I could have been the friend he needed—he
could have been the friend I need. . . . I have considered suicide
but . . . I couldn't do that. But there have been times when I've
wished someone else would do the job.*

*Well, thank you for listening. You might have saved my life.
But do not try to convince me to tell the world. . . . I can't han-
dle life. Bobby will be my beacon, my light of hope. I AM NOT
ALONE. . . . I'll never be happy. But I can struggle through it.
And, don't you worry, Mrs. Griffith. I shall not give up on love.*

But she did worry. No last name. No address. For weeks the
vision of Corey haunted her. She felt at once responsible and
helpless. If anything, letters like these increased her frustration,
her sense of urgency. How to raise the volume even more on
this crisis of silence and isolation that still beset gay kids? Why
weren't more people talking about it? What more could she do
to ferret out the Coreys, to reach a hand to them?

. . .

Events were conspiring to bring the subject widespread public attention. The issue of youth suicide had caught the imagination of the Reagan administration. At the time it seemed both a
worthwhile and noncontroversial subject. (No one had thought
to include *gay* youth suicide as a factor.) The Department of
Health and Human Services (HHS) held two national meetings
on the issue in 1985 and 1986. With the urging of Hank Wilson,
the San Francisco activist, and others, the dilemma of gay and
lesbian youths eventually got noticed. When HHS created its
Task Force on Youth Suicide and asked that body to produce a
report, it okayed the inclusion of a section on suicide among gay
and lesbian youth.

Paul Gibson, a psychiatric social worker who worked with
gay runaways in San Francisco, got the assignment. The task-

force report emerged in 1989, during the Bush administration and the era of "family values." The general findings of the task force were shocking enough: the suicide rate of *all* young people (ages fifteen to twenty-four) had tripled in the previous thirty years, and suicide was currently the second leading cause of death in that age range. But Gibson's results astonished even gay advocates. He estimated that three out of ten of those youth suicides may have involved gay and lesbian adolescents. Further, he calculated that between 20 and 35 percent of gay youth make suicide attempts, a rate three times the general youth suicide rate.

These were explosive numbers in an official government study. Gibson had cautioned that they were estimates based on the sparse research available up to that time. But the numbers immediately became widely quoted as fact and attracted the attention of gay activists, the mainstream press, and the right wing.

HHS had a hot potato on its hands. For the first time a government-commissioned study documented the scandalous history of rejection and isolation of gay teens. Gibson portrayed a woeful picture of life for gay and lesbian youth. They face the double jeopardy, he said in his report, of

surviving adolescence and developing a positive identity in what is frequently a hostile and condemning environment. . . . Lesbian and gay youth are the most invisible and outcast group of young people with whom you will come into contact. . . . With all of the conflicts they face in accepting themselves, coming out to families and peers . . . and confronting the haunting specter of AIDS, there is a growing danger that their lives are becoming a tragic nightmare with living only a small part of dying.

More pointedly, the Gibson report urged the government to promote several reforms. Among its suggestions: the passage of antidiscrimination laws, the legalization of gay marriage, and the creation of massive education efforts directed "especially to those who have responsibility for the care of the young, including families, clergy, teachers, and helping professionals."

In that most sensitive of domains, the schools, Gibson urged an ambitious menu that included providing positive information about homosexuality to *all* students; offering family-life classes that would present being gay as a natural and healthy form of sexual expression; developing curricula that would include a variety of historical and social references; offering sensitivity training for teachers and staff; and instituting penalties for harassment or abuse of gay youth.

To a far-right congressman like William Dannemeyer, this effort to "legitimize" homosexuality was the worst form of blasphemy. In this view, advanced by Dannemeyer's fundamentalist backers, the mere mention of homosexuality in any official way was tantamount to promoting it.

In September 1989, Dannemeyer, then a congressman from Orange County, California, wrote President Bush importuning him to "affirm traditional family values," to denounce the portion of the report dealing with homosexuality, and to "dismiss from public service all persons still employed who concocted this homosexual pledge of allegiance."

The administration was heading into an important midterm election year and could not have been eager to alienate the large, wealthy, and powerful voting bloc of the religious right. Within a month HHS secretary Louis Sullivan sent a reassuring and ingratiating reply to Dannemeyer, saying "the views expressed in the [Gibson] paper do not in any way represent my personal beliefs or the policy of this Department." He hastened to add, "I am strongly committed to advancing traditional family values. Federal policies must strengthen rather than undermine the institution of the family. In my opinion the views expressed in the paper ran contrary to that aim."

Decoded, the message from Sullivan, one of the few high-ranking blacks in the Bush government and the man answerable for the health of all Americans, was that the definition of traditional family excludes those that happen to include gay or lesbian children. The subtextual message to Dannemeyer and the factions he represented was "not to worry"—this report was not going anywhere. In fact, the government retired it to bureaucratic obscurity, and the two thousand copies of the first and only printing became collector's items.

But the genie was out of the file cabinet. The press got wind of the controversy with the help of an alliance of gay lobbying organizations, including the Human Rights Campaign Fund, the National Gay and Lesbian Task Force, and national P-FLAG. (Mary Griffith allowed her name to be signed to letters sent to the administration and members of Congress. The letter to Secretary Sullivan in her name urged him "to investigate the true facts concerning homosexuality.")

The debate moved in October 1989 to the floor of the House of Representatives, where Dannemeyer tried without success to attach a rider to an appropriations bill that would have cut off school districts such as Los Angeles's for involvement in gay-friendly programs. (The effort did not end: five years later a similar bill, spearheaded by North Carolina senator Jesse Helms, nearly made it through Congress.)

Controversy over gay teen suicide, plus the startling statistics and other details of the Gibson report, circulated in the gay press and gave the topic enough sizzle to penetrate the mainstream media. Soon stories on gay teen suicide were showing up in most of the leading metropolitan newspapers, with reporters playing up local angles in smaller venues.

The daytime talk shows were next to discover the topic. Their needs were different: they had to have live "heads" telling dramatic stories. Program directors turned for help to the well-connected national office of P-FLAG in Washington, D.C., which was continually fielding requests from the national and local media, both electronic and print, for interviews, articles, and talk-show guests. National P-FLAG was just beginning to realize that it had a significant asset in Mary

Griffith. The organization began recommending her when inquiries came in.

The opportunity for a national audience for her message excited Mary. When the call came to appear on "The Joan Rivers Show," she jumped at it. Over the next two years, Mary appeared on "Sally Jesse Raphael," the "Today" show, "Oprah," "Maury Povich," "Ricki Lake," "The Cristina Show," and a segment of ABC's "20/20." In addition, at least six video projects—including Pam Walton's extremely affecting forty-five-minute film *Gay Youth*—revolved around Mary or included major segments on her story.

Mary turned out to be quite telegenic in a nontelevision kind of way. The plainspoken appeal she had in person translated to the small screen. Her craggy, frontier-woman face, punctuated by worry lines around the mouth, communicated honesty and grit. Her voice, deliberate and flat-toned, was reassuringly American. Her words had the authority of a survivor of almost unimaginable tragedy. She told the same story again and again, yet each time it seemed real and new, from the heart.

SALLY JESSE: *Mary, talk to the parents.*

MARY: *Our gay and lesbian children need to have their self-esteem and self-worth restored. I believe in order for this to happen parents need to be open-minded. They need to be open to the special information that's available. Your child needs to know that he's an equal, lovable, and valuable person. Not only the parents, but the school administrators [her voice breaks], President Bush and Mrs. Bush and members of Congress and our religious leaders—let them not be, as I was, an unwitting accomplice to an innocent person's death.*

SALLY JESSE: *Where is Bobby now?*

MARY: *I believe Bobby's in a time and place that he can be himself. He can be accepted . . .*

SALLY JESSE: *Will God accept him?*

MARY: *Oh, yes.*

Television brought Mary wide exposure to a new audience—straight people who might never before have seen close-up the very human tragedy of gay suicide but who could identify with the horror of losing a child, any child. Mary evoked a powerful, universal empathy. On-screen images of studio audiences weeping each time she told her story persuaded the gay youth movement that it had a powerful asset in Mary Griffith.

P-FLAG framed a major national direct-mail appeal around Mary and Bobby in late 1990. It included a four-page solicitation letter in Mary's name and a mail-back insert with Bobby's photo prominently displayed, with the legend: "Dear Mary, In memory of Bobby and the other gay and lesbian youth lost to suicide, I'm making this gift."

Reacting to suppression of the report on gay youth suicide, P-FLAG also launched a national awareness campaign called Respect All Youth and invited Mary to address the press conference kicking off the effort in Orange County (Dannemeyer-Sheldon country). Respect All Youth would be a nationwide education program providing informational materials and training counselors to fight gay youth suicide.

Wearing her button with Bobby's portrait, Mary spoke to a crush of reporters and photographers at the Hyatt Regency in Anaheim. "I am here today because I have learned in the most painful way possible that ignorance, hatred, bigotry, and prejudice lead to violence and tragedy. . . . And I have learned that love, honesty, support, and acceptance . . . lead to health, wholeness, and self-esteem for our children."

When not racing off to television appearances and press conferences, Mary continued making the rounds of school districts with Rob and overseeing her P-FLAG chapter, which was growing as a result of her developing public persona. School districts were slowly responding: two of them agreed to receive literature and video materials, and another pledged to update its sex-education curriculum. But at least three districts still refused to meet with her and Rob.

Through Rob, Mary discovered two people who would become her mainstays in P-FLAG.

Joe Torp and Con Smith were retired schoolteachers who had been a couple since 1952. In every respect but gender, they lived the prototypical suburban existence in a handsome tract home with swimming pool in Concord.

For several decades, Joe and Con had lived closeted lives as schoolteachers. After retiring, they felt free to get involved, and were attracted to Rob's BANGLE organization. Soon they offered their home as a meeting site and began running the organization's phone tree and coordinating its newsletter mailings.

Through BANGLE they met Mary. Joe, now in his seventies, is soft-spoken and professorial, in contrast to his more whimsical partner. (Con Smith died in late 1994.) Joe was drawn to P-FLAG because of an incident that occurred during his teaching years at Antioch High in Contra Costa County. It involved a star student, lettered in three different sports and president of his senior class, who developed a crush on one of the male teachers. The boy went to the teacher and blurted out his passion. But the teacher, fearful for his job, refused to discuss the situation or counsel him. Some time later, the young man drove his car into a eucalyptus tree at eighty miles an hour and died. The teacher gave up his post at the end of the school year.

The tragedy stayed with Joe, and he wondered whether he would have had the courage to do anything differently had the youth approached him. Now there were still kids out there struggling with their sexual identity, and there was a chance to do something to help them. Joe and Con joined Mary's chapter. They became regulars, helping keep Mary organized and serving as her favorite role models for parents newly wondering what gay life was about.

Mary's role was unique in P-FLAG in that she was at once a counselor and a symbol. No matter how distraught parents who came to the meetings might be, no matter how guilty, angry, or bitter, they could look at Mary and be reminded that, as bad as they believed things to be, they still had their child. Mary was anointed by her tragedy—a living, vibrant argument for good sense and reconciliation.

In a way she *was* her story, and she used it to nurture desperate families and children back to reason and love.

. . .

Jenny and Jim Spinello lived a contented middle-class existence in Alamo, California, ten miles south of Walnut Creek. Jim Sr. was a civil engineer, and he and his wife shared a tolerant view of individual differences. Then they accidentally discovered a love poem from their son, Jim Jr., to another man. Jim, twenty-four, had never dated much, and Jenny and Jim Sr. had allowed themselves some suspicions, but with their discovery of the poem there were no doubts left.

Jim Jr. was living at home at the time, but was spending the night at a friend's. Jenny called him. "Jim, you need to be here tomorrow night. There's something we have to talk about."

Jenny spent an anguished night. When her husband left for work before dawn, she collapsed into hysterical weeping. She desperately phoned a county help line and was given Mary's number.

Mary listened calmly to Jenny's rantings and then told her her story. Jenny listened tearfully. When Jim Sr. came home, she related what Mary had told her.

"Whatever happens," the elder Spinello said, "we will not lose our son over this."

Jim Jr. arrived home and Jenny confronted him with the poem. "Yes, I'm gay," he acknowledged. "I was going to tell you this weekend. Now that you know, you should know I've met somebody special and I'm in love for the first time in my life."

Something cracked in Jenny. She began shouting. "How could you do this? Do you know what you are doing, with all this AIDS out there and everything else in the world? What are people going to say?" Jim Jr. was stunned. He had expected his mother to be supportive. They had been a close and loving family. For a moment he had the surreal feeling that Jenny would throw him out or stalk out herself.

But his father was firm. "We will get through this," he insisted. "We don't want to lose you, Jim." He turned to his wife. "Jenny, we are not going to lose our son over this."

Jenny cried all night. The next morning she called Mary again and arranged to see her immediately. Mary's low-key response calmed her somewhat, and she agreed to come to the next P-FLAG meeting. There, she met other mothers and other sons. The boys looked like her idea of normal kids, not stereotypes, and that reassured her.

Jenny became a regular. Soon her son and husband joined her in attending meetings. It took her six months to work through the heartbreak and shame. Gradually, she "came out" to her closest friends and was amazed at how accepting they were.

Throughout the Spinello family's struggle, Mary's presence was key. She remained nonjudgmental, no matter how angry or emotional Jenny or the others would get. She explained that sexuality was not a choice, relieving Jenny's guilty feeling that somehow she was responsible. She explained that it was not gay children that were wrong, it was society. Mary helped her understand that their struggle was not the end of the world. She provided perspective.

And when Jenny would feel most sorry for herself, or most alienated from her son, she would remember Mary. Jenny still had a son at home; Mary had to be content with a diary and photographs. This reality sank in and hastened Jenny's process of acceptance.

Finally, she was ready to meet Jim's young man. They met at a restaurant in San Francisco, with her husband and son. To her delight, Jim's boyfriend arrived with a bouquet of flowers for her. They got on beautifully.

The rest was easy. Jenny and her son grew closer than before. The crisis was over, but mother, father, and son remained active in the chapter. The more Jenny learned, the more angry she became at the injustice she saw in society's rejection of gay people. Jenny felt that those who had been helped must be prepared to help others. Obviously, many others felt this way, too: attendance at chapter meetings on the first Tuesday of every month in the Griffith living room swelled to more than twenty people, spilling over into the kitchen.

In June 1990, Diablo Valley P-FLAG and BANGLE announced the winners of the first Bobby Griffith Memorial Scholarships to a fanfare of press attention. The public had donated enough money (nearly six thousand dollars) to endow four five-hundred-dollar scholarships. Winners included a non-gay girl at Antioch High School, and the first gay person honored, eighteen-year-old Daniel Paul Layer, from Castro Valley High School in neighboring Alameda County.

· · ·

Daniel Layer knew he was gay from an early age. The product of a broken marriage, he had lived with each of his parents at different periods of his life. It was not until junior high school in the agricultural backwater town of Tracy, California (between San Francisco and Sacramento), that Daniel realized he was different in the eyes of others. He was not effeminate, but, like Bobby before him, neither was he given to fighting and roughhousing. Daniel was mercilessly persecuted, called "fag" and "homo" and physically attacked with regularity.

Once in biology lab, classmates threw dissected frogs at him. Another student held his head underwater and almost drowned him in a water-polo match. By the time he moved forty miles west to Castro Valley with his mother, Daniel was determined never to let that happen again. At Castro Valley High he did everything possible to blend in, playing a conformist role, stifling his natural inclinations. He made friends and became popular, but at a great psychic cost. The internal forces working within had no place to vent themselves; other than a schoolmate with whom he'd had a short fling, he had told no one and felt he could tell no one.

At sixteen, after breaking up with the schoolmate, Daniel became depressed. His grades dropped. He could see no hope for college or any kind of a future. He began to plot the most painless and least messy way to do away with himself. One afternoon, with his mother at work, he cleared the house of pets and plants, sealed the windows, extinguished the pilot lights, turned on the gas oven, and put his head inside.

Ten to fifteen minutes later the phone rang. In a dazed state, Daniel withdrew his head from the oven and crawled to the telephone. It was a girlfriend from school, intuitively calling to see how he was. Daniel hung up, turned off the gas, and cried for two hours. He cried at the realization that there were people who cared, that he truly wanted to live, that he had almost taken his own life. Had the call come three minutes later, he figured, it would have been too late.

Two years later, Daniel heard about the Griffith scholarship. By that time he had come out to his mother, and together they researched the history of the Griffiths. In Bobby, Daniel recognized himself, separated only by a fateful three minutes. He wrote in his winning essay, "It makes me physically ill to realize that other gay and lesbian people have gone through, or are going through, what I had to. Some succeed in cutting off a part of themselves by pretending it isn't there. Others simply cut themselves out of everything they could have had a chance to do with their lives."

He was astonished to learn he had won. It meant a lot to him, far more than just the money. He hadn't expected a reward for all the hell he had been through, for his ongoing struggle in an environment where few people knew he was gay. The scholarship was a recognition that somebody understood the pain and fear and, mostly, the strength it took to survive all that.

Mary and Joy attended Daniel's high school graduation ceremony and watched the lanky, slender eighteen-year-old proudly mount the podium to receive his diploma and the Bobby Griffith Memorial Scholarship. It was a moment of mixed emotions: to be witnessing the triumph of one gay young man emerge from the tragedy of another. Mary wondered if Bobby was watching. She decided he was.

At a reception afterward, Daniel grasped Mary in an embrace. "Thank you," he said. "You and Bobby have been an inspiration to me."

"You're the inspiration," Mary said. "And I want you to sign my program!"

Daniel wrote, "From you I can learn strength and courage. Even if it's only to survive."

A week later, Daniel had his fifteen minutes of national fame. *Newsweek* magazine had interviewed him months earlier for what he thought was to be a small story in a special edition on teens. The magazine came out in late June with a two-page spread and a gigantic photo of Daniel, as the symbol of America's gay teenagers. Days earlier, he had called his Seventh-Day Adventist grandparents and with a fear-choked voice told them he was gay and warned them about the article. They wept and told him, "We'll pray for you." He was surprised that it went as easily as it did.

Daniel went on to junior college, working part-time. By 1994, at age twenty-two, he was living in San Francisco, nearing an associate degree, and applying to Berkeley and Stanford, where he planned to begin studies leading to an international business career, with advanced degrees in business and philosophy.

"Life is incredible," he said recently. "Through all the pain, the one thing I've gained has been an appreciation for life.

There's no way I'd change anything that happened. I feel I have the opportunity to do anything in this world."

• • •

As 1991 approached, Mary, Joe, and Con began noticing a disturbing change in Rob Birle. He was losing weight. He tired more easily. In a kind of conspiracy of silence, nobody talked about it, even when Rob announced he was giving up the chairmanship of BANGLE on doctor's orders.

Rob was a man of prodigious energy and vision. He was action oriented, an idea person. Even after retiring as BANGLE chairman, he remained driven, spearheading a program to donate books on gay life to Contra Costa's twenty-three high schools, helping form a new coalition of gay activist groups in the county, and continuing to pursue his personal career as an artist.

What he knew, and others were beginning to suspect, was that he had full-blown AIDS. He had been HIV-positive at least since 1985. (He had taken the test the first weekend it became available.)

Tragically, his partner, Andy, was also ill.

While trying desperately to cut back on nonessentials, Rob was determined to work to his last breath to assert the right of gay youth to be protected in school. Ironically, as his work became more widely known, he himself was harassed at Antioch High School. One day he found the word *faggot* scrawled three feet high on his classroom blackboard. On other occasions, students would hurl epithets in his face in the parking lot. Exhausted, and stressed by the hazing, he resigned his post.

He and Andy took a studio loft in Emeryville, a town that sits between Oakland and Berkeley. There Rob could concentrate on the chalk and watercolor landscapes that typified his style. The works adorned the walls of the loft and were much admired by visitors, including Mary, who particularly liked his colorful depiction of an English garden.

In the summer of 1991, Rob developed an AIDS side effect that caused him to lose twenty-five pounds rapidly. It no longer made sense for him to be silent, and Rob began disclosing details of his illness to Mary and other friends. Allergic reactions to medication further weakened him. Clearly, some major changes were in the offing.

As Andy's condition also worsened, Andy's family in Kansas City begged the couple to move home to the Midwest, where they would have the benefit of a support network. (Rob was still estranged from his own family.) The decision made, Rob announced it with regret at a BANGLE meeting. Mary was distraught. She had come to love Rob.

Moreover, she knew that he was the engine that drove the effort in the schools, which was all-important to her. She would recall later, "Rob was the number-one sharpshooter, a one-man show."

In the fall, Mary, Betty Lambert, Andy, and Rob gathered for a farewell lunch in an Oakland restaurant. They tried to keep it light. Mary teased Rob and Andy about whether they were going by airline to Kansas (actually Missouri) or simply clicking their heels together three times.

Rob joked with Mary about her growing celebrity. "The only face I see more of on the tube these days is Zsa Zsa Gabor."

Mary returned, "Yeah, but I didn't have to punch a cop to get on."

"Mary, I hope you keep going," Rob said, now serious. "It's needed. And no one else can do it the way you can."

"I don't know how I'll manage without you, Rob," she said. She looked across at him, so thin, and restrained a sob. Both believed that when Rob left in a few weeks they would never see each other again.

Outside, in the parking lot, Rob lifted the latch on the trunk of his car and pulled something out. He unrolled a canvas, and Mary saw with a start that it was the English garden landscape she loved.

"I want you to have this," he said, "as a remembrance."

Mary, speechless, murmured a thank you, and they hugged for a long time. A few weeks later, Rob and Andy were gone. Mary matted and framed the landscape and hung it over the mantel in the living room.

As luck would have it, Rob's health improved in Missouri, and they saw each other three times over the next few years when Rob visited the West Coast. In Missouri, Rob continued his activism even as the virus finally began to catch up with him and Andy. He organized a books-in-school project that erupted in controversy when irate parents in some Missouri school districts held book burnings. Nonetheless, a number of districts persisted, and students in forty-two high schools now can read about gays and lesbians in a selection of educator-approved books in school libraries. (Rob's partner, Andy, died in 1994.)

With Rob many miles away, Joe and Con assumed leadership of Contra Costa BANGLE and, with Mary, undertook the book project Rob had started before he left. Mary was instrumental in getting a seed grant from United Way to purchase the books. With cooperation from most of the districts, such volumes as *Gay Men and Women Who Enriched the World, Positively Gay, Beyond Acceptance,* and *Fried Green Tomatoes* found their way to schools throughout the county.

But, once there, most of the books mysteriously disappeared—lost, misplaced, or dropped into trash containers. When the story of the disappearing books hit the local media, BANGLE was able to replace them, with assurances from schools that they would make it into the libraries. (There would be no book-burning parties in progressive California.)

Mary was especially gratified when she learned that Bobby's alma mater, Las Lomas High School, had placed the books in its library. It was more than ten years after Bobby had dropped out, mortified by his secret and feeling like an alien. Now, a decade late, there was at least a modicum of progress, she told herself.

Although her schedule remained busy, ranging widely from local community work to the responsibilities of her broader national role, she worried that the problem was far greater than the resources available to tackle it. She happily accepted the Community Service Award of the Bay Area Physicians for Human Rights, a group of lesbian and gay physicians, and, later, national P-FLAG's annual Humanitarian Award. But she constantly looked for ways to amplify her voice, or generate other voices.

In that respect, Mary worked closely with Pam Walton, then completing her documentary film *Gay Youth*. Walton, forty-four at the time, had been an English teacher for twenty years before turning to filmmaking. Once a repressed adolescent herself, she wanted to explore the lives of young lesbians and gays. The federal report on youth suicide had convinced her to include a suicide story, and she had read with emotion the *Examiner* account. Mary readily agreed to an extended series of interviews, and Pam offered to donate 5 percent of the film's proceeds to the Bobby Griffith scholarship fund.

Gay Youth tells parallel stories that dramatize the differing outcomes for two young people, one accepted and the other not. Bobby's history, recounted by Mary against a backdrop of photos and spoken quotes from his diary, unfolds in counterpoint to that of Gina Gutierrez, a California high school girl. Gina, a vivacious teenager, is seen in the context of a warm, nonjudgmental family that obviously holds her in high esteem. Gina's being a lesbian is not entirely easy for them, but it is depicted as a natural and minor part of the daily pulse of a busy, happy suburban household.

A high point of the film is a long scene showing Gina and her girlfriend getting ready for the senior prom with the help of Gina's sister and her boyfriend. Gina's parents then give the radiant couple a send-off at the door. The contrast with Bobby's story is powerful.

Gay Youth was a success, selling to schools, colleges, and nonprofit groups around the country with an accompanying study guide. PBS stations in Los Angeles, San Francisco, Detroit, Denver, and Kansas City ran the film. It was used on behalf of gay teen reforms in Massachusetts and other states. The Griffith scholarship fund realized two thousand dollars in royalties.

Another opportunity surfaced when the *Advocate,* a national gay newsmagazine, ran a cover story on teen suicide in the fall of 1991, prominently featuring the Griffiths, with a separate article on the government's behavior in quashing the HHS report. The piece again fanned the interest of the mainstream media, which watched the *Advocate* as a bellwether of important trends in the gay community.

The *Advocate* article convinced David Sloan, a producer at ABC's "20/20," that the issue of gay teen suicide was ready for prime time. Sloan and reporter John Stossel traveled with a crew to Walnut Creek in spring 1992 to interview Mary for a segment that would range from Bobby's story to that of a group of gay teens in Indiana and of a fundamentalist mother in Virginia. The twenty-minute segment, a frankly sympathetic account of the price of rejection of gay young people, aired in early May.

Barbara Walters, in her introduction, called it "an incredible and tragic irony" that suicidal gay teens "are pushed over the edge by the most important people in their lives." Mary told Stossel the tale of her son's tragic journey, to the poignant strains of piano accompaniment, while some 25 to 30 million viewers watched across the country. "What Bobby needed was for me to say, 'You're okay just the way you are.' How simple it would have been just to tell Bobby that we loved him and want to understand."

In contrast, Stossel interviewed the Virginia mother, Ellen Shepherd, who had pulled her child out of school when a class on homosexuality was introduced. She argued coolly that rather than "recruit" homosexuals and "then try to keep them from killing themselves," people should be working to prevent homosexuality in the first place. Besides, she added, there were "very few gay children out there."

Stossel told her of Mary's conviction that she had made a mistake with her son, that she should have accepted him.

"That's her choice," Shepherd said. "I wouldn't do that."

A portion of the segment focused on gay youngsters at the Indianapolis Youth Group, a tiny agency that provided telephone and on-site reassurance to lesbian and gay youth. In the course of panning, the camera paused briefly on a flyer listing the group's hot-line number. Within minutes after the close of the program, IYG's hot line was jammed with calls from teenagers across the country. Accustomed to absorbing up to fifteen hundred calls a week, IYG received an average of three thousand a day over the following month, almost breaking the organization financially.

Many of those who could not get through sent letters that challenged Ellen Shepherd's assertion that there were "very few gay kids out there." In fact, the IYG hot-line response to "20/20," reflected in tens of thousands of calls and hundreds of agonized letters, provided a spontaneous poll of lost gay youngsters reaching out from hamlets and towns across the nation.

A boy from Alabama wrote: "I really need your help. If you refuse me all I have left is suicide. . . . When my friends found out, they all disowned me. Some even come together to beat me up. I am so alone, even my own father will have nothing to do with me. . . ."

A fourteen-year-old boy from Pennsylvania: "I would like to congratulate you on being the only person I have ever talked to about my problems without being made fun of. It meant the whole world to me. . . ."

A seventeen-year-old boy from Missouri: "My dad was saying stuff like, 'Look how you're dressed like a fag, little faggot boy.' I got so upset, that night was the first time I tried to kill myself. . . ."

An eighteen-year-old girl from Wyoming: "You are the only ones I can turn to. I am . . . in a small town which only has rejection to offer me. My family and friends all reject me. . . . I already feel tired. Tired of dealing with everything alone. . . ."

A boy from Mississippi: "I just watched the "20/20" story. . . . I am thankful there is such a thing as IYG. Because of you, I did not commit suicide. . . . As I sat on my bed and looked at the bottle of sleeping pills, I felt so alone. I decided to get some help. I called the Boys Town Hotline and they gave me IYG. . . . I talked for almost three hours. In that time I learned it was okay to be me. . . .

"In the segment on "20/20" one lady said that she didn't think there are a lot of gay teens. . . . How can anyone be so blind? . . ."

Mary heard about the phenomenal response from "20/20" producer Sloan, who added that hundreds of letters about the program had poured into ABC's offices as well. She was elated that so many youngsters had been reached. There was no way to tell how many lives had been saved or how much isolation had ended in those few minutes. At the same time, the enormity of the problem was never clearer. It frustrated and saddened Mary that for every youngster who called or wrote there might be hundreds or thousands of others who hadn't been reached.

• • •

A month later Mary had a chance to interact directly with such kids. She traveled to Austin, Texas, where a group of lesbian and gay youngsters had elected to name their drop-in center in honor of Bobby. As she entered, she saw a framed portrait of her son over the doorway and a matted version of the *Examiner* story. A legend in large letters read: "The Bobby Griffith Memorial Drop-in Center." Mary felt a lump in her throat.

Inside, Lisa Rogers, the director of the teenage help agency OutYouth/Austin, introduced her to a roomful of about fifty young people. They applauded wildly and immediately surrounded her, vying to speak with her, ask questions, and thank her. They all seemed to know the story of Bobby. Living with a variety of problems ranging from parental rejection to drugs and AIDS, they saw in Mary a parental figure they could trust, one whose compassion had been forged by tragedy. She afforded a glimpse of what can be if those who reject and belittle come to accept. She was a champion, fighting to win them an equal share of society's benevolence.

It was a powerful two days. Mary spent time at the center, drove around the city with the young people, grabbed smokes with them just outside the street entrance of the center, and took some of them to dinner. She came home energized and hopeful.

. . .

Mary plunged immediately into preparing testimony before the California Board of Education, which was considering a controversial proposal that would for the first time add the topic of sexual orientation to health-education curricula in California public schools. But its significance went beyond California. Because of the state's large population, such a revision would influence the content of most textbooks for the next decade at least, in effect introducing the curriculum in classrooms nationwide.

This prospect attracted a broad band of interests, including the religious right, which depicted the plan as an insidious effort to intrude the "homosexual agenda" into public schools.

Mary, one in a long list of speakers, would have three minutes. She worked for days to condense her story and then practiced her work silently in front of the microwave while making dinner. She finished polishing her speech the day before the hearing and waited impatiently for Joy to come home so she could read it aloud. As she read it to Joy, and reached the passage about Bobby's suicide and the silence of the schools, she began to weep.

"What if this happens tomorrow?" Mary asked, sniffling.

"Go ahead and cry, Mom," said Joy. "Don't worry about it."

. . .

Joy drove Mary to Sacramento. The large hearing room was a noisy, crowded arena of disparate interests: the gay and gay-friendly; the fundamentalist opposition; and the panel of educators, most of them Republican appointees.

The Reverend Lou Sheldon was there, a surprisingly innocuous-looking squat man spreading his gospel in a high-pitched voice. He held a mini–press conference in the hallway, citing statistics that he claimed explained "the driving need for the homosexual community to convince people of their sexual legitimacy and to recruit young people into the lifestyle."

Mary waited her turn, listening to the testimony and bristling at the rhetoric of the Christian right. One witness—a young missionary barely out of his teens—spent his three minutes citing a survey that purported to quantify the percentage breakdown of perverse sexual acts performed by gay people: ". . . and 45 percent engage in anal fisting. . . ."

When he finished, Mary could not restrain herself. With Joy trailing behind, Mary rose from her seat and accosted the young man. "Thanks very much," Mary said, with obvious sarcasm. The young man recognized her.

"Look, I didn't write this stuff," he said. "It's a legitimate study."

"You need to think twice before you preach your politics," Mary shot back. A small crowd was gathering. "My son and most gay and lesbian people live respectable lives. You have desecrated my son's memory."

"I wasn't talking about your son."

Mary said, "My son is gay. But you could have dug up the same hateful things to say about heterosexuals."

The young man was getting uncomfortable. "I wasn't talking about *all* gay people."

Mary started to leave, then stopped, turned around, and fixed upon him the sternest stare she could muster. "You have a lot to learn about your Lord," she said, and walked away.

Her heart was pumping hard. She was not good at confrontation, especially in public. But Mary was mad, and the adrenaline flowed. It carried her through lunch (coincidentally, she sat at a table adjacent to Sheldon's) and back into the hearing room to claim her three minutes. She had to make this count, she thought, for Bobby and all the children who suffer because they are different.

She traced Bobby's early history. "Alone, frightened, ashamed, Bobby could not turn to his parents, brother, sister, scout leader, friends, Sunday school teacher, or pastor. Without hope for the future, he dropped to his death over a freeway overpass. Today Bobby's grammar school, junior high, and high school still remain silent, giving consent to the ignorance, discrimination, and homophobia that destroyed his life."

Too agitated to cry, Mary leaned forward, her voice gaining intensity. "This silence has deprived our children of an equal education . . . that provides knowledge vital to their health and welfare. To remain silent is blatantly to give consent to suicide statistics, consent to the mental, emotional, and physical abuse suffered not only by my son but countless [others]. . . ."

In closing, she took on the church, thinking of the young missionary. "If no one had ever challenged religious authority there would be no democracy, no public schools, women's rights, pursuit of science, medicine, abolition of slavery, and no laws against child abuse."

Mary passed out copies of her statement and retreated from the podium. Hers was just one of fifty testimonies. Too little time. She wasn't pleased with her delivery. Would any of this make a dent in that bank of impassive figures ranged before them?

It would take five months for the board to decide. In the interim both sides furiously lobbied board members. P-FLAG, the Gay and Lesbian Alliance Against Defamation (GLAAD), the National Gay and Lesbian Task Force, and other organizations held a candlelight vigil in August to dramatize the issue of silence about gays in the schools. Lou Sheldon teamed with other national groups such as Phyllis Schlafly's Eagle Forum in a national effort to influence the board to vote against the change.

But in December 1992 the board approved the inclusion of lesbian, gay, and bisexual references in health textbooks. It meant that future textbooks would for the first time carry references to lesbian and gay teen suicide, family structures, and puberty. More important, it formally recognized the existence of gay and lesbian young people in the schools and acknowledged their right to affirmative information about themselves.

It was a victory, if a cautious one. The guidelines called for a "factual, substantiated" discussion of homosexuality and decried name-calling, saying that "instruction in this content area should affirm the dignity of all individuals." Conversely, pressure from the right had succeeded in reducing a passage on suicide rates for lesbian and gay students to little more than a phrase, and a reference to "children of gay and lesbian parents" was changed to "alternative families."

Mary got the news from Joe and Con. The silence in the schools had been broken. But, she would think sardonically, why are they just whispering? Still, there was meaning to it. Mary thought of the kids in Indiana and Austin and elsewhere living in total isolation. If even one of them sees herself mirrored in a text somewhere, then this is good.

Her thoughts turned to Bobby, and she recalled the wonderful days before he had labeled himself, when his spirit ran free. He would bring drawings home from school and proudly display them. He wrote poems and compositions. Then, when he knew he was gay, school became a prison. His dream of flying ended abruptly. Her heart ached for Bobby and all the children whose soaring spirits had been thwarted.

That evening she rummaged through her files for Bobby's essay about his flying dream and reread it.

Peaceful darkness surrounds me like a comforting friend as I quietly lie in bed. Then, slowly, without even noticing, I drift off to adventure.

Standing outside my bedroom window in the night air, a tingly feeling of intense excitement rushes through my body. I see the stars up in the sky, like glittery sequins against a background of black satin. All is quiet and still. But my heart is pounding like a thousand drums. Then, with a sudden swoosh of exhilaration, I'm off flying through the air. I see the wind blowing through the giant eucalyptus trees, making the branches sway. I feel totally free and alive as I never have before. A smile dominates my face, and laughter bubbles inside. . . . Soon the trees, my house, then the whole world becomes minute, as I reach for the stars.

THIRTEEN

Born Again

I exit Interstate 680 South in the heart of Walnut Creek and head down South Main Street, then left on Rudgear, as I have done dozens of times in the last three years. The air is full of limestone dust and clashing steel from the endless highway project that seeks to untangle the ganglia of concrete ramps so they can accommodate even more commuter traffic.

Once on Rudgear the racket recedes and I am driving past a row of ranch-style homes with flowered hedges and attached garages. I turn into the driveway at the Griffiths' modest wood-frame stucco house and pull up next to Bob's 1988 Escort. Mary greets me at the door with two ill-tempered miniature poodles, mother and son, who like to snap at pant legs. "Janie! Bo! Now, you stop that. What's wrong with you today?" Mary admonishes, as if it were the first time this had ever happened.

Inside, I settle at the kitchen table next to a pair of windows. Nearly all family business is conducted here. There is a Silex of strong black coffee constantly warming on the stove. The windows command a view of the generous backyard, including a good-sized swimming pool.

A lot has changed since I first entered the Griffiths' lives in late 1991. Bob Griffith retired from his electrician's job, underwent a serious ulcer operation that cost him half his stomach, and turned sixty. Now he keeps up with handiwork about the house, reads, plays with a computer, and wonders how he'll keep busy and productive for his remaining years.

Joy and Nancy, both unmarried, have left the nest. For a time they were sharing an apartment about two miles away. Now Nancy has moved in with her boyfriend and Joy is apartment shopping. Ed and his wife, Linda, bought a home in Fairfield, an exurb twenty miles north, and have a baby girl, Christina. He has settled into a police job in Lafayette, a bedroom community between Walnut Creek and Oakland.

I look around and try to imagine for the tenth time the interior as it was a dozen years ago when Mary's life was absorbed with the paraphernalia of religious devotion. Gone since 1985 are the tattered Bible (stored away for reference only), the crucifix with the ceramic infant, the Scotch-taped Bible verses, the Norman Vincent Peale calendar, the copies of *Guidepost*, the bookcase stacked with Christian books and tracts (since piled into the car and delivered to Goodwill). It is as if a squad of God busters had roared through the house under orders to obliterate any trace of religiosity.

The family is scheduled to come together today at my request. My research is drawing to an end, and it is time to sum up. Mary and I begin early. We settle down over coffee and I ask, "What do you believe in? Do you retain any of the old beliefs?"

"I believe there is a spirit that goes beyond our capacity— something in the universe stronger than us. I don't understand its workings, but I no longer believe that Christianity is the key to the afterlife."

I ask, "Is there a hell in this universe?"

Mary considers, then replies, "I don't believe in hell anymore. That's just a way to keep the troops in line."

"Do you pray?"

"No, not anymore. I hope for the best in a person's life. I hope they have the faith and the strength to rely on their abilities and their good judgment. I believe in the inherent good in humanity."

"Sounds like you've become a humanist in the classic mode," I suggest.

Mary grins. "If that means I feel good about myself and not guilty like I used to, you're right. I was brought up believing that it is my nature to be sinful and that it is for *my* sins that Jesus Christ had to suffer on the cross. In that way of thinking you're just as guilty as if you had nailed him on the cross yourself. There wasn't anything I could rely on myself to do or accomplish. I had to rely on Christ. I was nothing.

"I feel since I've been able to really put the Bible in the proper perspective, I have the freedom to think and reason without being afraid. That is a wonderful feeling—to know that I am responsible for my life. I am responsible for what happens. It's not because God is punishing me for something. And I can't say, 'Here, God, you take care of it.' I would rather be where I am today because I feel I'm in control. I'm not evil. I love myself. My self-esteem has leaped a hundredfold."

She adds with a chuckle, "I've been born again!"

I can't resist suggesting, "Would you say it took Bobby's death to give you new life?"

She pauses to think about that. "I wouldn't state it that simply. I'd gladly give my life in a minute to bring Bobby back. But it's true that when I realized Bobby came into this world a beautiful and innocent child, even though he was gay, it was like a thunderbolt to me because I was able to project it to all people, including myself! I didn't have that burden any longer of being a bad person in a realm outside my control."

I remark that learning self-esteem is a lifelong project. "You're right," she says. "I constantly felt I had to measure up to my husband, my God, and my mother. The diet pills I took temporarily helped me raise my self-esteem levels. It was only when I got the courage to question that I suddenly realized,

'Wait a minute. I am a good decent human being, and always have been!'

"And that's how most people are, including my own mother. I've realized, like me, she has done a lot of things out of ignorance. I don't hold her ignorance against her.

"So many things have come out of Bobby's death. Emotional and mental freedom, and not being afraid of life anymore. That's the big burden taken from me. I'm just not afraid of tomorrow."

Mary pauses to sip her black coffee. "Once my beliefs were my reality," she says. "Now my reality forms my belief." It is one of those sound bites with the ring of truth. But it moves me to ask, "What if Bobby had lived? Would you have changed?"

Mary sighed. "You know, I think I would have still thought he had to repent. I don't think I would have relented." The answer takes me aback, although I know it is perfectly logical. It makes me wonder if it will take a figurative land mine in each case to make other people change.

"You talk about self-responsibility, yet you still cast blame on the church for the way you used to be," I say.

Mary answers, "Yes. I'm aware that I have that anger, and I try very hard to keep it under control. I'm afraid of scaring people off who really need that anchor of religion. Whatever path people choose, I can respect that now. I obviously don't any longer view non-Christians as damned—atheists, agnostics, Buddhists, Muslims. But I can't deny my feelings that the church knew more than I did. I was ignorant, and I think I might find a little excuse for my stupidity. But if there is blood on my hands, there's blood on the church's. They're far more intelligent. They know more about Bible history, about how those cultures were, and they have the facts available today. Why didn't they share it then, and why aren't they sharing it now?

"I feel a certain amount of guilt, but the church doesn't seem to have any. And I find that odd."

I remind her that many churches today seem to be facing up to these issues and struggling with them. "Yes," she responds, "some are looking at it. I'm by no means trying to imply that Christianity and tolerance are incompatible. I'm simply for the notion that Christianity should not leave anybody out, including gays. Love doesn't draw a line in the sand. Yet I still read a lot of rhetoric. You know, at one time the Presbyterian Church forbade divorce. Then the rule was changed, but Walnut Creek Presbyterian wouldn't go along with it until there were so many divorces that they had to change their tune or half their congregation would be gone. I look back and think, 'They compromise on divorce, and here my son is gone and they're still mouthing the same old bullshit.' It annoys me."

"So, no more guardian angels?" I ask.

"*We're* the guardian angels," she says. "We are the power. And we have a responsibility to do what we can in this life. It's part of an evolutionary process. Everything has gone through an evolution, including how I felt about God. History is full of stories of people who forge ahead to improve their lives. Determined to make life better, we search through trial and error until we find the right way. You know, with all the brutality in the world it's not enough to leave it to God. Too often the God we've known looks the other way."

If salvation is no longer the driving force, what gives life meaning?

"You mean, why are we here? I believe we have a responsibility to educate and make the world a better place. I truly believe one person can make a difference. I got fascinated with the story of Florence Nightingale. It's amazing what she accomplished single-handedly. She convinced the generals that fighting men needed R and R, time to write letters home, better sanitary conditions. They told her, 'These men fight better when drunk.' She said, 'They wouldn't be drunk all the time if they had other things to do.' And she succeeded in getting the army to overhaul that entire aspect of treatment of GIs. Now I realize of course that one hundred years later the military is still a place where gays are persecuted. But that makes my point. That's changing, too—all part of the evolution of things.

"I believe what I am doing now is going to make a better place for Ed and Joy and Nancy and their kids. Maybe homophobia will disappear through education. *Everything* starts with education."

· · ·

We take a break, and while Mary prepares lunch, I graze through old family pictures. Almost invariably in those photos, Mary is serious or seems to be forcing a smile. "I don't like me as a young person," she says. "I don't like the person I was when I married. Frankly, I'm embarrassed and ashamed of that person. I was always conforming to somebody else's image. I had no idea who I was."

Bob joins us. At sixty, he's still a fine figure, with a full head of graying hair and a slender frame. He is an introvert—uncomfortable, it seems, around deep emotions or feelings. He is slow to speak; when he does it's only after long pauses while his mind curls around an idea. Then he might sputter and spill the sentences out, groping for the right words and raising his voice and gesturing violently. One can understand that on occasions his children and his wife have found him scary.

I ask him how he thinks Mary has changed. He replies with characteristic understatement. "Well, she's changed, yeah, she's definitely not the same as before Bobby's death. Obviously, she's changed about religion, but now she has the same intensity in all that she's doing for the gays. It's unsettling only in the fact that she may ultimately get hurt again. She's still dealing with people, and people are going to fail—although I think she's standing on her own two feet pretty well. The TV stuff, it's been a positive note. I worry that if somebody knocks the pins out from under her she'll be struggling again."

"And how have you changed?" I ask.

Bob ponders for a while. "I guess the biggest thing for me is I've tried to come forward a little more. All those years when the kids were growing up, I didn't like to interject my thoughts. I'd rather see them grow on their own; then it has meaning to them. But I think I went overboard. I would do the fatherly things, teach them how to swim and so on, but I didn't like to interfere in their lives when it came to decisions and stuff like that. I think the kids interpreted it as me being angry at them or something or in a bad mood. I have a bad habit of taking things for granted. I'm extremely guilty on that score. I'd come home tired and grouchy and after a hard day's work and not say a lot, and I would take it for granted that people would understand. I should have been more communicative.

"I wish now I would have put more guidance into Bobby. I was as ignorant as he was about homosexuality. We were living in the Stone Age then as far as I was concerned. I assumed it was like other problems. You come to grips and find a niche that's going to work. I should have explained that more to him—that he was going to have to find his niche, that everybody goes through this and everybody has to work it out. I could have helped him, but I'm a very quiet person. Even *I* don't like it, but that's the way I am."

Mary offers, "You're doing better; the kids say so, too." Then she turns to me. "But he's a hard nut. It sometimes feels like it would take a big hammer to crack him open so he'd say what he's thinking or feeling."

Bob is not going to discuss it, but it seems clear that Mary's radical change affects how they relate. Bob is now the homebody and Mary the one who is engaged, on the road with a cause. This is not the traditional model for a 1950s family. The timid, submissive Mary has given way to a more assertive, self-realized model. A man of that era, whose wife spent most of a forty-year marriage focused on getting hubby off to work, raising kids, and cleaning house, might be expected to feel neglected under these new circumstances.

. . .

By now Joy, Ed, and Nancy are assembled, and we are all seated at the kitchen table. Ed, at thirty-two, is growing into the responsibilities of marriage, fatherhood, and adulthood. A mustache now softens the lantern-jaw look of his youth, while a police regulation close haircut casts him in a military mode. His inherent gentleness makes him seem an unlikely policeman. He resembles pictures of his father at that age.

Joy, barely a year older, is a large woman whose long brown hair frames a full, attractive oval face curving to a prominent chin, which, while less pronounced, accents a resemblance to her brother Ed. Nancy, now twenty-four, has luminous eyes and a glittering smile; more than anyone else in the family, she evokes Bobby.

What difference has the loss of Bobby made in their lives?

Nancy, who has very long blond, naturally curly hair, is in transition from a dead-end job as a mail clerk. She yearns to apply her artistic talents professionally, perhaps in computer graphics. Regarding the impact of Bobby, she says, simply, "I came to believe that people have a right to think for themselves and be who they are. It affects the way I treat them. I would hate to put anybody through what Bobby went through. I'm not the one to judge somebody."

Ed is sensitive enough that exposure to the criminal underside of life can be depressing for him. He hopes in the near future to leave on-the-street policing for an assignment in court services.

"I look back on myself and laugh because I thought I knew it all, and realize I didn't know anything," he says. "I'm a lot more cautious. You just can't come up to me and tell me anything now and expect me to believe it."

He plays with a wristband, looking thoughtful. "There was a time I thought being gay meant you're going to hell. I certainly don't any longer think it's a sin of any kind. I'm no longer afraid of gay people. I understand them, because of Bobby. If nothing had happened to him, I don't know where I would be. Playing around in the same field, I guess.

"I don't believe in hell anymore. I do believe in a hereafter. Possibly even reincarnation. I believe that the holy spirit of God is in everybody, even the worst crooks I meet in jail. And those people who wrote the Bible, I don't think they're any different than me. I have no problem with the American Indians and their religious beliefs or those of any others. As long as you're loving people and trying to help others along in life, you're okay."

Ed spoke with characteristic Griffith reserve, yet the enormous dislocation of his belief system propelled by Bobby's death was inherent in his words. He, Joy, Mary—all are still grappling with the dimensions of their spiritual lives.

Joy, too, is in transition. After working as an accounts supervisor for the same boss for nearly fifteen years, she is contemplating getting a college degree and pursuing a career as a child psychologist.

"I'm taking a class at JFK University and want to take more in the future. I'm leaning toward counseling—of children, maybe future parents of children. Some of it is due to my little niece, Christina. She stirs a lot of emotions for me." Joy pauses, apparently in the grip of some of those feelings.

"Christina has mirrored for me some of the important aspects of human nature, in regard to how a child comes into this world, thinking and feeling it is a very wonderful and special person. It's the adults that screw that up. The parallels with Bobby are obvious. But watching a child, and watching how slowly the spontaneity gets stifled and stepped on, really brings it home."

She looks at her brother Ed, Christina's father, and turns to glance at the portrait of Bobby on the armoire in full view in the living room. "I think about Bobby every day. When I spend time with Christina I think about him even more," she says. "The holidays are particularly rough. Bobby was always big on holidays."

We are all silent for several moments. I look around at this congregation of Griffiths and can feel the current that binds them. They are a family forged by love, tempered by tragedy and hard lessons. They are bonded by blood and genes and a melding of spirit, ineffable, unquantifiable, as powerful as life or even death. They have long since given part of themselves to one another, unconsciously and naturally, a merger born of self-lessness and generosity. The Griffiths are going to be all right.

. . .

Later, Mary and I drive up the long winding hill of Oakmont Memorial Cemetery to lay two white roses on Bobby's grave, almost exactly eleven years after he was laid to rest here. It is a magnificent, cloudless day, with the same penetrating blue sky of that other afternoon. The Garden of Peace sits on a crest, commanding a spectacular view of Mount Diablo's graceful arch.

Bobby is buried in a neat row of graves, with strangers ranged on either side. (When someone dies so unexpectedly, there is no time to think of family plots.) A simple bronze plaque marks the space. It shows a pastoral scene of mountain, lake, and forest. At the bottom, per Mary's instructions, an inscription reads, "See You Later," a favorite expression of Bobby's, with cosmic con-notations in this context.

The setting is parklike, with lovely rolling hills, a well-kept lawn, a splendid oak tree, pines and maples. Except for the un-obtrusive grave markers, one would not know this was a ceme-tery. In fact, a jogger in white shorts trots by at one point. Each site has a receptacle, filled in most cases with colorful summer flowers and/or an American flag. The cemetery seems to be non-sectarian; there are no religious symbols in evidence.

Mary bends to put the roses on the marker. About seventy feet away, a middle-aged woman sits on the grass next to a grave site, her legs straight out in front of her, apparently communing with her departed.

"I guess she finds solace from visiting," Mary says. "I don't. Bobby's body is here, yes, and I think about that sometimes when it rains. But his spirit is not here. It's like an old house you've always known and have left and shouldn't go back to.

"I'm slowly but surely learning to live with Bobby on a spiritual level, which is quite different. I experience his spirit with my own. I'm learning to accept that kind of relationship."

She rises and stands peering at the marker. "I know I can't have Bobby back, and that never leaves my mind. I think about it every day. I don't think anything else could happen to compare with that loss. I've walked through the fire and I've survived. I don't think there is anything that could destroy me now."

We turn to head back to the car. "You know, when Bobby died, I wrote in the last page of his diary, 'Bobby gave up on love.' That was another revelation to me. He killed himself because he gave up on love—love of himself and love from others. That's the bottom line. That's what we all live for."

It occurs to me that one of the victories in this tortuous saga is that Mary, who had given up on love as a child, learned to love herself in the course of grieving her son's loss.

We walk on the gravel road past the woman we'd seen, who is still sitting silently on the grass next to the grave site. Mary says, "I remember when we first started this, you asked me why I chose to do what I'm doing. I have it clearer now. It wasn't penitence. It was to right an injustice, to let gay kids know they are equal to all other human beings.

"I will go wherever I can to deliver that message. I worry, 'Am I spinning my wheels? Are the kids listening? Is it getting through to them that they are okay?' Don't give up on love. That's what Bobby did."

At the car, she turns for a final glance. She looks quite beautiful in the tailored celery green linen dress her children gave her for Mother's Day, her silver hair neatly framing her face. In this moment, Mary seems at peace.

Gay Youth

1996

> On reflecting about homosexuality, I've learned that: my
> religious tradition taught me to believe that my son was a
> sinner; my medical support system taught me to believe
> my son was sick; my educational system taught me that
> my son was abnormal; my legal system views my son and
> his partner . . . without legal rights; my family . . . pro-
> vided no support for having a gay relative in its midst; my
> major communication sources treated homosexuality as a
> deviant.
>
> *Testimony of James Genasci, father of a gay son,*
> *at public hearings of the Governor's Commission on*
> *Gay and Lesbian Youth, Boston, Massachusetts, 1992.*

If Bobby Griffith were an adolescent of high school age struggling with his gay sexuality in 1996, he would find that not
much had changed in his community; his school and his church
still offer little or nothing in the way of outreach to gay young
people. This picture is duplicated across America, where the
isolation and estrangement of gay youth remains epidemic.
Some major and encouraging strides have been made, most no-
tably in Massachusetts, where gay youth are protected by state

law making it illegal to discriminate against public school students on the basis of sexual orientation. Moreover, largely driven by one or two obsessively dedicated adults, services for gay youth are proliferating—from local drop-in clubs in unlikely small places to on-line linkups that allow youngsters to get information via the privacy of their PCs.

Such advances as these are a ripple in the sea of neglect and fear confronting gay and lesbian adolescents. The situation grew even more intense in 1996, a presidential election year, as right-wing conservatives turned many school boards and schools across the country into battlegrounds over issues of support for gay and lesbian youth.

At Las Lomas High School today Bobby Griffith would find some books on gay subjects in the library, thanks to the efforts of BANGLE and P-FLAG. There is also a part-time crisis counselor available two and a half days a week to serve those among the school's twelve hundred students who request help. And Las Lomas's three staff counselors are said to be sensitive professionals.

But there is no outreach to gay and lesbian youngsters, no proactive effort to signal a hospitable environment. The curriculum is void of references to the subject (although AIDS is discussed in health class). Training programs for teachers and counselors in the school district include no component dealing with problems related to gay and lesbian identity. There is nothing in the school regulations that provides penalties specifically for antigay slurs or gay baiting.

The school's head counselor, Carolyn Procunier, says teachers and counselors are sensitive when individual issues arise. But that approach is passive rather than proactive. Someone like Bobby, highly vulnerable to peer pressure, would be loath to risk exposing his sexual nature.

Procunier finds that high schoolers are more tolerant these days, but "you have your exceptions." The school has grown more heterogeneous in the past fifteen years as interdistrict-transfer rules have been relaxed. The student body has far less of a suburban-clone look to it. Still, words like *faggot* and *queer* are used interchangeably to mean "stupid" or "nerd." Homosexuality is, if anything, a subterranean topic on the Las Lomas campus, where sexual conformity is still largely the vogue. The rare gay youngster with a strong ego and parental support might do well in such an environment. Someone like Bobby would find little solace there despite the passage of time.

Crisis counselor Dale Russell says about fifteen to twenty students have come to him in the past four years with issues relating to homosexuality. But he acknowledges that the approach at Las Lomas is a passive one, dictated by what he calls the "politics" of this issue. "There is a bottom-line paranoia among administrators, who wonder, 'How many angry parents would I have on my head if I got too out-front on this?' " He noted that the situation is complicated by a large number of students from Mormon families on campus.

Similarly, Bobby's church, Walnut Creek Presbyterian, continues to be inhospitable to any open discussion of same-sex orientation. The church's enormously ambitious outreach program, which encompasses heterosexual singles, children, youth, the disabled, people of color, and the foreign born, fails to include an approach to gays and lesbians of any age. The pastor in charge of youth programs, Shawn Robinson, rebuffed my requests for an interview. Another pastor, the Reverend Carl Hamilton, suggested I try a "more condoning church," like Metropolitan Community Church, when I asked (without identifying myself) if gays were included in the singles program he conducts.

And, as Mary Griffith indicated, lacking the life-changing impetus of Bobby's suicide, she and others in her family might to this day have remained unflinching in their hostility to his way of life.

．．．

School, church, family. They remain largely ranged against gay young people like a fortress of enemy figures in a video game. This might seem a contradiction when one takes into consideration the remarkable advances in gay and lesbian civil rights that have taken place over the last decade. The fact is that those advances, while they benefited gay adults, have failed to translate (with some dramatic exceptions) to the protection and nurturing of the most vulnerable segment of the gay community—its youth. Being young and gay for most people still means being invisible, alienated, and largely ignored.

This situation constitutes one of the major unmet social challenges of our era, one glaring manifestation of which is the high rate of HIV infection among young gay males. Another is the frequency of suicide among gay youth. Though the statistics may be subject to political manipulation and debate, what is incontrovertible is that lesbian and gay adolescents are in a very high risk category not only with regard to suicide and HIV, but as victims of a social order that is still capable of punishing sexual difference with medieval-style venality.

The issue of gay youth has received considerable press attention. And grassroots services are springing up throughout the country at an impressive rate. (The latest compilation shows more than two hundred gay-youth-oriented programs nationwide, although one-third are concentrated in California and New York.) Most of these are mom-and-pop entities that scramble for funding. (One of the more advanced programs operates in San Francisco's public schools, as might be expected. A Bobby Griffith of today fortunate enough to be living twenty miles west of Walnut Creek would find an array of services at his disposal.)

Despite a flurry of interest, the high-profile gay organizations have given scant attention to the concerns of gay youth. Until recently gay youth struggled silently and alone, lacking the political muscle or sophistication to make their concerns heard. Lonely efforts such as the automobile odyssey of Mary Griffith and Rob Birle characterized the movement into the early 1990s. That is changing. In fact, the issue appears to be reaching the critical mass that tends in this country to command attention and response—as well as backlash.

Frances Kunreuther is the executive director of New York City's Hetrick-Martin Institute, one of the success stories, with a $2.5-million budget and seven projects including the renowned Harvey Milk School for problem gay youth. She relates what the gay youth movement is up against: "The institutions have not changed dramatically—schools, church, families, foster care, psychiatry, communities. And public opinion has not changed that radically. There's a lot of nonacceptance out there. Most youngsters still feel very isolated. Adults can go to support groups, or move to another town. Young people can't leave. They need school, relatives, and families to nurture them into adulthood."

Her predecessor, the institute's late cofounder, A. Damien Martin, described the situation in 1982 in words still relevant today: "In adolescence, young homosexually oriented persons are faced with the growing awareness that they may be among the most despised. They are forced to deal with the possibility that part of their actual social identity contradicts most of the other social identities to which they have believed they are entitled. . . . The adolescent realizes that his or her membership in the approved group, whether it be the team, the church, the classroom, or the family, is based on a lie."

Virginia Uribe, founder of the successful Project 10 in Los Angeles, wrote nearly a decade later that "cultural taboos, fear of controversy, and a deeply rooted, pervasive homophobia have kept the educational system in the United States blinded and mute on the subject of childhood and adolescent homosexuality. The paucity of literature, intervention, and understanding in this area is a national disgrace."

Available studies are few, and are often hampered by the difficulty of obtaining scientific random samplings of a population that is highly invisible. Nonetheless, the body of research, taken cumulatively, makes a strong case that a major social problem exists. For example, a 1984 study by the National Gay and Lesbian Task Force (NGLTF) found that 45 percent of gay males and 20 percent of lesbians of a sample of two thousand had been harassed verbally or physically in high school. Twenty-eight percent of those people dropped out as a result. A 1992 survey of four hundred students in a Massachusetts high school found that 98 percent had heard homophobic remarks. Sixty percent of those students said they would feel afraid of peer reaction if it were thought they were gay.

A Hetrick-Martin study in 1990 found that 41 percent of its sample were targets of violence, nearly half of the violent incidents being related to gayness and perpetrated by family members. A later NGLTF study found that one-fourth of the gay youth surveyed had been forced to leave home because of gay-related conflicts.

On issues of suicide, Gary Remafedi, a pediatric physician and researcher at the University of Minnesota, has produced a number of studies demonstrating a disposition to suicide attempts by gay adolescents. His 1990 study of 137 young gay and bisexual males, done in collaboration with University of Washington researchers, found that one in three had attempted suicide at least once. He concluded that, despite limitations of the sample, "the unusual prevalence of serious suicide attempts remains a consistent and disturbing finding in the existing reports of young homosexual males."

Other studies confirm those trends. But suicide statistics have become a political football, with some academics and the religious right contending that figures derived from limited, self-selected samples are being generalized to lobby for pro-gay causes. The estimate by Paul Gibson in his report for the Department of Health and Human Service's Task Force on Youth Suicide that three out of every ten youth suicides is committed by a gay or lesbian is indeed based on available studies, but none of them drew on scientifically based samples. Yet the figure has become accepted as authoritative, a government-certified factoid cited by advocates.

The bottom line is that precise statistics may make academics more comfortable, but they are less than relevant when lodged against the empirical reality that gay youths *do* kill themselves and that most suicide-prevention programs—local, state, and federal—ignore them. Gibson wrote passionately and accurately of the plight of lesbian and gay adolescents, and proposed some serious and practicable remedies. But his words fell victim to the right-tilting "family values" strategy of Bush's advisers.

The Clinton administration has quietly resumed interest in gay and lesbian youth, largely through individual efforts within the Department of Health and Human Services (HHS) and input from a new consortium of gay and straight service organizations—the National Advocacy Coalition on Youth and Sexual Orientation.

The Advocacy Coalition took form in late 1992 and early 1993, the impetus provided by the Hetrick-Martin Institute, which raised three hundred thousand dollars from the Joyce Mertz-Gilmore Foundation to fund the new organization. Based in Washington, D.C., the coalition is essentially a special-interest lobbying group, advocating for gay and lesbian youth. What is unique is that for the first time it conjoins gay-operated service groups with nongay mainstream agencies like the Child Welfare League of America, the National Education Association, the American Psychological Association, and several others.

The clear message is that those groups are recognizing that the safety and well-being of gay youngsters is not a parochial issue but one that transcends sexual-identity barriers. It also means that gay groups understand their need for the heft that coalition brings.

Frances Kunreuther, Hetrick-Martin's executive director, acknowledges that "we cannot have an insular movement anymore.

We realize that we will never have national clout merely as a gay youth agency going it alone."

The Advocacy Coalition brings to bear the cumulative weight of its 110 member organizations, which include national gay rights groups and regional and local youth service organizations. In November 1993, the coalition began a dialogue with people working in various agencies of HHS.

Perhaps for the first time, a national administration is at least opening its doors to discussion on the subject. "Representatives of HHS have been very receptive," said Rea Carey, the executive director of the Advocacy Coalition. "I'm encouraged by the individuals who seem to be truly committed. We're talking to them about their funding streams, how to make them more accepting to servicing gay youth agencies. We've asked specific agencies to establish goals."

The response has been encouraging yet cautious, perhaps out of political necessity. "In terms of national leadership, I would agree," said Carey, "that we need more visibility from the president, from governors, from mayors, all the way down the line."

What is really needed is acknowledgment at the highest level that suicide, drug abuse, harassment, and violence involving gay youth constitute a national health and public-safety problem. It requires an initiative by HHS and the Centers for Disease Control for a national policy to protect gay youth from discrimination and violence, to establish a range of services that reach out to this neglected sector.

This is unlikely to happen in the climate that exists at this writing. The political takeover of the Congress by conservative Republicans in 1994 emboldened the religious right to launch a major assault against services for gay and lesbian youngsters. Communities across America—from Merrimack, New Hampshire, to Des Moines, Iowa, to Palmdale, California—witnessed brutal battles aimed at taking control of school boards and blocking the very mention of homosexuality in the school context. Rev. Lou Sheldon helped engineer a two-day Congressional hearing in late 1995 that provided a national platform deploring the so-called gay agenda to make homosexuality an "acceptable lifestyle." (Mary Griffith was on hand to testify for the other side at that hearing.)

In another manifestation, conservatives in Congress with the backing of the Christian right managed in 1996 to push through legislation to control "indecent" matter on the InterNet. One consequence of this development is the possible squelching of many gay youth chat lines that have become virtual lifelines for thousands of gay and lesbian youngsters. Under the legislation, which was certain to be challenged in the courts, discussion of homosexuality on-line could be discouraged or banned.

Despite these developments, or because of them, the debate over gay issues in general and gay youth in particular has heated up, commanding public attention and resulting in some victories for youth advocates. For example, the Gay, Lesbian and Straight Teachers Network, organizing traditionally closeted and career-threatened teachers, has watched its membership explode from a few hundred in 1994 to three thousand in early 1996. In other cases, straight and gay youth have formed in-school alliances and defended teachers who went public and faced the wrath of the Christian right.

The right wing's strategy involves exploiting misplaced fears among parents that programs designed to aid gay youngsters are in fact subtle efforts by homosexuals to recruit impressionable children. Indeed, according to this belief, "normal" youngsters fall prey to homosexuality if it is presented as an acceptable way of life. The corrosive attack that killed the Rainbow Curriculum in New York City—which would have mandated instruction about homosexuality in city schools—was based on that premise.

The case against such a premise need not be repeated here. But such arguments can be and have been countered effectively when evidence of the pain and injury to gay adolescents is presented in dramatic human terms. People who recoil at implications of indoctrination respond to demonstrable arguments for justice and fairness.

. . .

Massachusetts, a liberal state with pockets of deep conservatism, is the prime example of a place where gay youth advocates have accomplished major social change with a canny mix of politics and emotional appeal.

The groundwork was laid by an advocacy group, the Massachusetts Coalition for Lesbian and Gay Civil Rights, which in 1990 endorsed a liberal Republican, William Weld, for governor. The endorsement gave the group access to Weld, and it used that access to educate Weld about the dilemma of gay and lesbian adolescents. Among those influential in this effort were gay Republicans organized as the Log Cabin Club, a national group attempting to blunt right-wing influence within the party, and David LaFontaine, the coalition's lobbying director.

They designed their approach to emphasize legal and constitutional protections guaranteed to all but gay youth, who were subject to harassment and violence in public schools. They presented evidence, from the HHS study and elsewhere, that discrimination in schools—by faculty and counselors as well as students—contributed to dropouts, drug use, depression, and suicide attempts by lesbian and gay youngsters. Presented as a fairness and *safety* issue, it won Weld over.

Almost immediately after Weld's election (with support of gay voters) the coalition filed legislation to create a state Commission on Gay and Lesbian Youth. Conservative reaction paralyzed the bill, but Weld established the commission by executive order in February 1992, urging statewide public hearings to assess the needs of gay and lesbian youth.

The commission orchestrated the hearings, drawing on several constituencies, including the strong regional chapter of P-FLAG and gay and lesbian teachers' groups. But students were the primary focus: a network of young people from around the state were ready to go public at the prospect of their government recognizing their right to be protected in their schools. More than one hundred of those young people, as well as parents, teachers, social-service workers, and others, testified at five well-publicized hearings, building a body of evidence that would lay the foundation for profound advances later on. Most impressive was the testimony of gay and lesbian youth, whose chilling accounts of harassment, suicide attempts, and literal terror made the case that the state indeed had a serious public-safety issue on its hands.

The commission produced five recommendations in a report titled *Making Schools Safe for Gay and Lesbian Youth*, with sixteen thousand copies distributed around the state and the rest of the country. Despite a growing clamor from the right, Weld endorsed the findings. Within three months, the governor-appointed state board of education approved four of the recommendations:

- the creation of policies to ban harassment, violence, or discrimination against gay and lesbian students;
- the training of teachers, counselors, and staff in crisis intervention and violence prevention;
- the creation of school-based support groups for gay and straight students (gay-straight alliances);
- the development of collections of educational literature, videos, and films, and their wide publicizing via displays, posters, and so on.

Significantly, the state board steered clear of a fifth recommendation addressing the need to revamp the curriculum to incorporate gay issues. It was a strategic decision that made sense, since curriculum "tampering" hits the hot button of the Christian right as well as middle-of-the-road parents.

David LaFontaine, who was named chair of the governor's gay-youth commission, told the *New York Times:* "The approach we're taking in Massachusetts is very different from the . . . Rainbow Curriculum. If we had tried to force a particular curriculum on the school system, I think the results would have been disastrous."

He later told me, "We've taken control of the issue. We reached millions and put a human face on the suffering of gay and lesbian youth. People realized their own child could be involved. We took the high road, making it clear that we are taxpayers and our public schools were shirking their responsibility. We merely insisted that they live up to their obligations."

By skirting the curriculum issue, the Weld administration could aggressively implement the fairness and safety provisions.

And it did. Weld personally launched a series of fifteen regional workshops in the fall of 1993 to train educators to oversee teams of parents, students, school personnel, and community representatives in each participating school. Involvement was voluntary, but within the next six months 143 of the state's 300 high schools signed on. "Every student," Weld said, "is entitled to pursue an education . . . that is safe and free of discrimination, abuse, and harassment. The concept of schools as safe havens must apply to all students, including gay and lesbian teenagers."

Such an extraordinarily open and visible commitment to so volatile an issue by a state chief executive was unprecedented. (Weld easily won reelection in 1994.)

The state dubbed its implementation program the Massachusetts Safe Schools Program for Gay and Lesbian Students and charged it with providing resources to help local units develop a host of activities. Its menu included:

- grants of up to two thousand dollars per school for student-developed programs and support groups such as gay-straight alliances (now existing in thirty high schools); video, film, theater, and photography programs; field trips; conferences; and so on;

- contracts with a network of mental-health providers to counsel gay and lesbian students and their families, and to develop plans for the internal training of school counselors;

- on-site faculty and staff training in violence and suicide prevention;

- resource guides for students and families to mental and physical health services, crisis lines, and so on.

If it lives up to its promise, the Safe Schools Program could have a long-range impact beyond measure. Nowhere else in the country had such a comprehensive and inclusive approach been integrated into the body of school policy. (The city of Seattle recently held a series of public hearings on a program modeled after that of Massachusetts.)

A second development, perhaps more impressive than the first, moved along a parallel track in Massachusetts during 1993. The state had been one of eight nationwide to declare discrimination against gays illegal. But the state's legislation excluded people under eighteen. To repair that exclusion, the Student Advisory Council, a statewide network of more than seven hundred students, filed a bill with the state outlawing discrimination against gay and lesbian students in public schools.

The bill was bottled up in committee for two years. Then, as the Safe Schools Program was gearing up in the summer and fall of 1993, gay youth activists felt the climate was right. They unleashed a drive to dislodge the legislation and get it passed. At the heart of the campaign was a cadre of hundreds of gay and heterosexual high school students who descended on the state capitol to lobby legislators, hold rallies, and talk with the press.

One of those students, Mark De Lellis, a senior at Belmont High School, kept a record of his lobbying activities. He gave legislators a firsthand account of harassment, telling them of his middle school experience when fellow soccer-team members "threw things at me, including dog droppings, called me 'faggot' and 'homo,' and spit on me until my shirt was soaking wet."

De Lellis was youth-outreach coordinator for the Coalition for Lesbian and Gay Civil Rights. He described in a memoir his work in helping to organize a massive rally at the state capitol, team lobbying of individual state senators, candlelight vigils while the bill wallowed in committee, press conferences, and, finally, last-minute efforts to assure passage: "The rally date came closer and closer. I continued to call different groups, trying to get as many as possible to endorse the rally. I was able to reach several community groups, gay-straight alliances, and political groups.

"The week before the rally, I designed the rally program . . . and did another two-thousand-piece mailing. The Department of Education paid for the mailing. The day of the rally finally came. It was October 13, 1993, at 3:30 P.M. in Nurse's Hall of the statehouse. . . . I was nervous. That day I stayed home from school so I could get ready and do some last-minute media outreach. I remember walking from the Park Street station to the statehouse along the Freedom Trail, thinking to myself how my pilgrimage was symbolic.

"I got up to the podium and looked around at the hundreds of students and student groups and their banners. I delivered my speech, observing all the dramatic pauses. 'Everybody has something unique to contribute to a public school education. No one should be harassed, attacked, or discriminated against, just because of who they are!' I was surprised by the amount of applause and energy.

"The week after, we held the lobby date. [The coalition had prepared for this by convening a training workshop for twenty-five student lobbyists.] We broke the [150] people down into ten lobby teams based on geographic location. We talked with aides to Senator Hicks, Senator Durand, Senator Mangani, and Senator O'Brien. At that point the bill was stuck with Senator O'Brien in second reading [and later, third reading]. I helped organize people to write letters. We organized candlelight vigils every Monday night in front of the statehouse.

"We decided to have a press conference and protest at the statehouse. About forty youth marched around the statehouse chanting about the bill. I found this particular experience very empowering—to hear the unified rage in our voices echo off the buildings."

The bill finally passed in early December, and Governor Weld signed it a few days later, making Massachusetts the only state to pass antidiscrimination legislation on behalf of gay young people. LaFontaine called it "the single greatest victory that gay youth in America have ever won. They now have a legal weapon to [combat] name-calling, hatred, and violence." The Massachusetts law simply adds the term "sexual orientation" to existing statutes outlawing in-school discrimination on the basis of race, color, sex, religion, and national origin. But it represents a civil rights victory of enormous potential.

It establishes a base for legal action against school systems that fail to protect gay students. It legally acknowledges the existence of sexual minorities in the schools, putting pressure on providers and giving them grounds to resist right-wing onslaughts. It puts unprecedented muscle behind initiatives to create and enforce antiharassment policies, amend current regulations, require training for school staff, and, ultimately, effect modifications to curriculum.

Moreover, gay and lesbian students now can claim the legal right to attend proms and other social functions as couples. LaFontaine said that at least eight same-sex couples attended their senior proms in June 1994.

The success in Massachusetts is attributable to several factors: a courageous and receptive governor; the influence of the gay vote on his election; the galvanizing of a youth alliance unique in the country; the raising of due-process and public-safety concerns, which resonated with citizens of a state that was a cradle of American democracy.

"Central to our victory was publicizing the problems in the mainstream media, and using the media to educate parents and teachers," said LaFontaine. "We reached the public first with our message and haven't let ourselves be put on the defensive. The right wing was in the awkward position of opposing safety initiatives and suicide-prevention programs. People in cities and towns rallied around us. It became a human issue."

Interestingly, active response to the Safe Schools Program has been concentrated in rural and suburban districts. Urban centers like Boston, Brockton, Lowell, Fall River, and Worcester have hung back. In those cities school boards are highly politicized, and battles over race and other sensitive issues can be public and ugly. But LaFontaine is confident that, with the strength of the new law behind them, school boards in those areas will implement changes as well.

. . .

Massachusetts is unique in its aggressive commitment to gay youth. But there are other significant efforts across the country worthy of note; space here limits discussion to only a representative sample.

Project 10, Los Angeles

Established in 1984 as a series of rap sessions for gay youth at Fairfax High School, Project 10 has proliferated to a multi-function support system, with outlets in three-fifths of Los Angeles's fifty high schools. It was founded by Virginia Uribe, a Fairfax High teacher whose intention was to develop a model counseling program that would include education, school safety measures, human-rights advocacy, and dropout-prevention strategies.

In addition to offering rap and personal counseling sessions that now reach several hundred students a year, Project 10 runs training workshops for teachers, counselors, and other school

staff and does outreach to parents of gay teenagers. It also operates a continuation high school for a small number of gay students with adjustment problems.

Although the target of intense opposition from the Christian
right, Project 10 has retained support of the Los Angeles School
Board, although funding is minimal. It has inspired similar programs in California and elsewhere around the country.

Uribe, a dynamic woman who describes herself as a lesbian,
warns that despite such efforts as Project 10, the problem requires much more aggressive and immediate intervention: "The
pain and hardship suffered by adolescent gay, lesbian, and bisexual youth is no longer invisible, and our lack of action is no
longer professionally or ethically acceptable."

Hetrick-Martin Institute, New York City

Founded in 1983 by a college professor and his psychiatrist
life partner, the Hetrick-Martin Institute has evolved into a
complex, multifunction institution with a staff of fifty-two. This
includes the two teachers and two aides provided by the New
York City Board of Education, which cosponsors, with the institute, the Harvey Milk School for outcast gay and lesbian students.

Hetrick-Martin originally focused exclusively on administer-
ing to the runaway, abused, and rejected gay and lesbian youth
of New York City, and that continues as the heart of its mission. In addition, Hetrick-Martin's services span on-the-street
outreach to homeless gays (said to make up 30 to 50 percent of
New York City's fifteen thousand homeless youth), HIV and
AIDs counseling, a drop-in center, individual clinical counseling, and training of young people and youth-serving professionals. Its clientele of about fifteen hundred youngsters a year is 85
percent nonwhite. As noted earlier, the institute, housed in handsome, newly refurbished headquarters in lower Manhattan,has
expanded its vision to the national stage with the creation of

the National Advocacy Coalition on Youth and Sexual Orientation.

In addition, Hetrick-Martin has begun to train professionals from other agencies such as the Salvation Army and the Child Welfare League to deal with sexual-orientation issues in their jurisdiction. "This is the future," said staff member Peter Webb. "We will train other organizations. We have the research and the clinical personnel and the foundation on the topic. I get calls from libraries and educational organizations. I send thousands of fact sheets out a month. The issue has moved into the mainstream."

Indiana Youth Group, Indianapolis

As with most gay youth grassroots organizations, Indiana Youth Group (IYG) is the creation of a few single-minded individuals.

Chris Gonzalez was a new graduate in journalism from Franklin College in 1987 when he began volunteering at a gay and lesbian switchboard in Indianapolis. He soon discovered that many of the calls to the switchboard were from young people desperate for help and contact, but there was no agency to which to refer them.

As a consequence, Gonzalez and his life partner, Jeff Werner, a tax accountant, began holding talk sessions for teenagers in their home twice a month. Before long, they had twenty to thirty-five people attending each time. The program expanded rapidly, moving to Damien Center, an HIV-AIDS center, and taking on the name Indiana Youth Group.

Casting about for funding, Gonzalez came to realize that the teen counseling he was engaged in had a direct tie-in with AIDS prevention. By providing self-esteem counseling, IYG was simultaneously encouraging young people to take responsibility for themselves and to avoid putting themselves at risk. The Indiana Health and Education Department agreed, providing financial backing that enabled IYG by 1991 to start its toll-free phone line, create chapters in nine other Indiana cities, and accommodate 120 to 150 young people at three meetings a month in Indianapolis.

The toll-free line is staffed by teenagers who take fifty hours of pretraining to qualify for phone duty. They usually process one thousand to fifteen hundred calls a month, primarily from within Indiana. (About a third of the callers mention that they have contemplated suicide.) But when the ABC network program "20/20" referenced the toll-free hot-line number in a segment that aired in May 1992, IYG was flooded with more than one hundred thousand calls in thirty days from every part of the country.

The calls and letters that followed were heartrending cries for help from isolated and frightened youngsters. But IYG was unequipped to handle them, and most went unanswered. Nonetheless, the responses represented unscientific but powerful testimony to both the quantity and the pain of gay and lesbian young people across the nation.

Since 1992 IYG has continued to expand. A local foundation helped the organization purchase its own building. Then, with passage of the Ryan White AIDS appropriation law, the U.S. government granted IYG $250,000. This money provided for increased staffing, including a nurse, a full-time individual and family counselor, and a case manager. Gay and lesbian youngsters now utilize IYG facilities for health, job, and education counseling.

Tragically, IYG's architect, Chris Gonzalez, died of AIDS in 1994 at age thirty. Jeff Werner undertook to carry on the work. "Chris had a vision and he went for it," said Werner. "We're proud of what we've done."

Despite Indiana's reputation for conservatism, the pairing of teen counseling and AIDS prevention enabled IYG to win establishment support. "Our primary focus was not to promote the so-called gay lifestyle," Werner said. "By pegging to AIDS we could do what we needed to do and make it palatable."

Why, Werner is asked, are so many youngsters still in such a state of isolation? "Even with all the resources, there are still large numbers of adults who don't understand homosexuality and who can be very hurtful."

"It gets better as the years go on," he said optimistically. "The next generation will be much, much better off."

Out Youth/Austin

Struggling on a budget of seventy thousand dollars, Out-Youth/Austin operates an ambitious program with a staff of one and a half and some fifty volunteers. It operates a youth drop-in center (named for Bobby Griffith) that is open five evenings a week, small weekly support groups with a facilitator, a toll-free help line, and training programs for school counselors and other mental-health providers.

The driving force of OutYouth/Austin is Lisa Rogers, a forty-three-year-old social-work graduate who in a previous incarnation obtained a seminary degree and worked as a chaplain. In social-work school at the University of Texas, she became interested in gay youth issues and discovered there were support groups sprouting around the country, but none in Austin. With a classmate, she began holding informal meetings for youngsters, at first in her home, then in the library. In 1991 the University YMCA became a mentor, arranging for Out-Youth to obtain a room the size of a small gymnasium to accommodate all its resources and activities, with space enough for a library, a pool table, and its annual alternative prom.

In the next three years, OutYouth grew, obtaining city money for HIV education and funds from private sources. Soon, fifty to sixty young people were using the facility each month. On its toll-free help line it received more calls than it could handle, from remote areas of Texas and other states—not unlike the Indiana Youth Group.

The organization gained legitimacy in the mainstream youth community. It was asked to participate in youth conferences, to do in-service training, and to take part in coalitions. In related advances, two of Austin's high schools have fostered support groups for gay kids, and a third has a gay-straight student alliance.

Increased visibility, however, also made OutYouth a target for Bible Belt backlash.

"We've had incredible struggles," said Rogers. "The religious right has taken over the school board. We used to be able to get ads in high school newspapers. Some principals are now so scared they won't run them.

"For every gain," she added, "a thousand preachers are condemning gay people and hundreds of thousands are sitting in the pews listening. It's like the sixties. Blacks got uppity in Selma and there was a backlash. It's two steps forward and one step back."

One of those backward steps occurred more than a year ago when a nineteen-year-old involved in the center hanged himself. The young man was estranged from his fundamentalist religious family. OutYouth held a memorial service for him at the Bobby Griffith Center and established a scholarship fund in his honor.

Gay, Lesbian, and Straight Teachers Network

Again, by virtue of the vision of a dynamic single individual—in this case, Boston-area prep school teacher Kevin Jennings—the Gay, Lesbian, and Straight Teachers Network (GLSTN) has grown into a nationwide body of thirty-five chapters with three thousand members in just a few years. Jennings was a teacher at posh Concord Academy. He began GLSTN when he discovered that most gay and lesbian teachers lived in frightened invisibility. His goals are to embolden teachers to come out, serve as role models for gay youth, and get involved in creating support systems for these youth in school environments.

Jennings believes in the concept of gay-straight coalitions as key to winning political battles at both teacher and student levels. To him, the problem is not homosexuality but homophobia, which he defines as "child abuse" in schools. "Teaching a kid to hate himself so much that he or she wants to die is abuse," he says.

. . .

In describing these five organizations I have merely skimmed the surface of the movement on behalf of gay youth. (For information about other organizations, see the listing in the appendix.) The level of dedication and vitality in so many of these grassroots efforts warrants that the movement will continue to persist in spite of ferocious opposition. There is a growing recognition in the education establishment that tolerance of homophobia is a social problem that also affects heterosexual youngsters negatively.

But the outcome remains unpredictable. Will gay and lesbian leaders elevate the issue to a stature sufficient to command the support and funding that such issues as gays in the military and AIDS have received? Will gay and sympathetic straight youth get organized in sufficient numbers to be a political force to be reckoned with? Will federal and state programs and dollars be sufficiently funded to address these issues in the face of right-wing backlash? The answers are yet to be known.

. . .

Any discussion on gay youth cannot be closed without reviewing briefly the situation in the churches. The question of homosexuality and the church of course goes beyond young people, but the outcome of the internal discourse now under way will profoundly affect younger generations to come. Most Christian denominations today are in the middle of a divisive—even monumental—debate over homosexuality, one that threatens the very cohesion of some of those institutions.

"This is not just another moral issue; this is *the* issue on which we defend or abandon the authority of the Bible," the Rev. David Seamands told the *Detroit Free Press*. Seamands, a retired pastor from Kentucky, was leading the fight to retain condemnation of gay sex within the 8.8-million-member United Church of Christ. Episcopal presiding bishop Edmond Lee Browning told the same paper that the issue of homosexuality is "tremendously explosive. It has the possibility of splitting our church." Browning was forced to close the public sessions of his church's national assembly when shouting matches over this issue disrupted the proceedings. Some traditionalist congregations have been discussing leaving the denomination.

This extraordinary debate reverberates in every denomination. The United Methodists voted in 1992 to retain their proscriptions against homosexuality, and tackled the issue again in 1996.

When the Presbyterian General Assembly voted 534 to 81 in 1991 to reject its own internally generated two-hundred-page report recommending softening the church's stance on gays, hundreds of Presbyterian protesters emerged from the crowd carrying an enormous wooden cross. They silently carried it to the center of the hall and hammered long steel spikes into the wood. Many in the audience wept. (It was a church of this denomination that Bobby Griffith attended!) Yet change is afoot. More than fifty Presbyterian churches across the country have declared themselves "More Light" churches, defining themselves as hospitable to gays. Another eighty list themselves as "inquiring churches," and many are committing ecclesiastic disobedience: a Eugene, Oregon, church recently ordained a gay and a lesbian as deacons.

The controversy in the church is a reflection of broad changes in the greater society. Urban churches are discovering large numbers of lesbians and gays in their midst as these people come out of the closet in today's more tolerant climate. Many demand greater acceptance, with the support of liberal-minded straight congregants. These are churches permanently touched by the civil rights movement, the women's movement, and other social currents. By necessity attuned to the pulse of change, they form the nucleus of the reform movement that has shaken old-guard traditionalists to their roots.

The struggle ostensibly revolves around varying interpretations of fewer than a dozen of the Bible's thirty-one thousand verses. At a deeper level, some argue, run currents of sexual phobia endemic to American culture. "Most devout, heterosexual church people are surprised, confused, and overpowered by their own sexuality, which they tend to see as dirty, as sin," wrote Duke Robinson, the liberal pastor of a Presbyterian church in Oakland, California. "While they regularly feel guilty about and confess to God their sexual thoughts . . . they ignore and refuse to confess as sin their hatred and demeaning treatment of homosexuals."

Mitzi Henderson, the mother of a gay son and the current president of national P-FLAG, has a family history deeply embedded in the life of the Presbyterian Church. Now a force for reform in the denomination, she was one of the earliest women elders, dating back to 1971. "The church is totally schizophrenic on the subject," she said, referring to the church in general. "It is split. Among Lutherans and the United Church of Christ it is such a hot issue, it could bring down the whole denominational alignment."

"What has made it such a combustible issue?" I asked her. "It's the outgrowth of the increasing outness of gay people. It's been brewing for a long time, and came to a head with the rise of the religious right, which has poured fuel on the debate. AIDS has been a factor. It has put the church smack up against its ministry of health care, forced it to deal with the issue. Some of their own congregants are ill, and it's become very hard not to see the connection. AIDS outed people and forced the church to choose between its commitments."

It is fascinating to compare the experiences of Mitzi Henderson with those of Mary Griffith. They both had four children. They both found out around the same time—1978–79—that their sons were gay (although Jamie Henderson was a junior at Harvard at the time, Bobby Griffith a high school student). Both women were intensely involved with their Presbyterian churches, Mary in California and Mitzi in the small community of Winona, Minnesota.

Bobby was struggling with his sexuality; Jamie was self-accepting. In each case, however, their families went into hiding. Both Mary and Mitzi were too mortified and fearful to discuss it with their ministers. (When Mitzi finally dared to bring it up, she was rebuffed.)

Both Mary and Mitzi began their "coming out" process around the same time, under very different circumstances. Bobby Griffith had died. Mitzi Henderson had moved to Palo Alto, California, a far more progressive environment. Mary's transformation, spurred by a tremendous loss, turned her away from the traditional church. Mitzi Henderson, struggling with her fear of rejection by the church that had nurtured her family for generations, found the courage to confront her religion from within.

In late 1985, while a few miles away Mary Griffith was taking her first hesitant steps toward advocacy, Mitzi Henderson "came out" to her church in a speech to the San Jose Presbytery. She said, in part: "It wasn't only our son who was at stake. It was and is fifteen of us in the immediate family, five of us elders who sit in Presbyterian pews . . . but outside it's love and care. . . . You as pastors and elders . . . can change that not only for us, but for other gays and their families who sit in your congregations, silent and afraid. . . . Until we are willing to listen to our gay members and learn about their lives, their dilemmas, their hopes and problems, we will never be able to minister effectively to them. . . . What counsel would you give our son, my husband and me, our other three children? What spiritual direction? What support group would you refer us to inside or outside the church?"

That was 1985. A year later her hometown church, First Presbyterian, in Palo Alto, became a More Light church. The enlightened congregation incorporated gay references into its liturgy and committed to ordain its gay or lesbian members elected to lay leadership. Simultaneously, Walnut Creek Presbyterian—Mary's old congregation—retained its traditional stance. The two institutions exemplify the modern schism that wracks the church.

As Mary Griffith became a spokesperson for P-FLAG, Mitzi Henderson rose in its ranks to become national president in 1992. Today they both continue to work tirelessly for the dignity, worth—and lives—of hundreds of thousands of children like their own.

Help Organizations

P–FLAG (Parents, Families, and Friends of Lesbians and Gays)
1101 14th Street NW, Suite 1030
Washington, DC 20005
phone: 202-638-4200
fax: 202-638-0243
E-mail address: PFLAGNTL@ aol.com

Where to Get Information on Lesbian and Gay Topics Confidentially

If you have access to America OnLine, e-world, CompuServe, Prodigy, or the Internet, you can receive a customized listing of lesbian and gay resources in your area by sending an E-mail to the National Coalition for Gay, Lesbian, and Bisexual Youth (E-mail address: ncglby@aol.com). You'll need to indicate your city, state, zip code, and area code.

There are also some outstanding forums for lesbians and gays, including youth, on both America OnLine and CompuServe. You'll find a wealth of information on coming to terms with your sexual orientation, coming out, social and political issues, and more. On America OnLine, go to keywords *GAY* or *LESBIAN;* on CompuServe, go to the Human Sexuality Forum, keyword *HSX100.* CompuServe also offers a special, limited-entry forum for lesbian and gay teens, but you'll need to provide the sysop for the limited-entry *HSX200* forum with an E-mail message stating your account name, your age, and the fact that you identify as a lesbian or gay teen.

To receive a customized listing of lesbian and gay resources in your area through the mail, send a large, self-addressed envelope, along with two dollars, to Lambda Youth Network, P.O. Box 7911, Culver City, CA 90233.

Appendix

National Lesbian and Gay Service Organizations

(The information given here comes from QueerAmerica, the database of lesbian and gay resources developed by the National Coalition for Gay, Lesbian, and Bisexual Youth.)

Bridges Project of American Friends Service Committee
1501 Cherry Street
Philadelphia, PA 19102
phone: 215-241-7246
fax: 215-241-7119
E-mail address: bridgespro@aol.com

The Bridges Project is one of the programs of the American Friends Service Committee's Lesbian, Gay, and Bisexual Youth Project. It has two major objectives:

• to establish a nationwide network of programs and organizations serving diverse gay and lesbian youth and to serve as a powerful national influence on public policy. Its activities in this area include the publication of *Crossroads* magazine, which supports lesbian and gay youth and links groups with similar challenges. The organization is now involved in the development of a national support line for lesbian and gay youth.

• to advocate that youth-serving organizations not currently serving gay and lesbian youth change their practices to do so. Programs in this area include gathering and sharing effective program and policy models, maintaining a list of lesbian and gay youth resources, disseminating print and audiovisual materials, and developing education packages.

Lambda Youth Network
P.O. Box 7911
Culver City, CA 90233

Lambda Youth Network is a nonprofit outreach and referral organization for gay, lesbian, and bisexual youth. It offers a national listing of youth help lines, youth newsletters, pen-pal programs, student groups, AIDS education and information organizations, P-FLAG chapters, and a wide variety of ethnic, professional, and cultural organizations in the gay, lesbian, and bisexual communities. If you are interested in information for yourself or would like to refer a young person (age twenty-three or under) to Lambda Youth Network, send a large self-addressed, stamped envelope, one dollar, and a brief note stating your age and where you heard of the organization, to Lambda Youth Network at the address listed above.

National Advocacy Coalition on Youth and Sexual Orientation
1025 Vermont Avenue NW, Suite 200
Washington, D.C. 20005
phone: 202-783-4165

The Coalition reflects nearly fifty local, regional, and national agencies dealing with youth issues. It serves as a lobbying and educational agency in support of youth who face discrimination based on their sexual orientation. It advocates for access to services, and educates policymakers, youth-serving organizations, and government agencies about issues confronting such youth. The Coalition is a referral source as well as a clearinghouse of the latest information on gay and lesbian youth issues.

National Coalition for Gay, Lesbian, and Bisexual Youth
P.O. Box 24589
San Jose, CA 95154-4589
phone: 408-269-6125
fax: 408-269-5328
E-mail address: ncglby@aol.com

The National Coalition for Gay, Lesbian, and Bisexual Youth provides referral services on an outreach basis to lesbian, gay, and bisexual teens, and tools and materials to youth-service providers. QueerAmerica, the organization's national database of lesbian and gay resources, is used to provide local referrals electronically through America OnLine, CompuServe, and the Internet, as well as through a nationwide network of direct-service organizations to put lesbian and gay teens in contact with local resources. Starter materials are available to groups and individuals interested in forming lesbian and gay youth-support organizations in their communities, schools, or community centers.

National Network of Runaway and Youth Services
1319 F Street NW, Suite 401
Washington, D.C. 20004
phone: 202-783-7949
fax: 202-783-7955

The National Network of Runaway and Youth Services provides technical assistance, training, and HIV/AIDS-prevention materials to member organizations, which in turn provide direct services for youth, including youth shelters, hostels, clinics, and alternative schools.

United Church Coalition for Lesbian/Gay Concerns
(National Office)
18 North College Street
Athens, OH 45701
phone: 800-653-0799

The United Church Coalition for Lesbian/Gay Concerns supplies youth and service providers with information, resources, and referrals on sexuality issues. Its services include homophobia workshops, a speakers' bureau, connections with other lesbian and gay programs, and the active encouragement of and provision of resources to people serving lesbian and gay youth.

The video *Scared to Death,* dealing with teen suicide, may be purchased by contacting The Lazarus Project, West Hollywood Presbyterian Church, 7350 Sunset Boulevard, Hollywood, CA 90046; phone 213-874-6646. The cost is $20, plus $3 postage and handling.

Canadian Lesbian and Gay Service Organizations

Pink Triangle Youth
Pink Triangle Services
P.O. Box 3043, Station D
Ottawa, ON K1P 6H6
phone: 613-563-4818 (Monday and Wednesday, 1–5 P.M.)
help line: 613-238-1717 (daily 7–10 P.M.)
E-mail address: an935@freenet.careltion.ca

The Lesbian, Gay, and Bisexual Youth Program
Central Toronto Youth Services
65 Wellesley Street East, Suite 300
Toronto, ON M4Y 1G7
phone: 416-924-2100
fax: 416-924-2930

Other Services in U.S. Cities

California

Gay and Lesbian Community Services Center
1625 North Schrader Boulevard
Los Angeles, CA 90028–9998
phone: 213-993-7450
fax: 213-993-7479
help line: 800-993-7475

Variety of services for youth, including emergency shelter.

Lavender Youth Recreation & Information Center (LYRIC)
phone: 415-703-6150
help line: 800-246-7743
infoline: 415-863-3636

Full menu of services for young people.

Project 10
7850 Melrose Avenue
Los Angeles, CA 90046
phone: 213-651-5200, ext. 244
phone: 818-577-4553

Project 21, The Gay & Lesbian Alliance Against Defamation
(GLAAD)
1360 Mission Street, Suite 200
San Francisco, CA 94013
phone: 415-862-2244
fax: 415-861-4893

Provides books on gay subjects for schools and libraries.

Indiana

 Indiana Youth Group
 P.O. Box 20716
 Indianapolis, IN 46220
 phone: 317-541-8726 (Monday through Thursday, 7–10 P.M.;
  Friday through Sunday, 7 P.M.–midnight)
 fax: 317-545-8594
 help line: 800-347-8336

Massachusetts

 Boston Alliance of Gay and Lesbian Youth (BAGLY)
 P.O. Box 814
 Boston, MA 02103
 help line: 800-42-BAGLY

Recorded message gives referrals for all of New England;
Boston has drop-in, youth support.

 Governor's Commission on Gay and Lesbian Youth,
  Boston, Massachusetts
 State House, Room 111
 Boston, MA
 phone: 617-828-3039

New York

 Hetrick Martin Institute
 2 Astor Place
 New York, NY 10003–6998
 phone: 212-674-2400
 fax: 212-674-8650

 Gay, Lesbian and Straight Teachers Network (GLSTN)
 122 West 26th Street, Suite 1100
 New York, NY 10001
 phone: 212-727-0135
 fax: 212-727-0254
 E-mail address: GLSTN@GLSTN.ORG

Texas
> Out Youth/Austin
> 425 Woodward Street
> Austin, TX 78704
> phone: 512-326-1234
> help line: 800-96-YOUTH

Washington, D.C.
> Sexual Minority Youth Assistance League (SMYAL)
> 333½ Pennsylvania Avenue SE
> Washington, DC 20003
> phone: 202-546-5940
> fax: 202-544-1306

Drop-in program, support groups, education, help line.

Copyright © 1994, National Coalition for Gay, Lesbian, and Bisexual Youth. Reprinted with permission.

(If you are interested in applying for or contributing to the **Bobby Griffith Memorial Scholarship**, write:

> Bay Area Network of Gay and Lesbian Educators
> P.O. Box 30482
> Walnut Creek, CA 94598

The Bobby Griffith $500 scholarships are awarded annually to one or more Contra Costa County high school seniors who demonstrate a commitment to equality for all people, including gays and lesbians. BANGLE is a nonprofit organization, and contributions are tax deductible.

Texas

Our Youth/A Youth
412 Woodward Street
Austin, TX 78704
phone 512-326-1234
Teen line 800-96-YOUTH

Washington, D.C.

Sexual Minority Youth Assistance League (SMYAL)
333 Pennsylvania Avenue SE
Washington, DC 20003
phone 202-546-5940
fax 202-544-1306

Drop-in program, support groups, education, help line.
Copyright © 1994, National Coalition for Gay Lesbian and
Bisexual Youth. Reprinted with permission.

If you are interested in applying for or contributing to the
Bobby Griffith Memorial Scholarship write:

Bay Area Network of Gay and Lesbian Educators
P.O. Box 30454
Walnut Creek, CA 94598

The Bobby Griffith $500 scholarships are awarded annually to
one or more Contra Costa County high school seniors who
demonstrate a commitment to ensuring for all people, including
gays and lesbians. BANGLE is a nonprofit organization and contributions are tax deductible.

Printed in the USA
CPSIA information can be obtained
at www.ICGtesting.com
LVHW031128310824
789807LV00003B/98